Lifelong Learning

Lifelong Learning

A Guide to

Adult Education

in the Church

EDITED BY REBECCA GROTHE

Augsburg

MINNEAPOLIS

ISBN 0-8066-2999-1

The paper used in this publication meets the minimum requirements of American National Standard for Information Sciences—Permanence of Paper for Printed Library Materials, ANSI Z329.48-1984.   ∞

Manufactured in the U.S.A.   AF 9-2999

01   00   99   98   97   1   2   3   4   5   6   7   8   9   10

Contents

Preface   7
Rebecca Grothe

Foreword   9
H. George Anderson

1 The Gospel Calls Us   12
  Margaret A. Krych
    Lifelong Learning—Through Two Thousand Years
    The Gospel Foundation
    Five Theological Themes of Lifelong Learning
    Pastor as Teacher
    Priorities

2 What Teachers Need to Know about Adults Today   33
  Robert L. Conrad
    Adults in Society and the Church
    Adult Development and Learning Styles
    Personality and Learning
    Life Stages and Learning

3 Principles of Adult Learning   58
  Kent L. Johnson and Nelson T. Strobert
    Theory of Adult Learning
    Formal and Informal Learning
    Motivation for Adult Education
    Learning Styles

4 Teaching Matters: The Role of the Teacher   88
  Luther E. Lindberg
    Teaching is at the Center of the Mission of the Church
    Five Key Factors
    A Solid Faith Base
    Openness to Life Experiences
    Teacher Preparation and Planning
    Cooperative Evaluation

5 Content Areas of Adult Education   121
   Donald R. Just and Eugene C. Kreider
      The Bible
      Church History
      Theology
      Ethics

6 Exploring Opportunities for Adult Education   143
   Mary E. Hughes and Diane J. Hymans
      The Web of Adult Education
      Elements of the Web
      Stories of Four Congregations

7 Making the Connections   168
   Norma Cook Everist and Susan K. Nachtigal
      Connecting Education and Ministry in Daily Life
      Connecting Education and Mission
      Connecting Education, Spirituality, and Worship

8 Organizing for Adult Education   194
   Norma Cook Everist and Susan K. Nachtigal
      Planning Together
      Inviting, Supporting, and Recognizing Teachers
      Educating the Educators
      Reaching Out
      Evaluating

   Notes   222

Preface

Lifelong Learning: A Guide to Adult Education in the Church is a unique book written by professors of Christian education at seminaries of the Evangelical Lutheran Church in America. The outline for this book was developed by the professors as a result of their annual meeting in 1995. These professors are:

Robert L. Conrad
Lutheran School of Theology
Chicago, Illinois

Norma Cook Everist
Wartburg Theological Seminary
Dubuque, Iowa

Mary E. Hughes
Trinity Lutheran Seminary
Columbus, Ohio

Diane J. Hymans
Trinity Lutheran Seminary
Columbus, Ohio

Kent L. Johnson
Luther Seminary
St. Paul, Minnesota

Donald R. Just
Lutheran Seminary Program of the Southwest
Austin, Texas

Eugene C. Kreider
Luther Seminary
St. Paul, Minnesota

Margaret A. Krych
Lutheran Thelogical Seminary
Philadelphia, Pennsylvania

Luther E. Lindberg
Lutheran Theological Southern Seminary
Columbia, South Carolina

Susan K. Nachtigal
Pacific Lutheran Seminary
Berkeley, California

Nelson T. Strobert
Lutheran Theological Seminary
Gettysburg, Pennsylvania

This group meets annually, and has a fine history of collaborative efforts, including a SELECT course on Christian education and a prior text. The writing task was divided among the professors by a task force of professors, editors, and adult educators in the church who refined the outline for this volume. These teaching writers share a common vision and commitment to adult Christian education, but each brings a unique perspective to the field. No one writer speaks for all; rather this book is a dialogue with respect for each other's work.

The writers and editor are aware of our use of Lutheran references and language, yet feel that this text makes points that are helpful to our ecumenical partners in adult Christian education. We invite readers from other traditions to enter into dialogue with the writers, defining those foundations and characteristics of adult education that are unique to their specific settings.

An important premise of effective adult education is providing learning opportunities that respond to key issues and questions in the adult learner's life. With this in mind, we invite readers to begin a study of this text with the chapters that fit best with their immediate priorities. Use this volume as a reference tool for adult education program planning.

Thanks be to God for faithful teachers of adults throughout the church—in our congregations and in our seminaries. Their commitment to lifelong learning is a gift that strengthens all teaching and learning in the church.

REBECCA GROTHE
EDITOR

Foreword

"People don't know the basics anymore."

"Everyone in my congregation comes with a different idea of what the church ought to be and do."

"Parents aren't supporting confirmation ministry like they used to."

"There's so much talent in the congregation nowadays—people have so many skills. I don't think we are using their gifts very effectively."

During my first year as bishop of the Evangelical Lutheran Church in America, I have visited almost all the synods of our church. I have asked leaders to tell me what changes they have noticed in recent years. The comments above represent a considerable portion of their responses.

The responses remind me of the results of a survey of the parishes in Saxony in 1528, shortly after the beginning of the Reformation. Reports lamented the lack of basic knowledge of the Bible and of doctrine. People had widely varying expectations of clergy and of the church itself. Their newly acquired freedom from church requirements, such as fasting, was leading to a disregard of all Christian duties.

Luther's reaction was to sit down and write two catechisms, one for parents to teach to their children and one for the parents themselves. Thus, education became the primary instrument for consolidating a church around the Word and sacraments. We need the same unifying and energizing emphasis today.

Leaders feel that it is harder to find common assumptions among the people in their congregations. References to biblical events draw blank looks. Members have come from other traditions or other parts of the country, and they are bringing a wide variety of experiences with them. Every decision must be negotiated out of near-anarchy. Time demands on parents and children have increased, so the church is constantly competing for the attention and interest of its members.

Adult education offers a response to many of these challenges. Today's members bring a variety of life experiences that hold the potential for invigorating parish life. The big question is how to integrate that variety into an effective program. As a result, congregational leaders are looking for resources that will help them create appropriate adult learning opportunities. As I tested out a number of possible churchwide initiatives with representative groups around the country, the vast majority put "adult catechesis" at the top of the list.

For most pastors and parish leaders the problem is that, although they have tried to get "back to basics," they have not found much interest in the congregation. Bible study courses do not draw well. Classes for new members encounter vast differences in the backgrounds and motivations of participants. So, often the expressed need for adult learning is followed by a shrug and a sigh of despair.

This book is a good tonic for the "been there, done that" syndrome. It offers an invitation to expand your thinking about adults and learning. It will move you beyond the typical Sunday morning Bible class or adult forum into a stimulating world of options for where and how adult learning can take place. The possibilities run from the liturgy itself into the workplaces and cars of members.

Here are new ideas for small congregations with limited budgets and for megachurches with numerous staff. And there are plenty of tips for those who continue to find Bible classes and adult forums useful in their congregational settings.

One of the most fruitful areas for adult education is in the ranks of the teachers themselves. These volunteers present a tremendous opportunity for nurturing future leaders of the congregation. Some years ago, many denominations encountered bitter conflicts over the authority of the Bible and its interpretation. Several of those denominations split over the issues. In our branch of the Lutheran church a division was avoided, and I believe that the reason we stayed together was that we had prepared a generation of Sunday school teachers to understand the Bible in a new light. We had given them intensive instruction in reading the Bible as a whole, centering in God's decisive act in Christ. Therefore, when the controversies came, these educated leaders—often council members—were not swayed by superficial arguments. When we work with teachers, we plant seeds that may bear fruit for several generations.

This book will highlight the many ways in which we can support those persons who accept our invitation to teach. The basic theme is to respect the need of adults—whether learners or teacher-learners— to participate in the shaping of their educational experiences. Attention to the needs of teachers will translate into attention to the needs of adult learners generally. Lay people are no different from pastors. They attend courses that they feel will help them in their lives and work.

It is the task of Christian education to probe so deeply into the issues of human life that the faith dimensions of those issues are revealed. We can welcome initiatives to set up courses in parenting or in dealing with stress, because serious discussion of those topics will inevitably lead to the investigation of more basic topics like vocation, stewardship, and sin. Ongoing conversation with teachers will help ensure that they and their fellow learners are plumbing these depths and seeking the resources of faith to address—and challenge—their needs. Such conversations also assure the teachers that they are not left alone to struggle with problems; the teachers can feel that their efforts are appreciated, their difficulties taken seriously, and their personal investment of time respected.

God has given us a rapidly changing world in which to live. God has also given us a solid promise and a steadfast Advocate. Just as adults are most sensitive and vulnerable to the changes of our age, they are also most eager to grasp the unbreakable bond between God's faithfulness and their own lives. It is to that discovery that we invite them through the educational ministry of the church.

H. George Anderson
Bishop, Evangelical Lutheran Church in America

chapter one

The Gospel Calls Us

Margaret A. Krych

"Join us on Sunday morning for Bible study, Jack."

"Well, I don't know, Sue. After I drop the kids off for Sunday school, I go home to read the paper before coming back to church. Besides, I learned plenty in Sunday school as a kid and then in confirmation. I think that'll do me."

"I used to think that too, Jack. But the last three years of Bible study have changed my mind. As a kid, I misinterpreted a lot, and some things I just wasn't ready for at all. Confirmation classes taught me plenty, but I was still too young to grasp many of the things in the Bible. I know now that I need to keep learning and reflecting on the faith if I'm going to apply it in my life."

"Well, I'm glad it works for you, but not everybody has to keep on."

"Jack, somehow I feel instinctively that everybody needs to continue learning throughout adulthood. But I don't think I can explain why."

Many adults share Sue's difficulty in understanding or expressing the reasons for adult Christian education. This chapter will explore theological roots of lifelong learning. Lifelong learning is rooted in the gospel —that is, in the message of a gracious God who puts us right with himself simply out of merciful love because of the work of Jesus Christ (*justifies* us.)

In other words, the gospel calls us to learn. The breadth of that gospel foundation may be spelled out further in five theological themes that arise from God's justifying work—Baptism, the priesthood of all believers, Christian vocation, the Word of God, and ministry in two kingdoms. These theological emphases were integral to the Reformation and are as pertinent today as then. It is now time to recapture them and state them anew, expressed in ways that the adults in our churches can relate to their own learning and can share with others.

LIFELONG LEARNING—
THROUGH TWO THOUSAND YEARS

Instruction and learning for all age levels is not a new idea. It is part of the heritage of the church. Before we examine the gospel foundation and five theological themes, let's consider the story of Christian learning that has brought us to this point.

Pre-Reformation

In the New Testament, *didasko* and *paideia* appear many times. *Didasko* ("to teach") is mentioned ninety-five times in the New Testament; two-thirds of the references are in the Gospels and Acts while ten are in Paul's letters.[1] The ultimate *didaskalos* ("teacher") is Jesus; his followers are learners, disciples. As teacher, Jesus expounds the Scriptures and deals with the ordering of life in relation to God and the neighbor. Jesus' teaching is not only what he says but primarily who he is: in his own person he brings people into direct confrontation with the will and Word of God.

Paideia ("upbringing" or "education") was a Greek notion. Originally referring to teaching, the term gradually came to mean education and discipline and eventually correction. In Ephesians 6:4, the Lord is the teacher through the father who is to bring children up "in the discipline [or training] and instruction of the Lord." And, in the Christian community, instruction (or correction) leads to repentance and to knowledge of the truth (2 Timothy 2:25).

The early church proclaimed the *kerygma*, the message of God's gracious act in Jesus Christ. New converts then received the teaching or *didache*, including interpretation of the Scriptures, the tradition, the confessions of faith, and the life and sayings of Jesus.[2]

In the early centuries adult education was a primary concern. The church engaged in a serious adult catechumenate up to three years in length in preparation for Baptism.[3] Learning after Baptism continued through instructive preaching. When infant Baptism became the norm, emphasis was placed on post-Baptism instruction of the baptized.

During the Middle Ages, clergy and university students had serious instruction in the Christian faith but the common people had little verbal or written Christian education. Liturgy, art, and drama were used as educational tools but the level of reflection and depth in learning were limited for most people.

The Reformation and Beyond

The Reformation saw a new emphasis on the education of adults as well as children. The ignorance of the people in the Saxony parishes in the fall of 1528 combined with the observation that "many pastors are completely unskilled and incompetent teachers"[4] led Martin Luther to entreat the pastors and preachers to assist him in teaching the catechism "to the people, especially to the young."[5] Luther's Small Catechism of 1529 was designed for use in families (households of plain people) so that the children could be instructed by the parents. In the same years, Luther wrote the Large Catechism, primarily for pastors, teachers, and adult laity. Other reformers also emphasized the importance of learning for both children and adults. Calvin in particular gave serious attention both to Christian education and to education in general.[6]

Following the Reformation, Christian education went through a series of phases. In the seventeenth-century period of orthodoxy, instruction became formal and repetitious, emphasizing correct doctrine. In the late seventeenth and early eighteenth centuries the pietist reaction was to place greater emphasis on personal faith, while eighteenth-century rationalism focused more on intellectual appropriation of the faith. In the first half of the nineteenth century, "revival" brought renewed interest in the Bible.

Gradually, catechetical instruction became less the role of family and more the prerogative of schools in Europe. In North America, in the early days parents and schools both contributed to the Christian learning of children. The Sunday school movement came from England to the United States toward the end of the eighteenth and into the nineteenth centuries, placing instruction in the hands of the Sunday school rather than the home, and parents began to assume a less important role in the Christian education of their children. In this way a major incentive for adult education may have been lost.

However, for some decades the Sunday school movement gave opportunity for adult learning as well as children's education. Adult materials such as the Unified Bible Lesson Series promoted ecumenical interest in learning in the late nineteenth and early twentieth centuries. Indeed the Sunday school movement has continued to educate many adults even up to the present. But in mainline Protestant circles, the Sunday school has become increasingly an agency for educating children and early youth.[7] In addition, while Protestant day schools have provided excellent Christian instruction, vast numbers of Protestant children attend the public schools and rely on Sunday schools, vacation Bible schools, and other congregation based programs for Christian education.

The Twentieth Century

Trends in Christian education theory directly influenced the content of Christian education in the twentieth century. In the 1950s James Smart built on Karl Barth's theology and emphasized biblical content in Christian education.[8] However, in the 1960s, small-group theory and the importance of affective learning—feelings—became a central focus. While rightly recognizing the value of group process, this trend tended to undervalue biblical and theological content.

In the 1970s Malcolm Knowles's theory of andragogy[9] deeply influenced adult education with an emphasis on self-directedness, the use of experience, and the need for adults to have a say in what and how they learn. (For more on andragogy, see chapter 3.) At the same time attention began to move from groups to a new emphasis on individualized education in the church, giving choice of activities and topics. Courses for adults in many congregations were offered cafeteria-style, based on wants and needs—an approach designed to motivate people to learn.[10] So courses on photography, financial planning, and auto mechanics might be chosen along with or instead of the Scriptures and theology.

In the late '70s and '80s imagination and the arts were emphasized,[11] as well as sociology and societal issues. Liberation education,[12] faith education,[13] life-transition learning, and cooperative learning were trends that followed. These drew from a variety of sources, some more than others, including biblical or theological study for older youth and adults. During this time, there also were signs that serious biblical and theological content were returning to the fore. The "back-to-basics" movement in secular education was mirrored in Christian education theory by a call for biblical content, not only at the children's level but also at the youth and adult levels. In the '80s and '90s educators such as Lawrence Richards, Olivia Pearl Stokes, Walter Brueggemann, and Sara Little[14] continued the emphasis on intentional biblical and theological learning for all age levels.

Current Calls for Lifelong Learning

More recently, Kay Kupper Berg has decried the biblical, doctrinal, and liturgical illiteracy in the church and in society in general and has called for a core curriculum within the urban church.[15] And Richard Osmer, in *A Teachable Spirit*, has proposed three tasks for recovering the church's teaching authority: the determination of the church's normative beliefs and practices; the ongoing interpretation of the church's normative beliefs and practices in the face of shifting cultural and historical contexts; and the formation and sustaining of educational institutions, processes, and curricula by which the church's normative beliefs and practices are taught.[16] Osmer deals with the education of all age levels in this transmissive and interpretive task. He calls for churches with a confessional heritage to teach that heritage, and argues that quality Christian education demands the cooperative effort of seminaries, colleges and universities, denominational staffs, congregations, and pastors.

These contemporary voices herald the return of an emphasis on teaching believers of all ages the central message of the Scriptures. However, although many educators encourage lifelong education, the bleak fact is that there is still little participation in lifelong learning opportunities in most congregations and by most adults. There may be many reasons for this, but it is likely that one contributing factor is that we have failed in recent decades to present convincingly, winsomely, and clearly—especially at the local level—the gospel foundations for teaching and learning that may persuade Christians of all ages to engage in biblical and theological learning. This brings us back to Sue's dilemma with which we began—how to articulate the need for lifelong learning.

THE GOSPEL FOUNDATION

The main reason for learning to be a lifelong disciple resides in the gospel itself. Paul, summarizing the good news of Jesus Christ, says that there is no distinction among believers, "since all have sinned and fall short of the glory of God; they are now justified by his grace as a gift, through the redemption that is in Christ Jesus, whom God put forward as a sacrifice of atonement by his blood, effective through faith. He did this to show his righteousness, because in his divine forbearance he had passed over the sins previously committed; it was to prove at the present time that he himself is righteous and that he justifies the one who has faith in Jesus" (Romans 3:23-26).

Justification

The cornerstone doctrine of the Reformation was justification by grace through faith, not only as a doctrine but also as a principle against which all other doctrines and all church practices are measured.

The reformers held that all persons are sinners from their conception, without fear of God, without trust in God, "setting up ourselves as God" and so making God into an idol.[17] Original sin is a deep corruption of the entire human nature, a continual inclination that permeates all that we do, even those acts that appear to be good.[18] Human beings are personally responsible for sin and stand under God's wrath.

The good news is that God has done something about sin! Christ in his obedience and suffering provides the means for our forgiveness.

In the justification of the sinner, reconciliation with God takes place, due to the work of Christ. This is solely a matter of grace—that is, of God acting graciously toward us. God freely chose to be reconciled with us because of God's unmerited love for us. Justification is due to the merits of Christ, never our own works, and is accepted by faith, which itself is a gift of God.[19] In justification, God accepts us in spite of our guilt, estrangement, rebellion, and self-centeredness. God pronounces us righteous for the sake of Christ, and this righteousness is applied, appropriated, and accepted by faith.[20] Faith is not a work that earns God's gracious forgiveness but rather a reception of that which God has already done for us in Christ. Since faith is the work of the Holy Spirit, it is not something for which we can take credit. God's gracious acceptance of us enables us to accept ourselves, to grow to our own potential, and to accept others; therefore, in being reconciled to God we are also reconciled to ourselves and to other people.[21] Free from worrying about our salvation, we are now free to serve the neighbor without thought of self, to live for others, to love, to do good works that flow from faith.

God's gracious love and forgiveness are extended to us continually. Christians are both sinful and saved, always in need of the Word, which both condemns and forgives, kills and makes alive. Daily we need to return to the proclamation of the word of promise in the gospel and receive forgiveness.

The Call to Teach and Learn

The gospel calls Christians to learn and to teach. Teaching is an important means of communicating this central message of the Christian faith. The Word is proclaimed in preaching and in sacraments, and it is also proclaimed in teaching. Theologian Paul Tillich articulated the faith in terms of question and answer, law and gospel, estrangement/sin and justification/acceptance. He argued that teaching is crucial to the life of the church and that in teaching one must follow a correlational method of question-answer, a law-gospel pattern, so that the Word might be heard and the Spirit call students to faith. To teach effectively the good news of God's activity in Christ means relating revelation to the learners' own existence, helping the learners grasp the correlation of God's answer in the gospel to their own existential questions of estrangement and sin. While the form of the answer will take serious account of the formulation of the question, the content of the answer comes solely from God's revelation in Jesus Christ. In this way the teacher seeks to communicate the gospel so that the learner is brought to faith.[22]

The teaching-learning situation gives opportunity to reflect on the Word, question and wrestle with meaning, hear and appreciate the gospel, and apply the faith to daily life. Teaching prepares the learner to hear more clearly the Word in preaching and to reflect upon it in depth. A wise and skilled teacher can help the learner hear the good news by approaching the Scriptures with the right questions and with a hermeneutic that will enable the learner to hear the Word of rebuke and of mercy addressed to him or her.

Luther expected that Christians should know what God has done in Christ for our reconciliation. He wrote the Small Catechism for use in households so that the young and uneducated could be instructed. He expected that heads of households—adults—would teach the catechism to the younger members of the family. The principle of teaching a large number of adults the basics and then having them in turn teach others is a good principle in adult education. Luther did not teach only a selected few; he wanted every household to have one adult well versed so that the rest of the family could be taught. Luther considered the catechism "the minimum of knowledge required of a Christian."[23]

Yet, Luther did not consider the Small Catechism to be sufficient. In the preface to the Small Catechism he urges those responsible that after teaching the Small Catechism they should take up a Large Catechism so that the people may have a "richer and fuller understanding."[24] Luther then was thoroughly serious on evangelical grounds about biblical and theological education for Christians of all age levels. For those who could not grasp more, the very basics of the catechism were acceptable, but he expected most baptized persons first to learn the parts of the catechism, then to be instructed in their meaning, and then to study a Large Catechism. Nor did he envisage merely a cursory glance at the Large Catechism. He encouraged serious study of it for as long as the person should live, as we see by his urging of pastors to study the catechism. Setting the example himself, he writes, "As for myself, let me say that I too am a doctor and a preacher—Yet I do as a child who is being taught the Catechism. Every morning and whenever else I have time, I read and recite word for word the Lord's prayer, the Ten Commandments, the Creed, the Psalms, etc. I must still read and study the Catechism daily, yet I cannot master it as I wish, but must remain a child and pupil of the Catechism, and I do it gladly."[25] For Luther, theology and Christian education went hand in hand: theology centered on justification was the impetus for lifelong teaching and learning, and also was the central content to be taught.

Of course, the Christian teacher does not teach so that others only might hear the gospel and reflect upon it. Rather, the teacher teaches himself or herself at the same time—in other words, the teacher has the same need as the students to hear the Word and be called to faith. Christian educators might well learn from Martin Luther's "attentive listening, with the utmost devotion, concentration, and self-criticism, to the word of the Scripture, which he was passionately concerned to understand, not from philosophical or historical curiosity, but because he was personally and intimately affected by its message. . . . He longed earnestly for only one thing: the redeeming and justifying word, and to receive for himself and experience in himself what it was his profession to teach."[26]

In addition to listening to the gospel, in the power of the Spirit the teacher and learning group can in fact be for each other, and do to each other, that which they teach: they can be a forgiving community, accepting each other in spite of who they are and what they have done. The operative phrase here is "in the power of the Spirit." Saved but also sinful, we by ourselves can never be truly "symbols" that point beyond ourselves to that of which we speak, but the Spirit of God can do great things. So it is appropriate that we pray to the Spirit that we may be transparent to the gospel that learners and teachers might communicate the gospel of mercy and forgiveness in deed as well as in word.

Evangelization and Education

In today's post-Christendom society, a theological foundation in the gospel is essential for the full breadth of Christian education. Rooting education in Baptism can be an excellent foundation for education of the baptized. However, the growing number of persons who are unchurched in our society calls for a broader foundation for the total educational work of the church, one that includes evangelization education for these persons. Justification by grace through faith provides a basis for teaching persons of all ages, the baptized and also those who have never heard or responded to the gospel. In fact, many congregations report that adults who are unchurched are coming to the church to learn. Teenagers who have no background in the church join catechetical classes. Adults are invited by a neighbor to join a class or small group. Some are seekers, inquirers—and some are not even at the inquirer level but are simply looking for friendship or support. What opportunities this gives the church for reaching out and teaching the gospel! Evangelization and Christian education belong together.

A foundation in the gospel calls congregations to offer a variety of levels of classes and groups—from the most basic introduction to the gospel and the Scriptures to the most advanced levels of reflection—so that the good news may be heard by all.

FIVE THEOLOGICAL THEMES OF LIFELONG LEARNING

1. Baptism

Whether persons are reflecting on Baptism that took place in infancy or are preparing for Baptism later in life, the Sacrament of Baptism has important implications for learning and teaching.

In Baptism the promise of God's forgiveness and salvation is proclaimed for the individual. Baptism is in fact a proclamation of justification by grace through faith. In Baptism, the Word of God connected with the water produces wonderful benefits: forgiveness of sins, deliverance from death and the devil, new birth as a child of God and an heir of salvation, dying to sin and rising to new life by the gracious action of God, eternal life. In Baptism, we participate in the death and resurrection of Christ and receive all the blessings of salvation and eternal life won for us in Christ's life, death, and resurrection. Baptism is not a work that we humans do but a treasure that God gives us and faith grasps.[27] So the benefit of Baptism is received through faith and Baptism, in turn, awakens and strengthens faith in the believer.

In Baptism God acts, graciously encounters us, giving his Spirit to us. God the Holy Spirit strengthens faith and calls us daily back to our Baptism, back to the word of promise and to the cross of Christ for the forgiveness of sin.[28] Each day in the life of the believer is a "daily baptism," a return to repentance, cleansing, dying and rising to new life in the Spirit.

Baptism is called the sacrament of prevenient grace (grace that comes before). It proclaims God's act in the death and resurrection of Jesus Christ for our salvation before we ever asked for it and even before we were born. Infant Baptism proclaims the priority of God's grace for helpless sinful children.[29] Persons who are not baptized in infancy and who later hear the Word and are called to faith in Jesus Christ may be baptized in later years.

Baptism incorporates us as full members into the one, holy, catholic, and apostolic church. The baptized assume all the blessings and responsibilities of belonging to the church, and the joy of such responsibilities and privileges unfolds first in childhood and then in adolescence and adulthood.

Baptism calls us to life in this world—a life of sacrificial service to our neighbor, ministering to the world and serving God wherever we are called to be. Baptism also points forward beyond this world to the time when what Christ accomplished on the cross will be brought to fruition and Christ will reign over all.

Lifelong learning is implicit in Baptism. The baptized need to learn of God's work in Christ proclaimed for them, of God's wonderful gifts given in Baptism, of the work of the Spirit in the life of the believer, of the daily return to Baptism, of the privileges and responsibilities of the people of God, and of the life of service to which we are called. Such learning is an opportunity to hear again the very Word proclaimed in Baptism and to respond in faith. Lifelong learning means being equipped to carry out the work of the baptized people of God. Through such teaching and learning the church is built up—encouraged and strengthened—in its faith and prepared for its mission. It is equipped to be the body of Christ in the world.

Learning is not optional or only for those who feel like it. It is incumbent upon all the baptized. Likewise, teaching is not optional for the church, which has a responsibility to ensure that all the baptized have opportunities to learn. Parents and sponsors, themselves baptized members of the church, promise to teach the newly baptized the Ten Commandments, the Creed, and the Lord's Prayer and to place in their hands the Holy Scriptures. They promise to bring the baptized to the services of God's house and provide for their instruction in the Christian faith so that, living in the covenant of their Baptism and in communion with the church, they may lead godly lives until the day of Jesus Christ. The responsibility for learning does not end with the parents bringing children to the church. Gradually, the baptized person assumes responsibility for his or her own continued learning throughout youth and adulthood.

We cannot rest content with children's education alone. As Sue sensed at the beginning of the chapter, much learning can take place only in adulthood. Research in cognitive development in the last few decades, following Jean Piaget[30], has shown that qualitative changes take place in thinking throughout the childhood years. Young children with preoperational thinking (from about two to seven years) will grasp some of the wonder of God's love. Concrete thinkers (about seven to eleven or twelve years) will be able to reflect on God's love and forgiveness in new ways. It will take the full development of abstract thinking (about twelve years and onward) to appreciate many of the ways in which the Bible expresses the gifts of salvation and the atoning work of Christ. And it will take years of personal reflection to tie those scriptural passages to one's life and draw out daily implications for living as God's baptized people. In fact, it takes a lifetime of learning.[31]

2. Priesthood of All Believers

Lifelong learning is also embedded in our understanding of our priesthood. In 1 Peter the whole community of believers is referred to as a "royal priesthood" that is to "proclaim the mighty acts of him who called you out of darkness into his marvelous light" (2:9). Martin Luther developed the notion of the universal priesthood of all believers as an important aspect of his understanding of the church.[32] The promise of justification by grace through faith lies at the heart of the understanding of our priesthood. As justified sinners, we proclaim the Word, we teach one another, we intercede for each other, we bear one another's burdens for Christ's sake, we serve each other. Our priesthood flows from the priesthood of Christ who intercedes for us and bears our burdens and who speaks and is the Word. All those who know God's grace in Christ have the right and the responsibility to teach and spread God's Word. The priesthood of all believers is rooted in Baptism, in which all Christians are called to announce the good news of justification by grace through faith and to intercede for others in the church and in the world.

Since speaking and teaching the Word are important aspects of priesthood, lifelong learning is a corollary. Believers need to learn the Word, reflect upon it, and then prepare to communicate it effectively to others. Believers also need to learn the many complex ways in which the gospel has been and can be spoken effectively and the Scriptures interpreted. They need, too, to learn the ways in which false ideologies and value systems challenge the faith, and how they may respond to misinterpretations of the faith. Study of church history, especially the early church controversies, can be very helpful since most modern heresies are simply new guises for centuries-old heresies. Many of these complex topics of study are not suitable for young children; they are, however, eminently suitable for adult learning and reflection.

Similarly, fulfilling the role of priest through interceding for others and serving others requires learning about prayer and service. The youngest child may pray for and help others, but adults will find their priesthood enriched immeasurably as they pray and reflect over a lifetime on bearing others' burdens.

3. Christian Vocation

The biblical record shows that God has always called people to serve God and to serve their neighbors. It also tells of God's call of persons to specific tasks and of God's presence with them to strengthen and aid them in fulfilling their tasks.

At the time of the Reformation, Luther emphasized the sense in which all Christians have a vocation, a calling in Baptism, which is expressed in daily living in family, work, or state. Justification by grace through faith means that all Christians have a vocation to speak the Word and serve the neighbor in daily relationships and stations of life. Christians speak the Word of forgiveness to each other. They also help each other discern and develop their gifts, which are used in their vocation in the home, school, workplace, or church. Vocation, therefore, is not to be identified with a job; by virtue of Baptism, a retired Christian and a child have as much vocation in the various spheres in which they find themselves daily as does the pediatrician, musician, or farm laborer.

Most people have a variety of settings for their vocation in daily life—home, family, congregation, wider church, workplace or school, leisure, volunteer organizations, and so on. In these settings the Word of judgment and mercy may be spoken by Christians one-on-one or to groups or institutions. Wherever Christians are, justification by grace through faith calls them to speak and work for reconciliation, justice, love, peace, and truth; to hear confession and to speak forgiveness; and to give caring service attentive to the neighbor's needs.

Clearly, teaching and learning throughout life are important preparation and support for vocation. The situations in which we find ourselves change as we grow older. We continually adapt to new spheres of daily ministry that demand studied reflection on God's call to us in those spheres. Again and again we perceive new instances of injustice and alienation in institutions and society that call for our biblically-informed address and action.

Of course, there are many opportunities for exercising one's vocation within the congregation as well as outside of it. All the baptized are called to use their various gifts in the church's tasks of worship, witness, and service in and through the congregation. Jürgen Moltmann reminds us that every member of the congregation has gifts that are to be recognized and used.[33] He discerns three kinds of gifts or *charismata* in Paul's writings: *kerygmatic* (gifts related to proclaiming the gospel, including teaching), *diaconal* (charitable), and *kybernetic* (shepherding). All these are "gifts and tasks connected with the building up of the community of Christ's people, which witnesses to the coming kingdom."[34] Lifelong learning that helps persons of faith identify and use such gifts includes preparation and training for vocation as part of the Holy Spirit's constant aid through our lifetime.

4. The Word of God

Another way in which we might approach the theological foundation of lifelong learning is to consider the Word of God which is God's self-expression, self-impartation, self-revelation. The Word of God, as Gerhard Ebeling reminds us, is an event, a deed by which God shows who God is.[35] The Word is creative and establishes an ordered world. It is also redemptive and re-establishes order out of chaos and sin. And the Word personally challenges humanity in history.

Jesus Christ the Word. The primary way in which God has spoken to us is in Jesus Christ, who is properly called the Word of God. John 1:14 speaks of Jesus Christ as the Word incarnate, made flesh. Therefore, any claim to be, or to represent, the Word of God must be measured against Jesus Christ as the ultimate Word.

We also refer to the gospel as the Word of God. It is the message about the enfleshed or incarnate Word, Jesus Christ, and of God's love and mercy shown in Christ for the forgiveness of sin. Of course the Word is not always one of comfort and reassurance. In Jesus Christ and the cross we learn of God's judgment and condemnation of sin, as well as of God's merciful compassion for us sinners. So the Word both judges and saves, kills and makes alive. The Word is sober and joyful news, both law and gospel. This Word will always be the heart of Christian teaching and learning.

The Bible. The definitive written witness to the Word in Christ is the Bible, which has its center in the gospel, the good news of salvation in Christ. Therefore, we also refer to the Bible as the Word of God. Danger arises when we short-circuit this understanding of the Word and come to think of a particular book or written document as the basic meaning of the phrase "Word of God." Such a book-centered understanding misses the dynamic and living quality of the Word who is active in history and in the lives of believers for salvation. If we give to a book the holiness and sacredness that belongs to the risen Christ then this seriously interferes with the proper interpretation of Scripture which measures all of Scripture by the living Word, Jesus Christ. So the Bible will be normative in all the learning and teaching of the church, but will be studied in order that the living Word may be heard.

When reading the Bible, we ask of every passage, "In what way is this text law? In what way is it gospel?" In these questions, we are asking how the passage functions; we are asking, What does it do to us? When we ask how it is law, we are asking how it presents God's demands of us, how it drives us to our knees to confess our sin and ask for God's forgiveness, how it reminds us that we can do nothing to earn God's favor but must trust only in God's grace. When we ask how a passage is gospel, we are asking how it is good news for me. In what way does it speak of a God who freely promises forgiveness of sin and who accepts me in spite of who I am and what I have done? In what way does it tell of the great saving works God has done ? How does it remind me that of myself I can do nothing but that God has done all that is necessary for my salvation?

This law-gospel hermeneutic, this way of interpreting the text, helps unlock the central message of the Scriptures. It acknowledges that all passages of Scripture may function in two ways; none can be categorized as solely law or solely gospel. At one time a passage might function as law and at another as gospel. It depends on what the passage does to us at any particular time—whether it convicts us of our sin or whether it comforts us with the assurance of God's free promise of forgiveness of sin. This interpretive key is crucial to hearing the Word in the Scriptures. Lifelong learning helps the believer grow in understanding that the law (the message of rebuke and condemnation) and the gospel (the promise of forgiveness of sins for the sake of Christ by grace through faith) are both Word of God. It helps the believer to distinguish law from gospel, yet see that the two are deeply interrelated. Learners will see that by revealing to us our sin the law drives us to the gospel message so that we can receive the assurance of forgiveness. But they will also see that the law is not itself gospel—salvation is through the Word of grace alone. In such Christian education, the Scriptures speak to us as the Word of God. The Word kills and makes alive. It grasps us by the power of the Spirit who calls forth faith in us.

The Bible brings with it a language that reflects a world not our own, and yet a language that can help interpret our own world and our own experience. Since the language reflects cultural and thought patterns of two thousand years ago and a history of God's dealing with people that extends over many centuries, learning the Bible is serious business and takes time. We may also expect that teachers will need to pay careful attention to the cultural and social situations of their students and seek ways to interpret Scripture in thought forms that connect with the worlds in which students live today. Tillich calls this "participating" in the situation of the students so that the gospel message may be communicated appropriately.[36]

Scripture is normative and is the standard of all that we learn and teach in the church and by which all liturgy, creeds, and catechisms are measured. Clearly, curriculum for all age levels will be measured by the Scriptures and will have the Scriptures as central content. Of course, not all age levels will explore every passage in the Scriptures. Careful attention to cognitive developmental stages will help curriculum developers and teachers determine which passages are most appropriately used with children and early teens. Much of the study of the Bible will be done in youth and adulthood. While adults who are new to the faith may need to begin with Bible basics, others who have studied the Scriptures for many years will be ready to compare the translations and interpretations of the scholars. Those who can use the original languages will find them a blessing in translation and understanding. With today's excellent translations, multiple commentaries of the highest quality from ecumenical scholars worldwide, and many denominational study guides and helps, adults have fine aids at hand to study the Scriptures and to relate them to contemporary life and societal issues. In many cases, we encourage serious students of the Scriptures to prepare in turn to teach others.

Congregations need to provide the tools, to give members easy access to quality resources. A good, up-to-date library is essential for all age levels. Some churches may cooperate in a joint library (including the latest computer resources) to save expense.

Proclamation Today. The Bible has its foundation in Jesus' own oral proclamation and that of the preaching of the early apostles. We acknowledge that the living Word, Jesus Christ, also comes to us today through proclamation (preaching), the Eucharist, and Holy Baptism. Christ is the real subject of Scripture, the real subject of preaching and sacraments, and the one who encounters us, who is truly present in the preaching and sacraments. Through this Word in preaching and sacraments today, God the Holy Spirit calls forth faith and gives to us the promise of forgiveness of sin over and over again. This same Word is spoken by pastors and laity to one another, not just in the pulpit but in mutual conversation—the consolation of one another. So learning in the church will help believers to prepare for and listen to sermons[37] and to participate in the sacraments. It will give opportunity for group members to speak the Word to one another and to reflect on ways to speak the Word outside of the class, too.

The Word of God is existential—that is, it affects the very core of our being, our very existence. It faces us with decision, forces us to acknowledge our need, challenges our unbelief, grasps us in judgment and promise, calls us to faith and to sharing the Word. So Christian teaching and learning are inevitably existential; when we study the Scriptures the Spirit speaks the Word to both learner and teacher and calls forth faith.

We are hearers and also proclaimers, or witnesses, of the text in daily life. The text of Scripture is the source of both witnessing and faith since both are rooted in the Word of God. It is the Word, Jesus Christ, who creates faith and who calls us to witness. So lifelong learning is also learning to witness, to share God's story with others.

5. Ministry in Two Kingdoms

Increasingly, the understanding of the term *ministry* includes the worship and mission of all the people of God: ministry in daily life. All baptized persons are representatives of the church wherever they are—at home or work or leisure. Wherever the baptized people are, there the church is engaged in witness and in service of the neighbor, and therefore in ministry. The variety of gifts that the Spirit gives to the people of God is used not only in the church but also in ministry in the world. The church is called to nurture and equip its members throughout life so that the ministry of the laity is effective and faithful.[38]

Martin Luther related education closely to his understanding of God's rule in two realms or kingdoms. All Christians live in two realms of which God is sovereign. One realm or kingdom is God's gift of creation. In this kingdom God has given the law to restrain wickedness and maintain order, justice, and peace, and thereby carry on civilization. The other realm is that of redemption and grace. We see in the cross God's promise of the world to come, in which God will rule through the gospel.

In writing to the city councilmen, Luther argues for education for service in both kingdoms.[39] For the sake of the gospel, he urges the teaching of biblical languages so that the Scriptures may be interpreted and taught correctly and the gospel preserved. He asserts that education is needed for good preaching that is not flat and tame, and that education in the gospel is needed for the salvation of souls. At the same time, the Christian must also be prepared to serve God in the other kingdom. Therefore quality education is needed for good temporal government so that Christians can perform the functions of the temporal offices. Since Christians serve God in both realms, Luther advocated education for girls as well as boys and education for the gifted who fulfill special roles of leadership in society and especially in the church. He also called for good libraries as sources for education.

Likewise, in "A Sermon on Keeping Children in School"[40] Luther argues for education both to prepare persons for preaching and also for governing, for serving God in both spiritual and worldly estates. Education in the gospel is essential so that Christians can snatch souls from the devil and speak the gospel to the neighbor. Luther also pleads for education for Christians who will establish law and peace and worldly government, serving God and the world.

While Luther was particularly concerned about the education of children and youth, his concern also sheds light on the importance of education in preparing adults for serving God in both realms today. Many adults nowadays engage in continuing education for the work that they do, often in order to retain their position or gain promotion. We can help baptized adults understand lifelong learning as preparation for serving God and others through daily work by ordering society and promoting justice and peace. This may put both education and work in a new light. Preparation for serving God in the family, community, church, and other settings of life in the temporal sphere is also an important part of promoting order, justice, and peace. Wolfhart Pannenberg calls responsibility for the social order and its justice as well as for the rational shaping of the individual life "a share in the activity of the divine world government that limits sin and its consequences."[41]

The study of the Scriptures is crucial so that adults can teach and speak the gospel to others. The church needs theologically literate adults who are able to lead the church on the local and wider levels, who can communicate the gospel, and who can support the pastor but also may call the pastor to task should she or he fail appropriately to teach and preach the gospel. Seminary education would be enhanced immeasurably if all students entered their seminary studies with solid biblical and doctrinal foundations already in place due to fine adult Christian education in the congregations from which they come!

PASTOR AS TEACHER

The teaching most likely to be relevant for adults will be done by the pastors and laity who are with congregations on an ongoing basis, who know the community and the people and their life circumstances. Pastors who preach the gospel and administer the sacraments on a regular basis know the people perhaps better than anyone else.

The church needs pastors and lay professional or diaconal ministers who are steeped in the Bible, catechisms, and other confessional documents and are eager to pass them on and reinterpret them for today's adults. It needs pastors who understand their role as teaching not only the recently converted, who certainly should be well introduced to both the Scriptures and catechisms, but also those who have been in the church all their lives. With good reason, Luther had harsh words for pastors and preachers who thought they were beyond the catechism because of their learning or who were simply too lazy to teach it.

Serious biblical and theological instruction is the right and heritage of all Christians and normally should be received in the local congregation. Believers of all ages need to receive the basics not just once but many times throughout their lifetime because retention of learning requires review and more review. In addition, adults need to wrestle with more complex and sophisticated theological issues as they are able. As "resident theologian" and biblical scholar, the pastor is in a unique position to teach and encourage this learning.

Luther was correct in placing the responsibility for congregational theological teaching squarely on pastors. There is no doubt that today, as in the sixteenth century, if pastors and other professional leaders give the impression that teaching really is not important for them, or that they are not equipped to teach, then a clear message is sent to the congregation that lifelong Christian education is a low priority. Those with seminary training are central theological teachers in the congregation and must be encouraged to see that teaching is one of the most important aspects of ministry. On the other hand, they cannot do it all. Competent and qualified volunteer lay teachers are also God's gift to the church and share jointly in the teaching ministry of the congregation. Most, however, do not have seminary training and many look to pastors and other seminary-trained congregational leaders for help with theological and biblical issues. Educational counseling is quite as important as other kinds of pastoral counseling.

The pastor also has particular opportunity to teach or to review the catechism in preparing persons of all ages for Baptism and for the

Lord's Supper, in receiving members by transfer, and in restoring those who have become inactive. New members will welcome an introduction to a denomination's theological stance, appreciating that which is important for the way in which the denomination understands God's self-revelation in Jesus Christ.

PRIORITIES

We should not be content until all of the baptized people of God expect to engage in Christian learning as a lifelong endeavor. For this to occur, there are four key actions that must take priority in our ministry as we move into the future.

Communicate the Basis

The first key action is to communicate the theological bases for lifelong learning to all members in the congregation. If adults do not know why the gospel calls them to learn, then it will not be surprising if they only engage in learning when they find it fun or have nothing else on. But understanding that the gospel itself has implications for lifelong learning and teaching will call for a different kind of commitment. Adults need to be challenged to take to heart justification—and this means taking seriously Baptism, the priesthood of all believers, Christian vocation, the Word of God, and ministry in two kingdoms, with all the implications for learning that follow. The role of the pastor and congregational leaders is critical in communicating this theological basis. Christian learning and teaching must be seen as part of the ministry of the whole congregation, who need to be informed about it, support it in prayer, budget for it, and participate in it because of the good news of God's forgiving mercy in Jesus Christ.

Equip Teachers

The second key action is to equip teachers in the congregation for their task. This includes integral training of teachers of adult groups and classes, not just those who teach children and youth. Teacher education is a must for those already involved in teaching and also for those who plan to teach in the future. Such education should include much more than craft and methodological tools, though these are helpful. Expect scriptural and theological study to be part of every teacher's training, and every teacher has the right to expect that opportunities for such study will be offered locally. Design training that balances process and content for teachers and adults. Design training that balances process and content for teachers and adults. Congregations that have few resources may find that joining with other nearby congregations for teacher education will be enriching as well as practical. Reclaim teaching as a high priority for the congregation. Choose members carefully and prayerfully for this important ministry, training them with the utmost seriousness, and supporting them with the prayers and encouragement of the whole congregation.

Reclaim Teaching as Part of Pastoral Ministry

The third key action is to reclaim the centrality of teaching in pastoral ministry. Today's pastors are often asked to be CEOs, counselors, financial advisors, psychologists, communicators, computer experts, social workers, and many other things. A return to the central focus of pastoral ministry—not only on the part of pastors but also on the part of the congregations who call them—is essential. There is only one reason for the office of the ministry of Word and Sacrament, and that is the proclamation of justification by grace through faith so that through the Word and sacraments the Holy Spirit works faith in those who hear the gospel proclaimed.[42] Proclaiming and teaching this gospel must always be the central focus of pastoral ministry. Teaching is not another task in the list of many duties. It is a priority of the call.

Offer Variety

The fourth key action is to offer in congregations a wide range of Christian education opportunities for all age levels so that all those for whom the gospel is proclaimed may learn about God's work in Jesus Christ. A variety of levels of learning and settings will enable all adults, both churched and unchurched, to learn. This does not mean that all adults will join study groups—although that would be a fine thing, too. Many adults today will prefer to engage in independent study on their own time using books, tapes, CD ROMs, videos, and other borrowable and buyable resources. But by whatever means possible, opportunity needs to be given to all baptized persons to engage in serious biblical, theological, and devotional study and to continue in learning throughout their lives.

A COMMAND AND A PROMISE

We go back to the beginning. Teaching was of prime importance in Jesus' ministry and in that of the apostles. It was critical in the ministry of the early church. It was reclaimed and highlighted in the Reformation because of the gospel. As heirs of the reformers today, as we look to ministry in the twenty-first century, we must reclaim our heritage of teaching and learning so that lifelong learning will be a top priority for the people of God in our time. Matthew ends his Gospel with a command and a promise to all baptized people as we recapture the gospel foundation for lifelong learning: "Go therefore and make disciples . . . teaching them to observe all that I have commanded you; and lo, I am with you always, to the close of the age" (28:16).

chapter two

What Teachers Need to Know About Adults Today

Robert L. Conrad

Today's adults are a diverse group. Adults vary from class to class and individual to individual. Those who work with adults in the educational ministry of the church know how important it is to have an understanding of the persons we strive to serve. We tend to assume others are like us in their level of understanding, their way of learning, and their situation in life. We are like fish swimming in water, unaware of our environment and unaware of the fact that other fish may not be swimming in the same water or swimming in the same way. Teachers who swim in very small puddles can frustrate and turn away people who swim in other ponds. We need to learn about adults in their settings so that we can begin where they are and help them embrace lifelong learning, growing in Christian faith and love.

In order to organize sociological and psychological information about contemporary adult learners, this chapter has two distinct sections. First, there is information about three groups of adults in our society and our churches—the cultural left, the cultural right, and the cultural middle—and strategies for learning ministry with each. Second, there is information on adult learning styles and the issues adults face in young, middle, and late adulthood, and Christian education strategies for each stage.

Helpful as the descriptions and suggestions may be, every teacher knows that they are only a place to begin. From that beginning, teachers go on to know and love people as the unique individuals God has made them to be so that they can be helped to grow in relationship with God and with each other.

ADULTS IN SOCIETY AND THE CHURCH

It is common knowledge that mainline Protestant churches in North America have had a difficult time maintaining their membership. Decline in numbers has been a distressing phenomenon for most churches. Many cultural factors contribute to that decline.[1] The level of people's education affects the intensity of their religious commitment: the higher the level of education, the less intense their religious commitment. Increased travel and the availability of mass media have made people more aware of other cultures and options. The resultant pluralism and mobility weakens congregational loyalty.

The increase of individualism affects the church. Robert Bellah and his colleagues in *Habits of the Heart*, a study of the white middle class, described the rise of individualism in the United States, an individualism that undermines community. Private gain is more important than the common good.[2] Individualism makes people think that church-going is optional. Many assume that one can be Christian without church affiliation.

Privatism is related to individualism. It results in lifestyle enclaves in which people live and interact only with persons like themselves. They retreat from public involvement. Faith and the church are viewed as helpful only to the extent that they contribute to personal success and fulfillment. Last, there is an anti-institutionalism that arises from distrust of authority and the institutions that depend on authority. A keynote of the counterculture movement in recent decades has been distrust of all authority and institutions, including the church.

Other researchers add to the chorus of reasons for this change. They note that there has been a massive shift in values from self-denial to self-fulfillment, mostly in the middle class. Self-denial is more characteristic of an older generation that denies one's self for the sake of the security and well-being of the family, doing whatever it takes to provide for the family. Self-denial also involves working hard for the necessities of life and, if there is anything left over, a few luxuries. Self-denial is concerned about respectability. People want a good family and responsible children so they can hold up their heads in the community.[3]

Self-fulfillment, on the other hand, views life as intrinsically valuable and, therefore, not to be denied for the sake of something else. It is not to be denied for the sake of family, community, or country. Secondly, life is to be creatively and emotionally expressive. Life is not to be subjugated to the wearing effects of hard and dreary labor. The third aspect of self-fulfillment is the psychology of affluence. Growing up in a post-war society, many young and middle-aged adults, for instance, feel that a person is entitled to affluence, and that the economy will provide the goods and services that guarantee that right. Self-fulfillment is a lifelong project that involves becoming as self-fulfilled as possible.[4] The ethic of self-fulfillment has consequences for the Christian community because the more one holds to an ethic of self-fulfillment, the less likely one is to belong to the church.

The effect of these cultural forces is felt in all social classes in the United States. Tex Sample, professor of church and society at St. Paul School of Theology in Kansas City, says there are three social classes: the cultural left, middle, and right. The cultural forces noted in the preceding paragraphs affect especially the cultural left. that has led to special attention to the cultural left. However, the cultural middle and right deserve attention as well. The following paragraphs examine each of these three cultural groups in greater detail.

The Cultural Left

Boomers. The cultural left, a group of about 33 million Americans, is mostly made up of baby boomers, those born between 1945 and about 1965. They are typically portrayed as being concerned about self-fulfillment, inner-directed, and marching to their own drummers. Sample says there are three lifestyles in the cultural left: the I-am-me's, the experientials, and the societally conscious.[5]

The I-am-me's are usually the youngest in this group and experience this lifestyle as a transition stage. They care little of what others think, preferring to look and act as they please. They are not usually concerned about social issues.

The experientials are a group committed to immediate, vital experience. They want hands-on engagement with life in a variety of ways. They love noise and excitement, but they also seek out the mystical through focusing on the inner self and its thoughts and emotions. They do not repress feelings, tend to distrust authority and institutions, and relate to things intuitively. These persons tend to be economically middle class and in their thirties. They are politically liberal and supportive of many innovative movements.

The third group in the cultural left is the societally conscious, a lifestyle that involves some 14 million persons committed to social issues and their solution. They have an average age of mid-forties and have high educational achievement. They are politically astute and active in order to achieve their ends.

Sample describes the way in which the church can reach this varied group of baby boomers. Church programming for the cultural left begins by looking for niches in their lives where the church can offer a ministry that provides an intrinsically valuable experience of worship, one that is emotionally expressive, that opens up the opportunity for new relationships, and that can deliver, out of this, occasions for short-term, hands-on servant ministry to the world.[6]

Helpful Educational Strategies. Offer short-term studies of issues vital to the life of the baby boomers both in personal spiritual development and social issues, leading to action that deals directly with the problem. Small groups are a primary means by which boomers learn not only about issues but about themselves and others. The groups benefit from a focus on relationships as well as issues, connecting with these theological themes of lifelong learning: Christian vocation, priesthood of believers, and ministry in two kingdoms. Relationships are important for people who sense a lack of family and community. Singles, as well as couples, can find caring relationships in small Bible study groups. There are 19 million people who live alone in the United States. They offer a great opportunity for the church to do ministry. The church can also offer quality education for the children of boomers. In fact, education for their children is a consistent demand by boomers. They may not have deep Christian commitment themselves but they insist on good education for their children.

The best way to reach boomers theologically is through a journey theology.[7] Such a theology has the advantage, first of all, of stressing that faith is a lifelong process, not a finished product. A journey involves strange twists and surprises as well as difficulties and hardships. There is hope that the journey will end well. Journey is also a metaphor for growth, movement, and development. The growth is both internal and external. It involves introspection and the search for inner meaning. Many boomers are interested in personal story more than official creeds. Journey also involves a profound sense of the inter- and inner-connectedness of all things. The journey is a walk through a world that extends beyond individuals and involves them in a sense of the whole. The final aspect of journey theology is related to the mystical, therapeutic, and experimental character of the spirituality of baby boomers. They seek to combine the inner and the outer, the visible and the invisible worlds.

The motif of journey is a familiar one in biblical theology. The Ark of the Covenant was carried along with the people in the journey through the wilderness. In the exile the children of Israel knew what it was to be removed from their homeland and forced to live in a strange place. In the New Testament the notion of being aliens is assumed in several places—for example, Ephesians 2:17-22, Hebrews 11:13-16, and 1 Peter 1:17; 2:11. This theme in biblical theology can be highlighted in a journey theology that makes sense to baby boomers.

Busters. The baby boomers have been followed by the baby busters in the cultural left. Some researchers describe the generations in memorable, if somewhat contrived, terms as seniors (those born before 1925), builders (1925-44), boomers (1945-64), busters (1965-80), and blasters (1980-present [the boomlet caused by boomers having late babies]).[8] Busters are those born when birth rates declined due to contraception and abortion. They have also been called "Generation X" by Douglas Coupland in his 1991 novel, *Generation X: Tales for an Accelerated Culture* (New York: St. Martin's Press). Some historians have determined that it is the thirteenth generation born since the U.S. Constitution, so they are referred to as the "13th Gen."

Kevin Ford, a former campus minister for Intervarsity Fellowship and a buster himself, insists that busters differ from boomers in significant ways. The differences may seem overstated but they are true from his perspective. Boomers, he says, are aggressive and want to change the world. Busters do not want to change anything. Boomers have things and want more. Busters are more interested in integrity than possessions. Boomers have hope while busters have little or none. In the view of busters, boomers have messed up the world, especially families, and the busters have inherited the mess.

Forty-six percent of busters are children of divorce.[9] They feel abandoned. Therefore, busters do not view the world as user-friendly. They view the world through dark glasses and just want to get by. Busters feel the world is not simple. They are overloaded with information, decisions, and problems. The problems are too complex to solve so busters tend to feel alienated and withdraw from the world. The world of the busters has no rules. Busters were raised by boomer parents who set no limits, no rules. There are things busters value, says Ford, such as simplicity, clear action, tangible results, survival through self-sufficiency, boundaries, friendships, and relationships. They do not like authority, systems, talk with no action, or symbols as a substitute for substance.[10]

Generation X can be reached best in three ways. The first is through a faith that works.[11] Faith can't be just talk; it must also be a walk that demonstrates authentic Christian commitment. Busters look for actions that show what Christians are all about in meeting the needs of people for homes, food, jobs, money, health care. The second way to reach the Xers is through process evangelism. Process evangelism is very patient and understands that conversion takes place over a period of time. Such evangelism involves authenticity, caring, trust, and transparency (allowing others to see us as we are). The third way to reach Xers is through narrative theology and evangelism. Narrative evangelism focuses on story. It is the collision of stories—the person's and God's. There are several reasons why narrative evangelism is appropriate. Narrative evangelism is biblically authentic because the Bible is a story. It is theologically appropriate because God is the center. It is culturally appropriate because it speaks to Xers who have lost the sense of a "megastory" that gives coherence and meaning to life. It is effective in building relationships because it speaks to the heart of people as does every good story.[12]

Helpful Educational Strategies. There are several important educational strategies for reaching Xers. The church must deal with the issues and questions that are part of the lives of Xers. Leaders should avoid easy answers and simple solutions. Life for Xers is not simple. The issues are best dealt with in small groups that are centered on relationship building rather than intellectually focused. Groups can be formed around any number of issues and in many settings: shared interests, recovery from addiction or illness, home or church settings. The best approach is "chat-discuss" rather than lecture; that is, the issue is presented in terms of someone's life story and then discussed by the group. This allows a group to deal with the experiences of persons and gives them a chance to express their feelings about the issue.[13] The gatherings should be those of "wounded healers," people who share their own struggles and faith. The groups are flexibly structured to meet the heavy time demands on the lives of Xers. However, group leaders are to be held accountable to help group members deal with more than relationships. The same fundamental themes of lifelong learning apply here. Leaders need to find ways to help young adults learn, serve, and reach out.[14]

The Cultural Right

On the other end of the spectrum is the cultural right. They constitute the largest group in American culture. Those who are working with adults in this group cannot use the assumptions or approaches appropriate for the cultural left. The cultural right is made up of the lower middle class, the working class, and the poor. The lower middle class and hard-working blue-collar folks are called the respectables. They struggle hard to be loyal to standards of respectability and are the carriers of the ethic of self-denial. The greatest number of church members are from this group.

A second subgrouping in the cultural right are the hard living. These are the people who have done a lot of heavy drinking, experienced marital instability, and are politically alienated and distrustful of institutions. A third sub-group are the desperate poor. They are the 6 million Americans who barely survive because they are part of a poverty underclass or they have suffered misfortune that brings them below the poverty line. Females make up seventy-seven percent of this group, a testimony to the feminization of poverty.[15]

The religion of the cultural right is largely evangelical or fundamental. Evangelicals are those who are born again, believe in the literalness of Scripture, and witness to others in an attempt to bring them to Christ. Evangelicals represent about one-fifth of the U.S. population or some thirty-five million people. Fundamentalists are characterized by separation from the world, dispensational premillennialism (Christ will come and establish his reign on earth for a thousand years before the judgment and destruction of unbelievers), and biblical literalism. It is estimated they constitute about one-third of the evangelicals in the United States.[16] The *political* and *economic* beliefs of the cultural right are not, as many would believe, conservative and reactionary. The stronghold of U.S. political and economic conservatism is the upper-middle class, of whom we shall speak shortly. The cultural right is *socially* conservative because of their commitment to traditional values of family and community. It is not a conservatism committed to capitalism.

People of the cultural right hold to the traditional values of family, home, community, faith, and country. The family is the central focus because cultural-right people do not have careers or professions that claim their attention. They are wary of any position that threatens the stability of the family. The community is an extension of the family. It is where people go to school, find their friends, attend church, and visit their neighbors. The country is an extension of the neighborhood. It is valued as a place of stability that makes it possible for individuals, families, and communities to thrive. People of the cultural right hold to a conventional morality. It grows out of the condition of people who live with moderate or stringent financial constraint. Drastic change is seen as threatening to an already fragile existence. Too much individual autonomy upsets the system and threatens to tear the fabric of society.[17]

The religion of the cultural right is popular religion. It is a way of life that involves belief in a God who is highly providential and involved in the events of the world. Popular religion is communal in character and is expressed in church suppers, worship services, and pious associations. There is a focus on devotional activities, especially prayer. Popular religion meets the needs of people who feel powerless and have the need to belong and have a sense of security. The theology needed for ministry with the popular religion of the cultural right is folk theology.[18] Folk theology is centered in Scripture. Scripture is the basis for sermons, studies, programs, and community services. Folk theology deals with identity for a people for whom identity is important but hard to come by. It has a deep communal expression that is reflected in the democratic organization of congregations and programs. It is a theology that is orally expressed and best captured in story. People get a chance to tell their story or give their witness. The sermon is very important in an oral community. It is the center of the community's worship and life.

Helpful Educational Strategies. The educational implications of a folk theology include attention to Bible study; supplying settings in which people can give their witness and share their story; a focus on life's meaning and purpose for people who often feel powerless; and the use of traditional values as the beginning point for exploring how the world can be a better place for individuals, families, and communities. An approach to the cultural right involves the following.

> It is first of all a complex interplay of traditional values, conventional morality, popular religion, and folk theology. To speak their language requires a sensitive working within these frameworks that reflects the significant relationships and concrete circumstances of their lives. Their understanding of meaning begins in the closest relationships with respect to a given issue or circumstance and works the implications of that in terms of the constraints imposed by low to moderate financial resources and the relative power and powerlessness of the person or group in question.[19]

The teacher of persons within the cultural right can do no better than to know and be sensitive to where people are and begin from there.

The Cultural Middle

The third sociological group of adults in the United States is the cultural middle. It is upper-middle class economically and includes the successful, the strivers, and the conflicted. The successful are those who have it made in economic terms. The strivers are those who would like to make it. This subgroup includes many African Americans and Hispanics. The conflicted are those torn between career and family. Yet, all three of these subgroups focus on career and strive for success. Individualism is strong in this group. There is instrumental (action-oriented) individualism, which focuses on success and status. And there is expressive (feeling-oriented) individualism, which features emotions and a sense of satisfaction. There is tension between the two and yet there is an interrelationship. Success brings status and allows a satisfying lifestyle. The tension is also felt in a public-private dichotomy because a career must be carried out in public and yet it is in private life that fulfillment and satisfaction are most deeply expressed.

Mainline churches relate well to the cultural middle. Many such churches are characterized as "civil" churches—that is, churches that have a high proportion of their members from the cultural middle, express a great interest in social issues, and yet confine their interest to study and discussion rather than political action.[20] Such congregations engage in human services to people in need but most do not upset things politically. Part of the reason is the protection of privilege of the upper-middle class. Cultural-middle people are not interested in upsetting what is comfortable for them. That is why they tend to be politically and economically conservative.

A ministry with people of the cultural middle deals with the issues of stress, the struggle for dignity through achievement, the fear of failure and pressure on the family. Ministry in the cultural middle needs to challenge the dominant ethos of that culture and help people achieve a different religious worldview that moves beyond individualism to compassion and a concern for the common good. A helpful ministry to this group is through an explanatory theology. It is a theology that attempts a critical and rational account of the faith and makes use of secular disciplines that provide important information. It is a theology that appeals to educated people as it tries to redefine the world and the place and mission of God's people in it.

> An explanatory theology that can counter the individualistic, privatistic, controversy-avoidance of cultural-middle lifestyles will be one that offers a more comprehensive account of personal and social issues and one that sets before the churches a vision more compelling than protection of privilege and shifts the ground on which the cross-pressures of business and professional life are usually adjudicated.[21]

The central focus of explanatory theology is a gospel of grace. It is the most powerful antidote for a competitive, achievement-oriented culture. The necessity of the powerful message of the gospel of God's grace in Jesus Christ is set forth in chapter 1 of this book.

Helpful Educational Strategies. Educational ministry for the cultural middle is a ministry that involves study at an intellectual level suitable to educated people. It makes use of information from the Bible, theology, and the secular disciplines. It focuses on a gospel that tells people they are accepted by God's grace in Jesus Christ and yet called to discipleship in the world, a world desperately in need of their ministry as God's agents for change. The result of such educational ministry can be a change of perspective on the self, the family, and the culture in the light of God's intention for the world.

Studies of Lutherans indicate that they struggle with many of the issues of the cultural middle. The research published in the 1972 book, *A Study of Generations*, showed that forty percent of Lutherans have a law orientation that involves salvation by works.[22] The more recent research published in *Effective Christian Education: A National Study of Protestant Congregations* shows that sixty-one percent of Lutherans have difficulty accepting salvation as a gift.[23] The challenge for Lutheran educators is immense. The research shows that only twenty-four percent of Lutherans have an integrated faith—in other words, faith that integrates the vertical relation to God and the horizontal relation to human beings. Integrated faith accepts grace as a gift. Thirteen percent of Lutherans have a vertical faith that accepts grace as a gift but lacks a relation to others. Seventeen percent have a horizontal faith and forty-seven percent have an undeveloped faith that lacks either a strong vertical or horizontal dimension. In both horizontal and undeveloped faith, grace is not accepted as a gift. There are similar findings for the other mainline churches involved in the study: the Christian Church (Disciples of Christ), Presbyterian Church (U.S.A.), United Church of Christ, and United Methodist Church.

The goal of Christian education is an integrated faith, and the research shows that the most important tool for achieving it is an effective program of Christian education that includes weekly classes for people of all ages, Bible studies, adult forums, family events, music and drama programs, new member classes, youth groups, and much more.[24] The challenge to educators is to take seriously the cultural place of the people in their congregations, determine which educational strategy works best in that setting, and put in place an effective educational program that helps people deal with their lives and their world in the light of God's intention.

This chart summarizes the cultural characteristics of the three groups and some theological approaches and educational strategies for working with them in adult education.

The Three Cultural Groups

	Left		Middle	Right
	Boomers	*Busters*		
Culture	Individualism	Alienated	Individualism	Conservative
	Self-fulfillment	Frustrated	Success-oriented	Value family
	Optimistic	Pessimistic	Political status quo	Stability
Theology	Journey	Narrative	Explanatory	Folk
	Lifelong journey of faith	God's mega-story for life	God's grace and relation to self and society	Scripture
				Worth
				Virtue
Education	Relational groups	Groups that focus on issues of "wounded" people	Intellectual exploration of the Bible, theology, disciplines	Bible study
	Personal and social issues			Witness
	Children's education		Social change	Social group
				Prayer

ADULT DEVELOPMENT
AND LEARNING STYLES

Having looked at adults in groups we now move to descriptions of adults as individuals. Adults develop over a period of time and in each phase of life they face crucial issues and find ways of dealing with them. The way in which adults deal with life at every stage is affected by personality type.

This section presents four personality types and their ways of learning followed by a discussion of three stages of adult development: young adulthood, middle adulthood, and late adulthood. The study of the emotional development of persons and the issues they face began with the pioneering work of Erik Erikson and continued with the work of others like Gail Sheehy and Daniel Levinson. The study of the mental development of persons began with the work of Jean Piaget and continued with the work of Lawrence Kohlberg in moral development and James Fowler in "faith" development. Information from all of these sources is used in the following descriptions.

PERSONALITY AND LEARNING

Personality type influences the way in which people learn and develop. In their book, *Please Understand Me*, David Keirsey and Marilyn Bates describe the learning styles of four personality types.[25] The first of these is the sensible/playful person. These persons need physical involvement in learning. They learn best through hands-on experience and activity. They learn from media presentations and other ways of visual and physical learning. It is very difficult for them to learn from written work or logical lectures. A teacher needs to involve these people in meaningful activities and help them reflect on the meaning of their experience. Sensible/playful persons don't usually stick with formal education beyond what is required. It is a real challenge for teachers in the church to keep such persons interested and involved in Christian education so that they don't become drop-outs.

The second type is the sensible/judicious person. These persons learn very well in classes and organized groups. They like and need structure and do best when lessons are presented sequentially and in increments that make sense. They are the people most likely to be in adult sessions that are structured for formal learning. There are many persons like this in congregations. They are also the ones who are most likely attracted to the stimulating biblical and theological studies found in lay schools of theology.

The third type is the intuitive/thinking person. This is the independent scholar. Intuitive thinkers have a hunger for knowing. They tend to be independent learners who track down information on their own. They prefer logical presentation of materials and will follow through on reading more about the subject. They tend to be loners who enjoy learning on their own. Teachers in the congregation can help these persons best by carefully presenting information and giving suggestions for further reading or by engaging them in an independent or guided study apart from class. They then can be called on to share the fruit of their study with the larger group.

The intuitive/feeling person is the fourth personality type. These persons enjoy interaction. They learn best in relation to others through discussion, role-playing, drama, and fiction. They prefer to focus on people rather than abstract subjects. Teachers can provide these persons with lots of interactive learning opportunities using teaching strategies in which people learn in groups—the "lots of talk" method.

It isn't possible to use educational strategies that appeal to all four personality types in any one learning situation. But, over a period of time, teachers need to make an effort to offer a variety of approaches that engage all four types of learners in effective Christian education. This chart summarizes the four personality types of adult learners.

Four Personality Types of Adult Learners

Types	Learning Style	Educational Method
Sensible/ Playful	Physical involvement Hands-on learning Informal setting	On-site physical activity Reflect on action
Sensible/ Judicious	Sequential structure Logical presentation Formal setting	Teacher presentation Well-organized lecture Classes in church
Intuitive/ Thinking	Individual learner Seeks own information Logical thought	Organized presentation Independent research Extra resources
Intuitive/ Feeling	Learns from others Learns by expressing ideas	Group interaction Discussion Small groups

LIFE STAGES AND LEARNING

Before presenting the three adult life stages and the emotional and mental characteristics of the development in each, it is helpful to deal with criticisms of both moral and faith development. Lawrence Kohlberg, the pioneer in studies of moral development, used males as his subjects.[26] Carol Gilligan noted that women had a different basis for making moral decisions. Women paid more attention to how other people were affected by a moral decision than by principles of justice and equality. Her research determined that women are governed by an ethic of care while men are governed by an ethic of justice. Gilligan says:

> While an ethic of justice proceeds from the premise of equality—that everyone should be treated the same—an ethic of care rests on the premise of nonviolence—that no one should be hurt. In the representation of maturity, both perspectives converge in the realization that just as inequality adversely affects both parties in an unequal relationship, so too violence is destructive for everyone involved. This dialogue between fairness and care not only provides a better understanding of relations between the sexes but also gives rise to a more comprehensive portrayal of adult work and family relationships.[27]

When considering the discussion of moral thinking at each life stage, teachers should temper it with the knowledge that women will more likely make decisions based on their concern for the welfare of others while men will more likely base their decisions on principles of justice and equality.

There are also criticisms of James Fowler's use of the term "faith" development.[28] There are many persons who feel that Fowler is not so much describing faith—that is, the way of *relating* to God—as he is describing ways of *thinking* about God. Many Christians define faith as that relation to God in which God's free grace and salvation is given without regard to worth or the ability to fully understand. Karl Ernst Nipkow points out the difference between faith as relation to God and faith as comprehension of God.

> If, on the one hand, God is acknowledged as the one and true sovereign in his work of redemption and liberation, he does not need higher stages of development on the side of human beings in order to give what he wants to give as *his* new life for us. Here is full *completion*. If, on the other hand, the perspective of *our*

grasping, comprehending, and construing the meaning of what he alone can do, has done, and will be doing, is taken into account, it makes good sense to speak of "faith" as something that can change and develop—although, in my opinion, it will always remain *incomplete.*[29]

Because *faith* most accurately describes a saving relation to God and *belief* best describes a way of thinking about God, *belief* development is the term used in the following descriptions of life stages. In each of the following life stages, emotional development is presented first, followed by mental development in terms of moral thinking and beliefs about God.

Young Adulthood. The first phase of young adulthood is what Gail Sheehy has called the "trying twenties," the time when persons try to find their place in the world.[30] This is a time of emotional development when Erik Erikson says young persons wrestle with the issue of intimacy versus isolation. If persons at this age have resolved the identity crisis of an earlier age, they are sufficiently secure in their own identity to forge close relationships in which they are willing to keep commitments without fear of losing their sense of self. This is related to one of the tasks of early adulthood, that of finding a loving relationship.

Daniel Levinson describes four tasks of early adulthood: forming a dream, gaining an occupation, finding a mentor relationship, and deciding on love, marriage, and family.[31] The first of these tasks, forming a dream, implies that each person needs a vision of their place in the world as well as a sense of fulfillment of that vision. Though Levinson's study focussed on men, Sharon Parks agrees that women also need a dream.[32] One of the most public dreams was that of Martin Luther King Jr., in his famous "I Have a Dream" speech. King never lived to see if his dream could be fulfilled. Christian adults struggle with the fulfillment of their own dreams. The issue for them might be, "I had a dream but it has never been fulfilled." Perhaps some have had their dream drastically altered.

James, John, and Paul had their dreams altered. James and John wanted right and left hand positions of honor but Jesus set them straight when he said in Matthew 20:26-28 that they were dreaming the dream of lords and not of servants: "Whoever wishes to become great among you must be your servant and whoever wishes to be first among you must be your slave; just as the Son of Man came not to be served but to serve, and to give his life as a ransom for many."

In the first chapter of Galatians, Paul tells his readers that he had violently persecuted the church of God and had tried to destroy it. But God called him to an entirely different vision of his place in the world. The experience of being called was dramatic (see Acts 9) but the full effect of that call was realized only after three years of thought and prayer and solitude. Then he was ready to begin life anew. The Christians' dream is their "calling." The writer to the Ephesians says, "I, therefore, the prisoner in the Lord, beg you to lead a life worthy of the calling to which you have been called" (4:1). The Christian's calling is to live life as God wills it to be lived. A dream consistent with the call of God can be pursued with energy. Paul puts it in terms of a race: "Run in such a way that you may win it" (1 Corinthians 9:24). We can help adults share how they have pursued their callings, no matter how their dreams have been altered.

The second task for young adults is gaining an occupation. An occupation is the place where the dream can be partially fulfilled. However, the dream is always larger than an occupation. Adults may feel that an issue for them is that their occupation has not helped them fulfill their dream. They can consider their options: change their occupation or change their attitude toward their occupation. Paul, in 1 Corinthians 7:17, says that Christians ought to lead the life that the Lord has assigned, to which God called them. We can help adults explore how they can use their occupations to carry out their calling by God. Or, if their occupation does not allow them to carry out their calling, how they can find other situations in which it is possible to do so. This theme of Christian vocation is a critical one in lifelong learning at this stage. Chapter 7 pursues the subject of making connections between faith and one's daily life.

Finding a mentor relationship is the third task of young adulthood. A mentor is someone who helps a young person attain certain goals and then moves on. A model is different from a mentor in that a model is someone to be imitated while a mentor is a helper. Some people have had helpful mentors and others have had to find their own way. Not finding a mentor can be a point of struggle for some young adults. For those who had a mentor and for those who lacked one, Paul's mentoring of Timothy is instructive. In 1 Timothy 4:6-15, he speaks to Timothy about the way Timothy should teach and live. Adult Christians can share the ways in which they have been mentored or have served as mentors.

The fourth task of young adulthood is deciding on love, marriage, and family. For some, marriage and family are the fulfillment of their dream. For others, occupation is the fulfillment of the dream. Whatever the dream, men and women in a marital relationship need to help each other fulfill their dreams. And those who are unmarried also need the relationship of a supportive person or persons who will help them realize their dreams. An issue for young adults could be: I know people need help in reaching their goals but I am reluctant to help someone else attain their goals. Within marriage husbands and wives are to help each other out of reverence for Christ (Ephesians 5:21) and in all relationships Christians are to recognize and value the gifts of others and their contributions to the common good (1 Corinthians 12:4-26).

The second phase of young adulthood is what Sheehy calls "catch thirty." [33] It has its own issues in emotional development. The primary one is the struggle to maintain stability in life while looking for new directions and relationships.

David Levinson says:

> To some degree everyone asks: What do I want from life? What do I give to, and receive from, my marriage, my family, my friends, work, leisure—every aspect of life that has significance for me? What do I need to change in myself, and in my situation, so that I can have a better life according to my values? What are my values? What is most important to me? [34]

We can help Christian adults share how they struggle or have struggled with the issue of keeping life together while seeking new directions. It is instructive to see the struggle of Jesus at age thirty as he faced temptations in the wilderness (Matthew 3:13-4:11 and parallel passages in the other Gospels). Adults can be invited to share how the struggle of Jesus informs the struggle of Christians.

We now turn to the *mental* development of young adults, which involves a transition, first of all, in the way in which *moral* judgments are made. Lawrence Kohlberg says that young people are usually in a conventional mode of thinking about moral choices—that is, they make choices governed by the people around them. The first phase of conventional thinking is restricted to the influence of peers. Adolescents are very aware of what other teens think about them and they do what pleases their friends. The second level of conventional thinking usually occurs in the twenties when the circle of influence expands to the larger society. Then young people pay attention to what society expects of them. Kohlberg calls this a "law and order" orientation. The law is the law and should not be broken. Persons do their duty and show respect for authority so that the social order can be maintained.[35] This is the point where many adults remain for a lifetime.

An educational strategy for helping persons examine their way of making moral choices is the moral dilemma. For example, use news stories involving assisted suicide and the moral dilemma involved in such an act. Present the story and ask them to write down whether the act was right or wrong. Writing the answer keeps people from being influenced by others before they have a chance to think it through themselves. In addition to whether assisted suicide is right or wrong, ask the reasons for the answer. Ask, "What are the Christian principles that play a part in your decision?" A person with a law and order orientation will usually say that assisted suicide is always wrong. A person who thinks in terms of the importance of the quality of life will usually say assisted suicide is okay. In both instances, probe to discover how the person's Christian faith relates to the decision. The ensuing group discussion lets persons hear other points of view that may help them reexamine their own. Moral development theory says that persons can only comprehend moral reasoning one level below or above their own but they will be attracted to the level above them.[37] Moral dilemmas help Christian adults think about their way of making moral decisions.

The challenge of dealing with moral dilemmas may help young adults to move to the next stage of moral thought. It is a stage that goes beyond conventional thinking to that of principled thinking—that is, moral decisions based on consciously chosen moral principles. Right moral action is defined in terms of individual rights within the standards of the society as a whole. There is a balance between what is good for individuals and what is good for society. Kohlberg refers to this as a social-contract way of thinking. Law is important but it does not override individual rights. It can be changed if it is seen to be harmful to persons. The law is not held as rigidly as in the law-and-order stage. Kohlberg says this is the level of moral thinking embedded in the U.S. Constitution, the official morality of the American government.[34]

Young adults also experience transitions in the way they think about God. Adolescents usually think about God in terms of the teachings they have learned in the family and in the church. James Fowler calls it a "synthetic-conventional" belief, one in which persons believe what they have been taught to believe. That belief stage is succeeded in the late teens and twenties by one in which persons compose their own belief system in contrast to that of others. Fowler calls it an "individuative-reflective" belief.[38] It is an age when young persons take

responsibility for their own commitments, lifestyles, beliefs, and attitudes. This causes tensions between their personal convictions and the
teachings of the group. So they construct their own set of beliefs, which
can be narrow in scope and involve rejection of a number of previously
held beliefs. The strength of this stage is the capacity for critical reflection on the self and one's outlook. The weakness of this stage is exces-
sive confidence in critical thought and a rejection of all other points of
view. Since there is the ability to think critically at this stage, persons
should be faced with life's issues, such as the questions raised by the four
tasks of young adulthood and how they can be dealt with in the light of
the Christian faith. They can be given challenging books to read and
asked to respond to them. They can be faced with moral dilemmas and
asked to resolve them in terms of their Christian principles. In these
and many other ways we can provide a setting for young adults to grow
spiritually.

In the thirties, young adults may move to a different stage of belief
development. It is a stage that comes after a lot of living and setbacks.
Life is no longer seen in sharply divided segments. It is viewed as
ambiguous and paradoxical. Fowler calls this the "conjunctive" stage—
the bringing together of opposing elements.[39] Earlier he called it the
"paradoxical-consolidative" stage, a term that is perhaps more descrip-
tive of the way of thinking at this level. Opposites are held together in
a creative tension that does not eliminate either side of the paradox.
The strength of this stage is the capacity to see the polarities of life and
to hold them together in creative tension. The danger of this stage is that
the struggle with paradox may lead to paralysis of thought and action.

Conjunctive thought is reflected in the nuclear crises of Erik
Erikson: the intimacy/isolation of young adulthood, the generativity/
stagnation of middle adulthood, and the integrity/despair of older
adulthood. Erikson holds both sides of the polarity together in a
creative tension. It is also the way of thinking about God implicit in
Lutheran theology, a theology that came out of the struggles of Luther.
Luther hoped to find a gracious God but all he found was a judging
one. He had been taught that he had to obey the will of God before
God would be gracious. Then, when he had attained a certain level
of righteousness, God would give him the full benefits of the gospel.
But Luther found that all he could do was sin. He could not obey the
will of God. He struggled with that issue until he gave up trying to
solve it rationally. Then the resolution of the struggle came to him
as a gift. It was the insight that the righteousness that God *demanded*
was the righteousness of Christ that God *gave*. Faith accepted God's
gift of grace in Jesus Christ offered in the gospel. It was grace, not works.

Out of his struggles, Luther came to understand God as the paradoxical one who does the alien work of judgment in order to do the proper work of salvation, as one who is hidden in wrath but revealed in grace, and as one who condemns through the law but saves through the gospel. Humans are paradoxical beings who are sinners by nature and saints through the Spirit, slaves to sin and yet free from it, active in trying to please God and yet passive when it comes to that which God freely gives. Both sides of the paradoxical nature of God and humans remain throughout life but faith makes it possible to live with paradox because it grasps the grace of God in Christ in the gospel.[40]

Middle Adulthood. Middle adulthood brings people to a reassessment of the tasks of young adulthood and the struggle of dealing with the polarities of midlife. The struggle is more true of middle and upper class persons who have many options than of other persons who have little or no chance for change. The dream of young adulthood needs reexamination and alteration. Midlife brings the realization that many things included in the dream are not going to be realized. One can either alter the dream or hold to it with great tenacity and carry it out at extreme cost. One's occupation can also be re-assessed and tested as to whether it has allowed at least a partial fulfillment of the dream. Midlife is a time when many adults change their occupations. Relationships are reviewed and renewed. Sometimes they are disrupted, especially when people choose to leave spouses and children in search of greater fulfillment. Midlife is the time to become a mentor. People who view younger persons as competitors will not become mentors. They are threatened by the coming generation. Erikson says this is a time of generativity or stagnation. Those who care for the younger generation will generate new ideas and energies while those who are threatened by them or ignore them will stagnate.

Daniel Levinson says there are four polarities to be dealt with in midlife: young/old, destruction/creation, masculine/feminine, attachment/separateness.[41] The major polarity is that of young versus old because midlife is the time when adults realize their mortality and have to face the fact that they will die. The tension can be expressed in the following way: I know I will die but I want to feel and act young. This tension increases when personal illness or the death of parents brings the threat of death to the forefront. Mortality brings with it a sense of limitation, the understanding that many things are no longer possible and the legacy one hoped to leave is less grand than that envisioned in the original dream. For some, there is a sense of desperation, a wish to turn back the clock and recapture parts of the dream. Desperate people do desperate things. They desert families and change spouses. They buy adult toys to make them feel young again. They do all these things, that is, unless they can come to terms with growing old and confronting death, integrating youth and aging, possibility and limitation. Integrating life and death is helped by Martha's conversation with Jesus in John 11. Lazarus has died. Jesus assures Martha that Lazarus will rise again. Martha says she knows that he will rise again in the resurrection of the last day. Jesus says to her, "I am the resurrection and the life. Those who believe in me, even though they die, will live, and everyone who lives and believes in me will never die" (11:25-26). Though there is the threat of death in the midst of life, there is also the promise of life in the midst of death. Christians in midlife can come through it with a more integrated and hopeful view of life.

The second polarity of midlife is destruction versus creation. It is somewhat related to Erikson's generativity versus stagnation in which persons either care for the coming generation or they stagnate in caring only for themselves. Levinson says that middle adulthood is the time for persons to realize that they have been both helpful and hurtful. They have been both creative and destructive. Those who are parents can readily understand this conflict. They have treated their children well in many instances but badly in others. The issue can be stated as: I want to be helpful and creative but I realize that I can also be harmful and destructive. Paul, in Romans 7:14-25, states how he struggled with this tension: "For I do not do what I want, but I do the very thing I hate. . . . For I do not do the good I want, but the evil I do not want is what I do. . . . Who will rescue me from this body of death? Thanks be to God through Jesus Christ our Lord." It is through the forgiveness and power of Jesus Christ that Christians can deal and live with this polarity.

The polarity of masculine versus feminine is the third tension. Levinson notes that "gender splitting" has four basic forms in our society: (1) The splitting of the domestic sphere and the public sphere as social domains for women and men; (2) The Traditional Marriage Enterprise and the split it creates between the female homemaker and the male provisioner; (3) The splitting of "women's work" and "men's work"; (4) The splitting of feminine and masculine in the individual psyche. (Daniel Levenson. *The Seasons of a Woman's Life.* (New York: Alfred A. Knopf, 1996). In middle adulthood, people realize that that which has been split should now be united. Males need to integrate their feminine side and females need to integrate their masculine side. How can the two be brought together?

Two Bible passages offer insight. the first is 1 Corinthians 13:4-7, where Paul speaks of the qualities of love: "Love is patient and kind; love is not envious or boastful or arrogant or rude. It does not insist on its own way; it is not irritable or resentful; it does not rejoice in wrong-doing, but rejoices in the truth. It bears all things, believes all things, hopes all things, endures all things." Is this the masculine Paul speaking of the need to be more caring in Christ? The other is 1 Corinthians 16:13-14, where caring and assertiveness are brought together: "Keep alert, stand firm in your faith, be courageous, be strong. Let all that you do be done in love."

Attachment versus separateness is the fourth polarity described by Levinson. Younger people need to be with others in order to be affirmed and supported. Older people need to learn to be alone, to be satisfied with themselves and find ways to be refreshed in solitude. The movement is from the outside to the inside, from being focused "out there" to being centered "in here." The tension is: I want to be active and related to others but I also need to be alone and let my spirit be refreshed. Jesus experienced the need to remove himself and his disciples from the crowd so that they could be alone. In Mark 6:31-32, he said, "Come away to a deserted place all by yourselves and rest awhile." The passage goes on to say, "For many were coming and going, and they had no leisure even to eat. And they went away in the boat to a deserted place by themselves." Later, in verses 45-46, after feeding the five thousand, he sent the disciples by boat to Bethsaida, dismissed the crowd, and went up alone on the mountain to pray.

The kind of moral thought that may have begun in the thirties is continued in the midlife forties and beyond. Kohlberg's postconventional social contract stage previously mentioned means that midlife adults recognize and bring together the good of individuals and the good of society. They recognize the importance of integrating the two and finding a balance. The conjunctive mode of thinking about God is also continued into and beyond midlife. It is obvious that Christian adults need to think about God and life in terms of the polarities and dialectics of human existence. We can be of great help to adults when we devise ways in which the issues implicit in social and personal life are raised to consciousness and the grace of the gospel is brought to bear on them.

Late Adulthood. Late adulthood brings its own issues. People in their sixties and beyond must deal with the tensions that arise from changing roles versus lifelong interests, aging bodies versus interesting activities, and a sense of integrity about life versus a feeling of despair. The first of these issues involves the struggle to find a balance between giving up many lifelong roles and accepting new roles and situations. The responsibilities of middle adulthood need to be relinquished. If the self has been defined only in terms of those roles, the task is very difficult. There is change in occupational roles, marital roles (sometimes) and living arrangements. The issue involves having to give up many responsibilities and still feel useful and worthwhile. Evelyn and James Whitehead speak of celebrating *uselessness*—in other words, in the Christian community one's worth does not depend on job or social status.[42] One does not have to *do* anything to belong to the Christian community. The words of 1 Peter 1:3-5 are encouraging:

> Blessed be the God and Father of our Lord Jesus Christ! By his great mercy he has given us a new birth into a living hope through the resurrection of Christ from the dead, and into an inheritance that is imperishable, undefiled, and unfading, kept in heaven for you, who are being protected by the power of God through faith for a salvation ready to be revealed in the last time.

Aged Christians need help in understanding that they are valued by God and other Christians even if they cannot do what they used to do. The second polarity of late adulthood is aging body versus interesting activities. As people age their bodies begin to limit them. They cannot do what they could do when they were younger. Some people suffer a great deal of pain, while others have only minor aches. Some people transcend their pain and limitations, while others are overwhelmed by them. They can only complain. They do not know how to resolve the issue of wanting to do interesting things while being limited by their aging bodies. Paul, in 2 Corinthians 12, speaks of the limitations he suffered and how he was helped to transcend them. He tells of a person in Christ who was caught up in an unspeakable vision of God. That person undoubtedly was Paul because he went on to say that in order to keep him from being too elated, God sent a thorn in the flesh. He asked three times to be relieved of it but the Lord said, "My grace is sufficient for you, for power is made perfect in weakness" (2 Corinthians 12:9). So Paul was content with his weaknesses so that the power of Christ might dwell in him. In his weakness he found strength. It is a helpful word for Christians who must deal with their "thorn in the flesh."

The final polarity is that suggested by Erik Erikson: integrity versus despair. Some people regret what they have done with their lives and wish they could start all over again. Others find that a review of their lives, even though faulty, leaves them feeling content with what happened. For most, life is a mixture of good and bad. They struggle with the tension of wanting to think their lives have been worthwhile even when they know some of it has been a waste. Paul, near the end of his life, reflected on what his life meant and the legacy he was leaving. In Philippians 3:4-16 he recounts his accomplishments as an upright and zealous Israelite. But he counts it all as loss because of Christ. He speaks of reaching for the goal of Jesus Christ and his willingness to press on until it is attained. In Philippians 4:8-9, he gives his benediction:

> Finally, beloved, whatever is true, whatever is honorable, whatever is just, whatever is pure, whatever is pleasing,whatever is commendable, if there is any excellence and if there is anything worthy of praise, think about these things. Keep on doing the things that you have learned and received and heard and seen in me, and the God of peace will be with you.

We can help older Christians review their lives through the recounting of their stories and seeing how God has been present with them. Then they can see their lives as more than just one thing after another. They can see their lives as a journey with God. We can encourage older adults to tell their stories in writing or on audio or video tape so that they can share their legacy with others.

Moral thinking can reach the "universal ethical" stage late in life. It is the stage in which what is right is defined in terms of self-chosen ethical principles of justice and equality of human rights for every individual.[43] The person who reaches this stage is unmindful of individual cost but seeks the unqualified good of others. Only a few persons reach this stage. The same is true of the final stage of belief development, that of "universalizing" belief as Fowler calls it. Only a few adults may reach the stage in which they become so immersed in seeking love and justice that they are lost in spending and being spent for the transformation of human existence.[44] No teacher can guarantee that Christians will reach any stage of development. It is the work of the Holy Spirit.

Life Stages and Learning

	Young Adults	Middle-Age Adults	Older Adults
Emotional Issues	The dream Occupation Mentor Loving relationship	Reassess earlier tasks Polarities of mid-age Young-old Destruction/creation Masculine/feminine Attachment/separateness	Changing roles/lifelong interests Aging bodies/interesting action Integrity/despair
Moral Thought	Conventional (what society expects)	Post-conventional (principled though seeking good of person within society)	Universal ethic (seeks the good of others)
Religious Belief	Individuative/reflective (personal belief system)	Conjunctive belief (life as paradox)	Universalizing belief (love that seeks good of other at cost of self)

REACHING ALL ADULTS

The descriptions in this chapter from sociologists about the way in which society has shaped different groups of people are important to consider in planning programs of lifelong learning because of the variety of adults our church serves in a variety of settings. To use inappropriate educational strategies with the people among whom we work is to risk frustration and anger. It is also important to know how people grow and develop in their individual intellectual and emotional life. God's people move through life's stages facing difficult situations and decisions. How can they be helped to put their Christian faith to work in those situations? How can they hear and receive gospel foundations of lifelong learning? The descriptions of life's stages and the suggestions for dealing with life's issues in a Christian manner are only beginning points for teachers. Their attention to and love for the people they teach will be used by the Spirit for the nurture and strengthening of God's people wherever they live and work and worship.

chapter three

Principles of Adult Learning

Kent L. Johnson
Nelson T. Strobert

Adult Christian education is an important concern for clergy, directors of Christian education, and volunteer leaders, as well as for adult learners themselves. Too often adult education opportunities are a process of trial and error, making the quick fix, or doing it the way it has always been done. These approaches can be frustrating and aggravating, giving limited, if any, satisfaction for the planners and participants in this area of the church's ministry. While such strategies may work from time to time, a purposeful and basic understanding of adult education practice will form a foundation for all who work with adults—those who are lifelong Christians and those who are new in the Christian community. This chapter introduces additional underpinnings for solid adult Christian education in the congregation: theory, formal and informal learning, motivation, and learning styles.

THEORY OF ADULT LEARNING

For quality Christian education to take place, there is a need for some common understandings about the adult learner. Such understandings or theory, while they cannot guarantee success of educational programs, can assist planners and teachers in considering adult education seriously and developing clear objectives for what is done.

The Starting Point

As the end of the twentieth-century approaches, we in the church continue to be challenged to strengthen adult Christian education in congregations. Recent research has indicated that only one-third of adults in our parishes participate in adult education.[1] Part of the challenge emerges from the general perception by many adults that Christian education is designed and intended for toddlers, children, and youth. Also, many contemporary adults have not been nurtured in the educational ministry tradition of the church during their childhood or adolescent years and are, therefore, limited in the knowledge of possibilities for adult learning within the church. Examples of these perceptions were expressed in a recent forum on a computer network as people posted their comments about adult Christian education:

"Pastor, I don't do Christian education."

"Teachers see no real need of participating in classes."

"The church is way off target in what it offers."

"People have become too comfortable sending their children to Sunday school."

While poor participation in adult education may be a source of discomfort for leaders in the church, adult education is flourishing in other areas of the society. One only has to look at the popularity of elderhostels, community college classes, or the abundance of learning-vacation tours.

The perception of Christian education as a program exclusively for children and youth certainly is not supported by many religious educators or faith communities.[2] Christian education is a lifelong activity that is essential to living as a baptized member of the Christian community. We are challenged, therefore, to take adult Christians seriously as thinking and reflective people of God. This means that we must see educational ministry as an integral component throughout the human life cycle. It also means that we must look beyond the images of childhood learning settings in order to take into account the unique elements of the adult years. Exploring the art and science of helping adults learn—*andragogy*—can help leaders and planners move beyond past images of adult Christian education.[3]

Background

For more than twenty-five years, Malcolm Knowles's name has been synonymous with the study of the art and science of teaching adult learners, *andragogy*. His seminal work in the field, *The Modern Practice of Adult Education*, posits a sharp distinction between teaching children and teaching adults. Since the publication of that work, there has been much discussion and development of andragogy, as well as challenges to it, by specialists, practitioners, and Knowles himself.[4] Given this, the concepts of andragogy continue to challenge adult education leaders, calling us to take seriously the adults we serve.

Who Is an Adult? Precisely, what do we mean by *adult* or *adulthood*? Leon McKenzie highlights several definitions:

- *Economic.* A person who is financially self-supporting.
- *Legal.* Someone who has reached the age designated by a governmental body.
- *Societal.* A person who has reached this status through cultural advancement. In some societies, teenage males and females are taught customs of the community with special rituals, and upon completion the young person is considered an adult.
- *Biological.* A person who is physiologically mature—able to have children.
- *Psychological.* A person who has reached post-adolescence and has begun to experience certain characteristic passages in life.
- *Educational.* Someone who has completed a certain amount of schooling designated by his or her society and culture.[5]

The definition of adult is not as clear-cut as one might think. It is difficult to say at what designated point in life a person becomes adult. Each of the above descriptions has limitations. When we reflect on the above descriptions, we are reminded that there are people we define as chronologically adult, but who cannot support themselves. This might be due to unemployment, physical and mental illness, or old age. When we reflect on the biological definition of adulthood, we know that there are high rates of pregnancies among the youth population—children bearing children. We are left to say that to be an adult is to be a part of the human life span. McKenzie points out that we can only differentiate the stages in broad terms.[6] Due to the various aspects of this long period in the life cycle, and the various elements that are part of these passages, one can assert that adulthood is the differentiation of experiences; it is a complex integration of the above characteristics.

What Is Christian Education? How do we define *Christian education*? A. Roger Gobbel asserts that Christian education is an activity of interpretation. More precisely, it is the "work of engaging Christians in an ongoing hermeneutical or interpretive task. As such, it necessarily includes instruction in the contents of the faith, but moves beyond that boundary. It strives to assist and to challenge Christians to interpret their lives and the world with its things, events, and people under the life, death, and resurrection of Jesus."[7] This definition is significant because it does not limit adult Christian education to any particular age group, but is explicit in making this a part of the continuing educational process in the church. As such, Gobbel affirms that Christian education is a lifelong activity within the Christian community.

Adult Christian education engages persons in reflecting, thinking, and interpreting the experiences in their lives. Adults' educational experiences must be sensitive to and reflective of their educational needs. Again, that means considering seriously the needs of each individual.

What Is Theory? What do we mean by *theory*? The very word produces a number of responses. Theories about adult learners can assist us in formulating objectives, planning educational experiences that are consistent with the objectives, providing a basis for using various methods, and providing criteria by which the results of the educational efforts can be measured.[8] A theory is evaluated on its power to predict behaviors or performances. Leon McKenzie states, "Prediction in education is not an exact science but it is certainly better than just emotive decisions." He adds, "The educational researcher is able to forecast the probability that one event is associated with another given certain conditions."[9] Using educational methods that are informed by the theory of adult learning will assist church educators in creating effective programs of adult education, as the theory gives them a frame of reference from which to work.

Historical Development of Adult Learning Theory

The Dutch adult educator, Ger van Enckevkort, has made an exhaustive study of the origins and use of the term *andragogy*. The term was first used in 1833 in an article by Alexander Kapp, a German elementary school teacher, to describe the theory of education of Plato, although Plato never used the term. Enckevkort observed that the word was used again in 1921 by the German social scientist Eugen Rosenstock, who indicated that the field of adult education necessitated special teachers, methods, and philosophy. Although the term was used in several other public occasions after this event, it was not widely recognized.

The word *andragogy* was used again in 1951 by the Swiss psychiatrist, Heinrich Hanselmann, in his book *Andragogy: Nature, Possibilities and Boundaries of Adult Education*. In the same year, another work in the area of adult education was written by Franz Poggeler, a German teacher, entitled *Introduction to Andragogy: Basic Issues in Adult Education*. Consequently, the term became utilized in other than German-speaking countries.[10]

Although many want to credit Knowles with inventing the term *andragogy*, this is not the case. It can be stated that Knowles was the first to introduce and popularize the term in the United States. In 1968, he published "Andragogy not Pedagogy" in *Educational Leadership* after being introduced to the term the previous year at a series of lectures by Dusan Savicevic.[11] In 1981, the word *andragogy* appeared in the addenda of *Webster's Third New International Dictionary* and thus became part of the official English language.[12]

Knowles acknowledges that the field of adult education has needed some adhesive to combine the various components of this level of education. With the differentiation of experiences among adults, andragogy may be able to be the unifying theme and theory.

Children and Adults: Pedagogy and Andragogy

Knowles asserts that much of what we experience throughout our formal educational years has to do with *pedagogy*, the art and science of teaching children. The roots of this term come from the Greek *paid*, which means "child," and *agagos*, which means "leading." Along with the term, Knowles notes that pedagogy implies that teachers are the transmitters of knowledge or information.[13] As such, teachers are feeding or giving information to students. The students, in turn, are the receivers or receptacles of information. In pedagogy, responsibility for learning is with the teacher. He or she makes the critical educational decisions for the students.[14]

Pedagogy carries certain assumptions that distinguish it from adult learning. Knowles describes these assumptions of pedagogy:

• *The child is a dependent being.* The child is dependent on other people for his or her subsistence or survival. This dependency is part of life at home, at play, in church, within the community, and at school. Adults have the deciding voice in the deliberating process.

• *The child has limited life experiences from which to draw.* Children more often have experiences happen to them than have an instigating role in the experience. Knowles sees that the experiences of children are of limited worth in terms of resources for learning. It is the experience of teachers, writers of texts, and the media producers that are important.

• *Readiness to learn.* Children learn in order to advance to another level of learning. In addition, the learning identified as important for advancement is determined by adults. This is particularly true in religious education settings that have confirmation programs.

• *Orientation to learning.* The child learns for the future. The child learns subject-matter; to learn is to acquire content. For many, the culmination of the elementary years of biblical study, Sunday school, is the entrance into confirmation instruction. The conclusion of confirmation instruction leads to the rite of confirmation and increasing possibilities and responsibilities in the faith community.

• *Motivation.* The responsibility of education is placed on the parents, guardians, and sponsors of the child. In the baptismal liturgy, adults promise to "bring them to the services of God's house, and teach them the Lord's Prayer, the Creed, and the Ten Commandments . . . and provide for their instruction in the Christian faith."[15]

In contrast to these six assumptions about the theory of childhood learning, Knowles offers these assumptions of andragogy:

• *The need to know.* "What is so important about this class for my life as a Christian adult?" Adults desire to know the reasons they need to learn before they commit themselves to an educational experience. Adults will also invest much energy in examining the benefits and liabilities of a learning experience. It is important for the adult educator, then, to present how a specific learning activity will improve performance or the quality of their lives.

• *The learner's self-concept.* "How am I going to grow or change from this educational event?" Knowles describes adults as responsible for their own decisions. They are more self-directed and, therefore, better able to determine their perceived needs. With a strong self-concept, adult learners struggle when they feel that others are imposing their wills or desires on them. This assumption is particularly important for adult education leaders to consider. Too often, participants in adult Christian education don't perceive the educational process as self-directing, even though they may be self-directing in other areas of their lives.

• *The role of the learner's experience.* "Do my past experiences count for anything?" Adults bring more years of life experiences to the learning event than do children or youth. Because of this, they bring a diversity to the classroom interaction among the students and teacher. At the same time, the multiple experiences of the adult might close him or her to new ideas and change. The role of the teacher is to develop ways to challenge adults to consider alternative perspectives. According to Knowles, not to acknowledge these experiences is to ignore the adult as a person.

• *Readiness to learn.* "I wasn't able to deal with this before but now I can." Readiness emerges from the adult's desire to interpret and confront his or her real-life circumstances. The resources for this readiness emerge as one moves from one developmental stage to another. Knowles states that leaders don't have to wait for this readiness to occur on its own. It can come by exposing adult learners to various experiences, such as models, simulations, or counseling.

• *Orientation to learning.* "How can I deal with so many changes going on in my life?" While the orientation of children's education is subject-centered, adult education is motivated by an orientation toward life—task or problem-centered educational experiences. Adults devote time to learn something when they sense that it will assist them in dealing with problems and issues they are confronting in their lives.

• *Motivation.* "I just know that I need to get a handle on my life and faith." Certainly, the external motivation toward increased pay, or the possibility of changing jobs, is an important impetus for lifelong learning. However, the most powerful motivation, according to Knowles, is the internal motivation of the individual adult learner.[16]

These assumptions of andragogy are important for all adult educators, and adult religious educators in particular. Andragogy takes the adult learner seriously and respects the adult learner's investment in his or her learning. Knowles's work and research is certainly indebted to earlier contributors in the field of adult education as well as contemporary supporters of andragogy.

In the 1920s Eduard Lindeman, in *The Meaning of Adult Education*, stated, "A fresh hope is astir. From many quarters comes the call to a new kind of education with its initial assumption affirming that education is life—not a mere preparation for an unknown kind of future living. Consequently all static concepts of education which relegate the learning process to the period of youth are abandoned."[17] Moreover, Lindeman affirmed curriculum that emerges in the adult educational arena as constructed by student needs and interests.[18]

Knowles's use of andragogy underscores or supports Lindeman's assertion that adults' experiences must be taken into consideration. Lindeman states, "The resource of highest value in adult education is the learner's experience. If education is life, then life is also education. Too much of learning consists of vicarious substitution of some one else's experience and knowledge. Psychology is teaching us, however, that we learn what we do, and that therefore all genuine education will keep doing that thinking together."[19]

Adult education is also indebted to the work of Edward Thorndike who, by using empirical research, helped to change popular thoughts about the adult learner. In *Adult Interests* Thorndike states the following:

For thousands of years it was an avowed or tacit assumption of human education that learning belonged primarily to infancy and childhood. People did and should learn then most of the facts, principles, habits and skills which they used in later years. The young were supposed to amass a store of information and ability, the income from which supported them through life. . . . The assumption was shown to be false by the experiences of everyday life and of schools for adults.[20]

Thorndike also made a significant contribution to the field "by experimental evidence and [by measuring] roughly the changes in the ability to learn up to age 45. [He] showed that the ability to learn increased from childhood to about age 25 and decreased gradually and slowly thereafter, about one percent per year. Childhood was found to be emphatically not the best age for learning in the sense of the age when the greatest returns per unit of time spent are received. The age for learning that is best in that sense is in the twenties, and any age below 45 is better than ages 10 to 14." [21]

Leon McKenzie affirms Knowles's assumptions and asserts that if a theory cannot take into account pragmatic considerations it cannot be put into practice. He states that adults follow their felt needs and interests in regard to participation in education, adding, "They will respond favorably only to programs that they perceive as relevant to their concerns. Moreover, with the desire to address individual needs and interests of the adult parishioner, pastors and religious educators must meet the agendas of the adults before they can address their own educational agendas for the adult membership."[22]

Critiques of Andragogy

While educators generally affirm the need for a distinctive approach to adult education, andragogy has its critics. Some educators have critiqued this theory, and these concerns must be addressed in order to strengthen and build on Knowles's work.

Daniel D. Pratt asserts that andragogy inspires strong individualism.[26] The values espoused in andragogy position the individual at the center and the community at the periphery, affirming the goodness of individuals and learning to one's potential. Self-direction is an indicator of adulthood in the democratic environment. He goes on to state that societal change can be a by-product of individual change, but that societal change is secondary to that which is primary, individual change. In this regard the Christian educator must facilitate a delicate balance. While the educator wants to affirm and assist adults in their growth in faith, he or she also wants to assist the learner as a member of the faith community. The learner is part of the gathering of believers.

Sharan M. Merriam states that while andragogy has been important to our understanding of the adult learner, the distinction between pedagogy and andragogy must be seen in context. Each of these two approaches must be used where appropriate for children and adults. Merriam further asserts that andragogical theory must come to grips with critical social theory, which focuses on the social context of adult education. Here, the objective is to uncover oppressive forces that hinder the individual from developing fully. Moreover, andragogy must also take into account feminist scholarship. Particularly, she asserts that one must consider how women's learning needs might be different from those of men. This would include looking at the learning environment and the empowerment of women in the education setting.[24] Merriam also reiterates the concern that adult education cannot just be described in psychological terms, but that the learner must be seen in terms of his or her relationship to the world and how he or she is affected by it.[25]

John Elias has critiqued the notion of andragogy on several grounds. He asserts that Knowles's assumption has little research support, has introduced artificial jargon, and that it takes little account of older adults who become more dependent persons in terms of their self-concept.[26] At the same time, he says that andragogy has focused on some learning assumptions about children and adults that needed to be examined.

R. E. Y. Wickett affirms Knowles assertion that adults will see education as a means of building competency in order to achieve their full potential in life. He reminds us that adults also look to others: "It is a part of reality to affirm that each person will experience the presence of something or someone beyond the self in some way."[27]

In *Understanding and Facilitating Adult Learning*, Stephen Brookfield comments that Knowles does not develop andragogy from an empirically based theory—one derived from a number of experiments resulting in assertions that can be generalized. He states that Knowles's work should be only used as a set of assumptions, and that "the role of past experience in affecting how adults interpret their current personal and social worlds is central to andragogy and to effective facilitation."[28] Furthermore, he states that there have been extraordinary interpretations made of Knowles's assertions that must be addressed: that self-directedness is an innate characteristic of adulthood, that adult learning efforts are generally problem-centered, and that adults always seek immediate application with their learning.[29]

K. Patricia Cross recognizes that andragogy has been successful in raising important issues about adult education and has received considerable attention by practitioners, but she is reticent to acknowledge whether andragogy can be the basis for a unifying theory on adult education. In addition, she does not see the contrast between pedagogy and andragogy as one that is sustainable by research.[30]

While the debate continues on the development, direction, and appropriateness of andragogical theory, it is important for leaders in educational ministry to consider the needs of the adult learner. While it is often convenient, and at times expedient, to dispense information in class settings, it becomes a challenge for leaders to examine, listen to, and use the unique experiences, thoughts, life successes, and struggles of the adult learner. Andragogy demands dialogue between the student and the leader as well as the student among his or her peers. Some of the most exciting forums or Bible studies with adults in a Sunday or weekday class occur when the participants share their reactions, experiences, and previous learnings with the group. When women and men share the concrete crises in their lives and their faith with honesty, they are able to reflect on the role of other Christians in their lives during these critical periods.

One other important component to consider when examining andragogy is its role in helping education leaders address some of the critical social issues in North America, including racism, poverty, womanism, feminism, human sexuality, and inclusiveness. As we hear the diverse voices and concerns, education methods based on andragogical assumptions take adults' experiences seriously and give opportunity and respect for the various issues involved. For example, as we encounter persons of color in the classroom or group setting, the openness of the teacher and others to listen to their experiences and raise them before the group indicates that those experiences are important and can be shared, respected, and valued.

Implications

Margaret Fisher Billinger states that "in order to increase knowledge of adult learning concepts, I encourage educators to pay attention to what is going on inside learners. Adult religious educators who are aware of the principles and conditions for effective learning usually design programs that are faithful to these principles and that are sensitive to the needs and backgrounds of the learners."[31] If this is the case, then it is essential for the Christian educator to pursue these priorities:

• *Be faithful to the gospel.* It is imperative that the responses of the educator are theologically and confessionally grounded by the tradition of the faith community. As teachers, root the emphasis in the gospel story of Jesus—good news for humankind. It is within this context that adult learners will find "mutual conversation and consolation of brethren [and sisters]."[32]

• *Consider the learner as a partner.* Effective adult Christian education works with adult learners, helping them to cope with the joys, crises, changes, transitions, and passages they experience in life.

• *Become acquainted with the learners.* For adult Christian education to be effective, the teacher must be sensitive to the needs and the background of each learner. Take time for students to share who they are with you and with the others in the group. This is more than introductory exercise at the beginning of a class. It is an ongoing process that continues as learners are involved in the questions, issues, and topics of their study.

• *Be open to myriad issues.* To be the leader of an adult Christian education group calls for openness to new and emerging issues that develop in people's homes, community, the church, and society. At this same time, the religious educator must be aware of his or her own faith journey. This recognition reminds the leader that each adult's story is unique. For example, in an adult class on death and dying, participants may talk not only about their past experience with the church and death, but also how they are changing as they come to grips with the meaning of Christian hope as more and more relatives and close friends die.

• *Create a hospitable and inviting environment.* The education environment must be one that the learner perceives as safe, caring, and open for dialogue and interaction with one's fellow Christians and those who are seeking.[33] For example, during a study on poverty, would a participant feel comfortable enough to share that, because of divorce, he or she has to rely on welfare to survive?

• *Create opportunity for individual and corporate remembering.* Adults have memories and stories from their lives that assist them in their life together. Again, these are unique to the individual and to the congregation, but these stories help people to have a sense of being part of the community. The adult educator is called to help adults incorporate their personal stories into the church's story of salvation.

• *Respect the adult learner's experiences.* All learners come with experiences that influence their educational experience. The leader of adult events must assist the learner in the best ways of using those experiences for learning, being aware that not every experience will contribute to the specific learning activity.

If the church's religious educators, pastors, and lay directors of Christian education acknowledge and address these priorities, they will be better prepared to face the challenges of adult religious education in the twenty-first century.

FORMAL AND INFORMAL LEARNING

What experiences in Christian education have been part of your adult years? Perhaps you participate in a class offered by the Christian education committee, or perhaps you think you haven't been involved in Christian education at all since your high school years. Christian education occurs in many ways. While the schooling model of an adult class may be most familiar, our growth in faith also takes place in other arenas of the congregation's life, and these are as important as what takes place in the classroom.

Adult religious education occurs in a variety of ways within and beyond the congregation. It happens in small and large groups, between generations and genders, in one-to-one conversation, as well as in the adult forum. Nancy Foltz indicates that these kinds of settings are increasing as we come to the end of the twentieth century.[34] Each of these ways encourages adult Christians and inquirers to reflect on their lives as baptized Christians.

Formal Learning

Formal educational settings are those events that are organized, planned, and publicly announced within the congregation, ministerium, or cluster of congregations. These activities include Bible study groups, lectures, retreats, videos, printed material for home use, service projects, sermons, and the gathering of the community in Word and sacrament ministry.[35] For many congregations the formal educational setting is the Sunday church school with adult classes in biblical, theological, and social concerns. In addition, some congregations extend their learning activities to midweek with adult Bible study or community forums.

Linda Vogel suggests three categories of formal settings: instruction, inquiry, and participation.[36]

• *Instruction.* The instruction category uses a schooling model that can be designed for the individual or for small and large groups. Individuals can use study guides for Bible study. Small groups might be involved in studying a book or selecting a specific topic for investigation. Large groups might enjoy a series of lectures or a film series. The instruction model depends on clearly specified objectives. Many adult Sunday school classes fall into this category.

• *Inquiry.* In the inquiry category of adult learning, adults use their problem-solving skills and imaginations. This includes adults involved in brainstorming sessions, task forces, and individual and small-group exploration.

• *Participation.* In the participation category, adults are involved in reflection on their lives within the faith community. They can be immersed in simulations, field trips, and learning-by-doing activities. Think of the number of people in our congregations who are not only concerned about the homeless and hungry, but who also work at soup kitchens and shelters. These social ministry projects are also formal teaching and learning events.

It must be emphasized for the pastor or religious educator that planning for any of these learning experiences needs to consider andragogical theory. Take seriously the experiences of the learners, offer alternatives so that the learner has some choices, and make deliberate references to the objectives of the learning event so that changes in the process can be made if needed.

Informal Learning

Informal educational settings include those events that are not planned, deliberate, or publicized but that, nevertheless, involve adults in learning through the life of the faith community. This education occurs in the daily and weekly encounters of adults in various activities within the church. Through such informal settings, many of our parish leaders—church school teachers, church council members, and committee members—become examples of the faithful life. For many, their spouses are important teachers and examples of people of faith that help them in their own growth. Norma Thompson identifies these categories of informal learning:

• *Religious education centers.* These centers are usually cooperatives among several congregations and are places where adults can go for individual study and research.

• *Travel experiences.* These experiences often include an expert traveling with a group to various places of theological or biblical significance. An important component of such trips is the group interaction. With the number of partner-church relationships developing around the globe, this will increasingly be an important area of adult learning.

• *Intergenerational and family clusters.* These events involve projects, worship experiences, family enrichment programs, and family camping experiences for members of the faith community. Thompson states that the variety of programs indicates the creativity that can exist in these educational events.[37]

In both formal and informal settings, take seriously the adult learner as a thinking and interpreting person who has an interest in his or her educational venture. Honoring the varieties of education settings for adults invites creativity, imagination, and excitement for the adult learner and the planner in lifelong Christian education.

MOTIVATION FOR ADULT EDUCATION

Sooner or later, at any gathering of those responsible for adult education in a congregation, the question is going to be asked, "How do we get them to come?" It's a crucial question. Though there are exceptions, the number of adults who participate in worship services on any given Sunday far exceeds the number who attend classes. It's a nagging question because deep down in the bones of most congregational leaders there is the conviction, or at least the suspicion, that equipping persons for ministry through adult education is one of the most fruitful avenues by which to set loose the spiritual and missioning potential inherent in every church. How do we get them to come? It's a question of motivation.

The Importance of Motivation in Adult Education

No dimension related to adult education has been more thoroughly investigated than what it is that motivates adults to participate in formal education. With few exceptions, those who do study the subject are quick to point out—as discussed in the previous section of this chapter—that formal classes are, very likely, only a small part of the overall adult learning picture. Still, whether they are dealing with college, extension, community, or congregational programs, the majority of these researchers make strong arguments for a formal program for adults, and thus are concerned with motivating adults to attend them.[38] The fact that the research continues suggests that the source for that motivation is yet to be found. While admitting that the very notion of motivation is hard to define, and the role it has in determining participation in learning opportunities difficult to demonstrate, Raymond J. Wlodkowski argues that it is a key concept that must be attended to in developing any structured learning opportunities for adults. He writes:

Motivation is not only important because it is a necessary causal factor of learning but because it mediates learning and is a consequence of learning as well. Historically, instructors have always known that when learners are motivated during the learning process, things go more smoothly, communication flows, anxiety decreases, and creativity and learning are more apparent. Instruction with motivated learners can actually be joyful and exciting, especially for the instructor.

Learners who complete a learning experience and leave the situation feeling motivated about what they have learned seem more likely to have a future interest in what they have learned and more likely to use what they have learned. It is also logical to assume that the more that people have had motivating learning experiences, the more probable it is that they will become lifelong learners.[39]

As the above statement demonstrates, there is more to motivation than simply getting persons to attend congregationally sponsored adult education events. Motivation is a critical factor influencing the hopes and behaviors of those who plan for adult education. It is an imperative consideration when planning events in which adults will be invited to participate. Anyone who has been a teacher of adults knows that what happens in those planned events has a determining effect on whether adults are motivated to complete a course of instruction or interested in taking another. Each of these will be discussed.

Motivation and the Planners of Adult Education

"If we build it, they will come" is not an uncommon conviction (dream) that informs the planning of adult education in many congregations. While it may hold true when building a field for heroic ballplayers—and even that hasn't been demonstrated beyond fiction—it just doesn't work in adult Christian education programs unless a great deal of planning, commitment, tenacity, listening, and prayer go into the building. And these qualities are not going to be in the program unless those who plan for adult education are highly motivated. All of which is to say, developing and sustaining congregationally based adult education is hard, and sometimes discouraging, work.

Two decades ago Alan Knox identified one of the reasons why adult education is so challenging. He observed that the response of many adults to the invitation to classes was similar to what Elizabeth Kübler-Ross found as the emerging responses to the knowledge that a person was dying: denial, anger, bargaining, and finally acceptance.[40] Members of a congregation are not likely to deny the value of adult education as a generality. If Knox is correct, however, a majority are going to deny that it is *for them*, at least initially. Unaware of that reality, and not sufficiently motivated to get beyond that response, planners for adult education may pull the plug on their vision for adult education even before it has been given a fair chance to succeed.

Initially denying the need for attending a class does not mean that adults are not motivated to learn, or more specifically, to gain skills and information they desire or need.The reality is quite the opposite. However, in research reported in *Intentional Changes: A Fresh Approach to Helping People Change*, Allen Tough found that "with most intentional changes, it is largely the person himself or herself who chooses, plans, and implements the change. Intentional changes are largely "do-it-yourself" changes. The person often obtains significant help from acquaintances, but only rarely from professionals or books."[41]

Anticipating some change in participants must be part of the motivation for a congregation working to develop a program in adult education. That anticipation needs to be kept in tension with the reality that adults play a significant motivational role in choosing the changes they wish to pursue, planning how to accomplish them, and actually carrying out their plans. If planners for adult education in churches don't take into account this active motivational role on the part of the prospective adult learner, the likelihood of building a program to which adults will come is very low.

There are few short cuts to a solid educational program for adults. It takes more than enthusiasm for a good thing. Only those who value the laity's potential for service, who recognize the church's capacity for helping persons to create both a personal and community identity, and who are convinced that the adult journey of faith and life is immeasurably enriched by the Scriptures and the traditions of the church, will be motivated to invest the time, effort, creativity, patience, resources, and prayer needed in the development of an effective program. Chapter 8 in this text provides some specific helps with both planning and evaluation models that make these tasks easier.

Realizing the challenge, and at the same time being motivated to meet it, planners for adult education in a congregation are prepared to start at the right end of the program development continuum. For R. Wade Paschal, that's at the place of defining needs. The easy way to try to do that is to send out a questionnaire. A better way is to discover what those needs are by personally listening to and observing adults.

Once needs have been identified, the next step is to locate a nucleus of people who would be interested in forming a class to meet that need. The all too common way of doing that is through announcements in both written and verbal form. That's the low-motivational approach, based on the notion that most anybody *might* be interested in addressing the need that's been identified. There are a few, but not many, who are motivated by such an announcement to attend a class. It's just too easy to deny that the invitation was meant for *me*. A better way is to contact persons who are likely candidates for a class and ask them to commit themselves to it for a specified period of time. If three or more can't be found, it might be better not to offer the class. Nothing is so counter-motivational as offering a class to which one, two, or none show up. Once the nucleus for a class is identified, however, planning can move forward with the selection of teachers, curriculum, space, and time—followed finally by the class itself.[42]

This whole process is too often short-circuited by beginning where it should end: the building of a class to which adults may, or may not, come. When the latter happens, planners and teachers for adult education are likely to get discouraged and lose some of their own motivation.

One way to generate interest in adult Bible study is to bring into a congregation a carefully written and orchestrated program such as *Inspire, Bethel, Crossways,* or *Kerygma.* It's exciting to be in a congregation where the leadership is motivated to stand behind one or more of these offerings. In my experience, the congregational phase of these studies begins with a bombardment of information and enthusiastic personal invitations to motivate adults to join in. Then come the classes that enjoy a longer or shorter run as teachers and participants make their way through the prepared sessions. It would be difficult to overestimate the positive impact of these programs on the persons and congregations that have participated in them.

A downside to these efforts is that so much effort is focused on them, and sponsors are so motivated to have them go well, that once they are completed there is a tendency for adult education in the congregation to go into a period of stagnation. A comment heard too often is "We really don't have anything going in adult education now, but last year [or five years ago, or twenty] we did [*name of organized program*] and it was great." Those programs are great. But, they should not be allowed to drain away the motivation necessary for ongoing adult education.

No small part of the genius of the Bible studies like those named above is that their publishers insist on preparing those who will be the teachers using the materials. That very equipping is a motivational factor leading to the greater interest, participation, and effectiveness that Wlodkowski described. Recruiting and equipping teachers of adults in a general way, by the same logic, is one of the most important things that leaders can do to create and maintain a high level of motivation for adult education year after year in their congregations.

"If I don't do prospecting for clients," a friend who sells insurance says, "I'm out of business." You can be sure that he is motivated to prospect. A similar perspective needs to inform leaders of adult education. Not only do they need to be prospecting for those who will form the nucleus for the planned classes, they must be identifying and equipping those who will lead those classes. Without those teachers adult education is never going to "get into business." This is not the place to describe those who make the most likely candidates to be teachers, but it can be said that there should not be any time in the year in any congregation that someone isn't being prepared to teach adults—either through independent study, mentoring, or a class. Developing a cadre of teachers is, itself, adult education. And having such a cadre serves as motivation for drawing together a nucleus for new classes. There are many materials available to equip these teachers. "Developing Skills for Teaching Adults" in the *Teaching the Faith* series from Concordia Publishing House is among the most versatile, allowing for both independent and group-learning experiences.[43]

In its study on effectiveness in Christian education, Search Institute found that only eight percent of the congregations in the Evangelical Lutheran Church in America had sixty percent or more of their adult membership involved in formal educational events sponsored by them.[44] Other mainline denominations fared little better. No wonder the question is asked, "How can we get them to come?"

The place from which to begin to respond to that question is with the ones who plan and lead adult education programs, and not the users. Before attempting to motivate and change the attitudes of adults who don't participate, leaders must examine the level and the nature of their own motivation. Is it of the kind that is prepared to identify persons and to invite them one-by-one to commit themselves to a specific learning opportunity? Is it of the kind that will intentionally develop a cadre of teachers for adults? Is it of the kind that will consistently evaluate whatever is done in the area of adult education to determine both what motivates adults to participate and what stands as barriers to that participation? Is it of the kind that recognizes and welcomes, especially in smaller congregations, the potential for adult education inherent in events that are ecumenical and/or community based? In other words, is there the kind of motivation that will put a foundation in place to make adult education a significant part of adults' lifelong experience in the church?

Focusing on the particulars isn't the whole of the picture, however. Leaders also need a vision, a grand purpose, toward which the details are all moving. Enhancing a sense of belonging, enriching the understanding of what it means to be a people created, redeemed, and called by God, and enabling persons to serve others in God's name are a start in focusing that vision.

Motivating Adults to Participate in Congregationally Sponsored Learning Events

In order for leaders to build an educational program to which adults will come, the factors that motivate adults to participate, or serve as barriers to their participation, must be taken into account. In summarizing a great deal of research he has reviewed, Wlodkowski writes that learning how to do something, and then applying that knowledge to some level of competence, are two of the most predictable factors that motivate adults to learn. Thus, it can be said that adults, first, are motivated to learn in settings in which they have *strong expectations of success.* There is more to it than that, however.

Second, the learning must also *relate to what adults want to know,* or the skills they desire to develop. If they want to learn how to carve wood, and are convinced that they could be helped in learning how to do it by attending a class, there is good reason to think that they will enroll in the class. Wanting to learn, according to Wlodkowski, "is the most critical and basic level of positive adult motivation for learning. There is almost no limit to the number of specific reasons why an adult might *want* to learn something, but unless an adult feels a sense of choice, motivation will probably become problematic."[45]

Third, adults are motivated to learn when they *value what they learn.* Leon McKenzie has argued vehemently that much of adult education in the church has had its origins in what pastors have valued, and thus have wanted to teach, without taking into account what lay adults would value learning.[46] Certainly there is an important place in adult Christian education for the teachings of the church, but it should not be assumed that what the pastor values is identical with the priorities and values of all the adults in the congregation.

A fourth motivating factor for adults is *enjoyment.* While the first three dimensions are primary concerns for those who plan for adult education, the latter is definitely in the realm of the teacher and of those with whom adult learners find themselves joined in a formal classroom setting. It's a hard thing to say, but it must be said just the same: There are some folks who, no matter how hard they try, will never be able to make a class interesting and exciting—enjoyable. Unfortunately, there are some who can make a class enjoyable by virtue of their personal gifts but who don't discipline themselves in ways that allow adults to learn the information and skills they value. Those teachers who can make a class enjoyable, while at the same time satisfying the desire of the participants to learn and develop, are the ones who will motivate adults in the church to come back again and again to learn.[47]

Adults Are Motivated to Attend Classes They Enjoy. Learning information and gaining skills may appear to be motivating factors primarily for those desiring to enhance their careers, and are therefore left to the community and technical schools to provide. General texts in adult education could, indeed, leave one with that impression. It may be that participation in Christian adult education may not result directly in a job promotion, or the learning of technical skills needed for it, but congregational leaders must not underestimate the importance of what they have to offer and how they are able to respond to that which motivates adults to learn.

For example, if one starts at the fourth dimension named by Wlodkowski, that of enjoyment, there is no reason why well-prepared teachers of adults in the church can't make their classes enjoyable. One reason that is so is that the Bible, the most basic resource used in adult Christian education, is gracefully stimulating and exciting. And, though not all are ready to study it, there are few adults in the church who don't value the Bible highly. Given reason to do so, many adults are ready to study it if their experience in doing it has value and is enjoyable.

A few years ago a series of Bible studies for adults was held at a Bible camp. On the first evening together the teacher was asked to tell what the subject of the studies was to be, and when he said that it would be on the Psalms, he actually heard a few persons groan. During the next few days they explored several of the Psalms. By Thursday, one after another of the participants were telling how much they were "enjoying" their study and discovering the value the Psalms had for their lives. They were gaining the competence to make connections between their life experiences and what Walter Brueggemann calls the *Message of the Psalms.*[48]

Adults Are Motivated to Learn When Facing Life Transitions. Gaining information and skills leading to competence is an example of the single most common factor that motivates adults to pursue learning: coping with transitions. "Those transitions include: new job responsibilities, losing or changing jobs, marriage, the birth of a child, the aging of parents, divorce, and struggling with questions related to faith and values" as they are encountered at the various stages of the adult journey.[49] In all of these, adults recognize a need for information, skills, and nurture that will assist them through the transition.

As Tough has pointed out, a significant number of adults will identify those transitions for themselves, will work out a plan by which to gain the information and skills they think necessary to negotiate the transition, and will implement that plan on their own initiative. The church must be ready to meet its adults at these junctures where they are motivated to learn and make itself available as a valuable resource as adults formulate their plan for coping with them. What's at stake in many of these transitions is nothing less than the self-image and esteem of the persons experiencing them. No gathering of people is in a better position to affirm powerfully that image than the Christian community. And no word, no message, is more able to transform persons moving through those transitions than the gospel of our Lord, Jesus Christ.

Compassion, Service, and Community as Motivating Factors for Adult Education. There are more motivating factors that influence adults to participate in educational events that can be noted here, but we will focus finally on these three. Search Institute found in its study on effective Christian education that compassion is a stronger motivating factor influencing membership in the church today than is loyalty.[50] The same could be said for participation in adult education.

Though the data is anecdotal, seminary students who report on their observations of congregational adult classes more often than not comment on the age of the participants—that a majority are "older." They are the loyal ones, who have been coming to classes for decades and will continue to do so as long as they are able. Loyalty, a sense of responsibility or duty, is a motivating factor that must not be set aside when leaders make provision for adult education. It's just that loyalty isn't as powerful a factor as it used to be.

Younger adults often can be attracted to educational opportunities that have a service orientation. Put another way, service-related activities can become excellent opportunities for adult education. At least one community has developed an ecumenical car repair service for people who cannot afford to have it done by themselves.

Another has developed a far-ranging program that includes rehabilitation of housing units, English as a second language courses, and grooming classes for teenagers—all led by lay adults. Food pantries, shelters, and serving at dining places for the poor have become almost commonplace in congregations all across the country. There are forums aplenty on social issues such as hunger, violence, and care for families. All reflect the compassion for others that runs deeply in the hearts and minds of church members, both young and old. It is a motivational factor that must be taken into account as formal adult education is planned in a congregation.

Present North American society is often characterized as one dominated by individualism. *Habits of the Heart*, by Robert Bellah, seemed to demonstrate that beyond all doubt.[51] If that is the case, there is still a yearning in many adults for community, a sense of belonging. For some adults that yearning may be the primary motivation for their attending an adult class. For others, it is an expectation that they bring with them, whether it is consciously identified or not. Dick Murray notes that it is a myth that adult education and the coffee hour are in competition with each other. The trick is to bring the two together so that they reinforce each other.[52] R. Wade Paschal agrees. He recommends that classes begin with an emphasis on establishing relationships among the participants.[53] Classes need to be more than community building, but they can't be less if they are to respond to what motivates many adults to participate in them in the first place: the desire to find others to whom they can give themselves and be accepted as they are.

Another motivational factor can be associated with the phrase "adult education fares well when it sees itself in second place" to whatever else adults value. Most adults appear to place a higher value on worship than they do on education. If worship draws them to gather on Sunday mornings, or on weeknights during Lent or Advent, build educational offerings around those services—either in addition to or in conjunction with them. If parents are committed to instruction for their children at the time of their first Communion or confirmation, find ways to include those parents in the instruction. When her congregation decided to give Bibles to third graders, one director of Christian education made that an occasion for inviting parents to a series of classes, with their children, providing an overview of the Bible. A pastor in Tacoma, Washington, makes stewardship a context for doing adult education. Stewardship committees are selected a year in advance in that congregation, and for a year that committee studies the biblical basis for stewardship. Over the course of many years a significant number of the congregation has become well informed on the subject, and the congregation has grown. Interestingly, it is in this congregation that plans are being made for an academy for adult learning, with a building program centered around that vision.

What else in the lives of adults motivates them and can be connected to Christian education? acting? singing? dancing? building? painting? growing? giving? traveling? serving? The possibilities, the "ing" words, go on and on, limited only by the creativity, energy, time, and resources of those who recognize motivation as a key factor in adults' participation in education.

Motivation and the Classroom Experience

After all is said and done by those planning for adult education in a congregation, it is what happens in the class that determines whether adults will come a second time to the same course or be motivated to think of themselves as lifelong learners and the church as an agency for that learning. There are some guidelines that teachers need to keep in mind to create a positive experience for adult learners.

• *Honor the expectations that learners bring with them to a class.* Course titles and descriptions may carry different meanings for different learners. What learners thought they were signing on for may not be what the teacher had in mind when the course was designed. An open sharing of expectations, with the possibility of negotiations, is one way to create a positive climate for learning.

• *Respect the class members and their experiences.* If anything deserves the efforts of teachers of adults, it is working at finding ways to demonstrate respect for all persons without surrendering their own.

• *Both a teacher and a learner be.* It can be expected that teachers of adults know something about the subject of the class they are teaching. A decade or so ago it seemed that adult learners were supposed to be so much in charge of their education that teachers, who were called enablers, were expected to be silent, even if they did know something. Thankfully, that era seems to have passed. It is now essential for teachers of adults to be well informed about their subjects and not keep that information a secret. At the same time teachers are expected to think through a process by which teaching and learning are designed to occur, rather than waiting for the class to determine that direction. In addition, teachers of adults need to be aware that they are not the only source of information in the class. Each person has information to offer—about themselves and the subject—and it needs to be welcomed and appreciated. And when alternative routes are suggested for a class or course that hold greater promise than the one planned, there should be no fear of taking them.

• *Flavor teaching with a good dose of enthusiasm.* David Silvernail has noted that enthusiasm in teachers is a quality that grows exponentially in value as learners move toward adulthood.[54] Enthusiasm generates energy. It has a way of awakening the energy in others and putting that energy into motion. Enthusiasm sustains persons when the learning seems to get bogged down in details or in conflicting ideas and opinions. Enthusiasm doesn't have a single face. Not all teachers will express it in the same way. How it is communicated is not nearly so important as that it be present in a class, focused in the teacher. When it is present, along with the other guidelines suggested above, an adult class has come a long way toward being effective as a motivational factor for lifelong learning in a congregational setting.

Given that these guidelines are honored, Patricia Cross has argued that adults are motivated to continue in a class in which they have a sense of congruence.[55] *Congruence* is a far-ranging term that takes into account many things: Is the space a comfortable one? Does the participant feel welcome? Are the goals of the class consistent with the participant's expectations? More importantly, congruence has to do with the teaching and learning style employed in the class and the relationship that the teacher is able to create with the participants.

Dick Murray, in his characteristic down-to-earth approach to adult education, argues that there are basically two kinds of classes for adults in the church. One is predominantly discussion oriented, allowing participants to raise their questions and issues and to hear the responses of their peers. This type of class is generally gathered around a table, or in some other informal arrangement, which allows for the exchange of information, questions, and opinions. The teacher is primarily a facilitator of the process.

The other is more teacher directed. In these classes participants come to hear what the teacher has to say on the designated subject. Lectures are likely to be the most common activity employed in a class arranged for the participants to receive information and to raise questions addressed to the teacher, but not to each other.

It would be wrong to assume that the latter are for serious learners whereas the former are not. Both are intent on learning; they just approach learning in different ways. Adults take those approaches seriously. They look for congruence. If they are expecting lectures and, instead, are placed around a table with six or eight other persons and feel that they are expected to talk, they are likely to feel "incongruent" and probably won't return for the next session. It's no wonder that

Murray encourages all congregations to have at least two adult classes, one for each of the approaches described above.

While Murray comes close to over-simplifying the matter of congruence, R. Wade Paschal is in danger of complicating it. In *Vital Adult Learning* he makes the case that classes have "personalities." Adults will be motivated to participate in those whose personality fits their own. He has identified seven of them: the introverted class, the extroverted or social class, the missions and service class, the leader class, the supportive class, the experimenter class, and the traditional class. Participants in each of these classes bring with them expectations as to how they will relate to the teacher, the kinds of learning activities in which they will be involved, the setting in which they will meet, and the purposes for the class.[56] Paschal's design is, in reality, for homogeneous grouping for adult education. If classes could be organized along these lines, the matter of congruence would be addressed about as completely as it could be, and adults would, supposedly, be highly motivated to participate. A question, and a competing value, need to be set along side Paschal's recommendations.

The question is, how large a pool of adults is needed to even begin thinking in terms of seven categories of personalities? The response, of course, is that the pool would be far larger if leaders did think in terms of those categories. And, there is no need that all seven be in place at any given time. It is critical for the teacher to identify which personality is represented in the class so that the matter of congruence may be addressed.

The concern is not so easily dismissed. Public educators have long debated the positive and negative effects of heterogeneous versus homogeneous grouping as factors influencing learning. What may be at stake in Paschal's recommendation not only has to do with creating contexts that are congruent for teachers and learners, but also with what it means to be the church. In a study that made use of demographic information in an attempt to understand the history of a congregation and how it functions in the present, lay persons were asked if it was important for them to gather information about such things as age, or position, or income in coming to an understanding of their congregation. A significant majority responded negatively. Their reason was that the church should be one place where we don't emphasize our differences or our place in the world. Before God, and in our congregations, we are together.

Is that too idealistic an expectation for adult classes? Does what we know about congruence and learning theory militate against what we believe about the nature of the church? Are the social sciences to govern how we function in the church, and if not govern, how much influence should they have? Would it be too much to expect that younger and older adults could be motivated to learn together in the same class? Is it possible that extroverts and introverts could sense a level of comfort in the same class sufficient to motivate them to stay with it? Are mission action-oriented persons able to learn in the same setting with those who are pleased to examine every issue from a dozen different perspectives? Or the more important question might be, would the learning for each of these personality groups eventually be enriched by the presence of other personalities in the same class? If there is an answer to this, it probably will be found somewhere in the information about learning styles and how different ones can be accommodated in a single class.

LEARNING STYLES

Not long ago a congregational task force gathered to discuss possibilities for adult education. In the course of the discussion a young man blurted out, "We shouldn't allow one more class around this church until everyone who would attend it has gone out and done something practical." He had recently returned from Mexico where he had worked with a construction team building a school. Filled with enthusiasm for what he had done and learned, he wanted everyone to have a similar life-changing experience. Whether he realized it or not, he was also expressing a bias for a kind of learning that physically engages the learner.

The matter of congruence has been addressed. One of the most important dimensions of congruence is learning style. It's hard to imagine many teachers who have not had this experience: one or more adults in a class acting as though they were having the most fun they had had since discovering ice cream, and one or more in the same class convinced that they have seldom had a worse experience. Teachers can wonder what in the world is wrong with themselves, until they realize that it isn't so much a matter of the teacher as of learning styles. Participants are, as often as not, simply responding to the choice of activities designed to assist them in their learning.

Learning Styles—They Are a Reality

In one seminary Christian education course, students are asked to complete a learning-style inventory first devised by Bernice McCarthy and reprinted in Jeanne Tighe and Karen Szentkeresti's excellent manual *Rethinking Adult Religious Education*.[57] After the inventories have been completed, the hypothesis that all four learning styles are represented in the class has never failed to be validated. It is safe to assume that those four styles are present in every group of adults who gather to learn. While four seems to be the magic number for learning styles, there is more than one system for naming them. Consider the following: concrete experience, reflective observation, abstract conceptualization, and active experimentation. As these are explored, keep in mind how they relate to congruence and motivation.

Concrete Experience

Guided imagery is a favorite activity for concrete experiential learners. Warm up a class for it by asking them to pretend they are trees—rooted, then blowing in the wind (with sound effects), and then quieting down as after a storm. From there, move into the story of the ten plagues as described in Exodus 7-12. As you read the story, ask participants in the class to act out being gnats, or drinking from a river of blood, or hopping like frogs around the room. Finally, as you come to the death of the firstborn, assume the role of a parent who has lost a child. What begins lightheartedly ends in a hushed awe. It's a powerful activity that engages learners physically, mentally, and emotionally.

That's the nature of the concrete experiential learner and the activities that appeal to them. They appreciate doing role plays, dramatizations, going on field trips, playing games, or doing work projects. They value teachers who are innovative, who are not afraid to take some risks in their teaching. They are willing to be vulnerable. There is a risk in doing experiential learning activities with persons who do not have this as a learning style. They may either do the activity despite feeling very uncomfortable or stand aside while others participate. As adults learn to trust their peers and the learning environment, even those whose preferred learning style isn't concrete experience can be brought into class activities if not frightened away before that trust can be developed.

Reflective Observation

While concrete experiential learners are interested in participating in debates, panels, dramatizations, and role plays, reflective observers are content to watch and draw from those activities what has meaning for them. For all of that, they probably would prefer a well-organized lecture that communicates a great deal of information on which they can reflect. They might ask questions at the close of a lecture, but they are equally likely to get a little irritated if other learners interrupt a lecture with too many of their comments or questions.

As one observes the church, it seems that this is the learner most adult classes are designed to attract. The adult forum is an example. A guest speaker is enlisted to present a topic and a group of adults is gathered to listen. It's a good way to communicate information. Reflective observers are delighted to receive that information and process it for themselves. It must be remembered, however, that even the most die-hard reflective observer is not a tone deaf ear immune to the effects of boredom. Good lectures have anecdotes, humor, introductions, and summaries. They make use of visual aids, whether it be an overhead transparency, the chalkboard, or some other more modern form of visual communication. When the reflective observer is treated well, abstract conceptualizers are pretty happy as well.

Abstract Conceptualization

These folks enjoy all sorts of learning activities, as long as they are purposeful and well done. Adept at working with ideas, they have a way of imposing their own sense of order on whatever they do. They are impatient with ill-informed teachers or those who don't come prepared to provide leadership for a class. These folks are excellent at studying biblical texts. Questions for their use, however, must be carefully designed. They can't be ones with yes and no, or simple one and two word, answers. They want to probe, evaluate, express their opinions, engage the opinions and convictions of others. They may be even a bit argumentative. Others in class might be threatened by them.

Case studies in which adults work together in small groups to solve a problem almost always go well when working with abstract conceptualizers. "Where to Put the Baptismal Font" is an example. In this case, a congregation has a policy that no matter what the reason, the baptismal font will not be moved from its position in the center-front of the nave. A family planning a wedding asks that it be moved for the processional. Their request denied, the family takes it to the worship committee. The class dealing with the case study is organized into small groups, each designated the worship committee, and asked to define the problem, consider alternative responses, choose one, and then project the outcome of their decision. After thirty minutes in discussion, the groups are asked to give their solution to the problem. The response is wonderful. Not everyone comes to the same conclusion, but it's a delight to hear the rationales that are developed. It makes one wonder if there is a *single* resolution to the case study. Of one thing you can be sure: abstract conceptualizers will be arguing the case long after the class.

Active Experimentation

Some teachers like to do experiments in class. One example is the one alluded to earlier with regard to discovering the learning styles in a class. Another is giving participants two 3" x 5" cards and asking them to describe an issue they are dealing with on each card. After they have written on the cards, the teacher discusses stages in the adult journey and the kinds of questions asked at each stage. Participants are asked to see if they reflect the general research for their age group. The research isn't totally replicated, but it does work out with amazing predictability, and adults get more interested in the topic of the maturing adult.

Testing hypotheses, challenging old ideas, gathering information that is not presently available, exploring new areas and situations—all are things active experimenters like to do, as long as what is done is practical and represents a responsible use of time. This style of learning seems to be most at home in a laboratory, but a place can be found for it in adult Christian education. There are all sorts of things that people in the church accept tacitly without having any particular basis for thinking them to be true. A class could begin by naming some of those things and then devising a strategy by which to determine their validity. Like concrete experiential learners, active experimenters may not be pleased with the very activities that are most acceptable to reflective observers.

Unless we group these learners homogeneously as Paschal suggests, how can all these learning styles be accommodated in a single class? You may want to refer to the discussion of teaching strategies in chapter 4. Another way is by employing a structured teaching approach called *shared praxis*. It's described in chapter 5 of this book. When you encounter it, explore the approach in terms of its capacity to legitimately and effectively accommodate the four learning styles described here, all in the context of a single session.

SOME CONCLUDING COMMENTS

Psychology as a branch of the social sciences and the development of religious education as a specific dimension of pastoral theology began at about the same time—at the beginning of the twentieth century. It should be no surprise, therefore, that psychology has had considerable influence on religious education as it has emerged as an academic discipline.

Malcolm Knowles has had significant influence on the study of adult Christian education. Familiarity with his theory undergirding andragogy is a necessity for anyone working in the field of adult education. Research indicates that a great deal of adult learning occurs informally, without the help of a designated teacher or a classroom. Aware of that, those responsible for adult learning in a congregation can, at the minimum, be alert to what adults are learning informally as they participate, or don't participate, in the various dimensions of a congregation's life.

Much of the research in adult education focuses on what motivates adults to participate in formal learning situations. While there are no absolutes, there are things that planners and teachers in adult education can do to encourage adults to participate in the courses and programs congregations offer. One of the most fruitful of these things is to attend to the matter of learning styles, the ways in which particular adults prefer to learn. This chapter is finally a word about theory. As you now move to the more practical dimensions of teaching adults, and discovering more about how to organize and "do" adult education, don't leave the theory behind. Adults are theory makers. Those who plan educational opportunities for them can be no less.

chapter four

Teaching Matters: The Role of the Teacher

Luther E. Lindberg

No matter where we put the emphasis as we read the title of this chapter, we are zeroing in on two matters of vital importance in teaching and learning with adults in the congregation. If we say "*teaching* matters," we are making a statement about how important the teaching process is in both the life of the individual and the community. Teaching is a vital ministry that must be tended to if faith is to grow and the church is to reach out. Teaching makes a difference in how effectively the mission and ministry of the congregation are lived out. This chapter is an affirmation of the ongoing and even increasing importance of the ministry of teaching adults in the congregation.

On the other hand if we say "teaching *matters*," we are opening a door to the many things that go together to make the teaching of adults effective. How we go about the process of teaching adults can mean the difference between stagnation and transformation in congregations.

TEACHING IS CENTRAL TO THE CHURCH'S MISSION

Often we look back to Matthew 28 as our imperative to have a strong ministry of teaching in the congregation. We could just as well look further back into the Old Testament and the Torah, or not so far back to the early Christian church and its catechumenate. In the early church teaching was the central means for inviting persons into the fellowship of the church. The Apostles' Creed and the Lord's Prayer provided the words that made up the core of the tradition of the church. Although the process used was called "catechetical instruction" it was really a way to form the whole life and being of the convert through the lived faith of the members of the Christian community. This kind of formation was partly responsible for leading Martin Luther in 1529 to write his catechisms as summary of the essential teachings of the church. One cannot fail to note the influential role teaching has played in the development of the church.

When we look at recent books in adult Christian education, it soon becomes clear that there is a renewed concern for teaching in the church. To mention only a few of the most helpful of the recent books: Eugene Roehlkepartain's *The Teaching Church* (Abingdon, 1993); Richard Osmer's *A Teachable Spirit* (Westminster/John Knox, 1990) and *Teaching for Faith* (Westminster/John Knox, 1992); and Margaret A. Krych's book *Teaching the Gospel Today* (Augsburg Publishing House, 1987). Ours is a teaching church. The Protestant church was born in the university. Martin Luther was a teacher. Osmer worries that the church today has forgotten its call to teach: "What is missing from mainline Protestantism today is a vital teaching office by which the foundations of Bible and Christian doctrine are taught to the members of most congregations."[1]

While there is a tendency to think of teaching as relating first of all to children, it is the theme of this book that teaching adults is a first and fundamental task of the church. It takes prepared and committed adults to be models for children, youth, and those outside the church. While it is clear that adult learnings have their origin in earlier life, it is also true that reflection on former learnings and building on them must take place later in adult life. In the understanding of the Roman Catholic Church, adult education or *catechesis*, "including parent and family education and allied programs for the enrichment of married life, has become more prominent."[2] In fact it is the chief form of catechesis. We do not graduate from the need to learn or reflect on our learnings as we make the transition into adulthood. Learning is not only an ongoing possibility, it is an ongoing must. "Because of its importance and because all other forms of catechesis are oriented in some way to it, the catechesis of adults must have high priority at all levels of the Church. The success of programs for children and youth depends to a significant extent upon the words, attitudes, and actions of the adult community, especially parents, family, and guardians."[3]

Walter Brueggemann is known for his concern about teaching and passing on the traditions of the church. Tradition is another word for unanimity about fundamentals which have been brought into being by the trials, errors, and corrections of centuries; experience teaches. In his book *The Creative Word*, Brueggemann writes: "Every community that wants to last beyond a single generation must concern itself with education. Education has to do with the maintenance of a community through the generations. This maintenance must assure enough continuity of vision, value, and perception so that the community sustains its self-identity. At the same time, such maintenance must assure enough freedom and novelty so that the community can survive in and be pertinent to new circumstances. Thus, education must attend both to processes of continuity and discontinuity in order to avoid fossilizing into irrelevance on the one hand, and relativizing into disappearance on the other hand."[4]

Images of Teaching and Learning

Early in our discussion of adult Christian education, it is important that we note the importance of the image adults have of the teaching and learning process. All humans are governed by general images. How important is the adult's image of just what the learning group is all about? James Fowler, in *Becoming Adult, Becoming Christian,* argues that we grow and become adults in terms of some image or myth of the life story that defines for us what it means to become a complete human being.[5] In the same way adults operate with an overall understanding of what adult education in the church feels like. There are a number of common images or metaphors to be found. Conversation among participants in adult classes uncovers different images of adult learning:

• Our adult learning group is like a *class in school.* We come here to learn things we don't know and to be taught about the things we should know. We need an expert, someone who knows more than we do to tell us what we ought to know and do.

• We are more like friends having a serious *conversation* together. We talk about important things like the Bible and doctrine, and we discuss how life is going as we seek to be disciples in the world today.

• Ours is mainly a *fellowship time* in which we gather around a coffee pot ("Coffee—Grounds for Conversation," as it is called in one congregation) and discuss whatever comes up. We try to see the Christian angle.

• We are longtime friends in our group and we see ourselves as being on a *procession together.* This idea carries the powerful impact of seeing life as a journey not only together but leading somewhere. The idea of destination keeps the feeling of moving ahead and making progress alive. (Here the imagery of the Palm Sunday parade comes to mind—Jesus going to Jerusalem and the cross.) Our journey together is a lifelong moving from sin, death, and despair to reconciliation, rebirth, and hope. It's like the Easter story. We talk about where we have come from, where we are, and where we are going. We try to support and help each other as we move into the future. No matter what we study in our group, we see ourselves together as Israel moving toward the promised land, as a community of Christ moving forward.

• Most of the time we *tell stories.* We find that we are most interested when we read stories from the Bible and listen to each other's stories. A lot of our stories come from our teacher, to be sure; but we all tell our own stories as well. Learning becomes personal for us as we talk about my story, your story, and God's story.

• Our class seems most like a *theater* or *auditorium* or even a *lecture hall* where we sit and listen to the teacher. We can't talk much but we learn very important things. (In some congregations the image goes even further: When I come to our class I feel as though I am in a *sports arena*, where members are competing to control the topics and conversation. Most members just sit back and watch the vocal competitors battle it out with their words.)

While these metaphors may appear to be oversimplifications, it is true that the teacher plays a vital part in how adults picture the teaching process. Our images have been built largely by the teachers we have known.

Basic Motivations of Teachers

The initial basic mind-set of the teacher subtly controls much of what adult learners feel about the learning process and how the teacher handles teaching. Jack L. Seymour and Donald E. Miller have identified five approaches to teaching that seem to cover the basic *motivations* of most seasoned teachers in congregations, especially teachers of adults.[6] These serious theological categories lie behind the popular images just noted.

Some teachers are motivated by the strong desire to pass on the *tradition of the church.* Christian learning is primarily for the purpose of encountering God's self-revelation in the faith tradition. We must think deeply about the gospel and its implications for life. We must decide where we stand. We must believe. These teachers tend to stress the importance of content. Often they see the goal of the session as covering a maximum amount of content.

Other teachers of adults are motivated by a sense of the importance of the *faith community,* the church. The task of education is to help persons understand and embody the meaning of being God's people and a community of Christ in the world. Formation, rituals, and participation are very important. Togetherness in feeling is more important than what is being studied. The important concerns are those of the whole community. Personal interaction is important.

A third motivator for teachers is concern with faith development and *individual persons.* Fowler's *Stages of Faith* becomes very important in this approach. We educate in order to help individual learners participate in life in mature ways. Nurturing the natural unfolding of faith and helping persons through the experiences and transitions of life are important. In any given group of adults we are going to find persons who are at different stages in their faith development, or who are experiencing transitions between stages.

Another approach sees *the world as its arena* and works to improve the social, cultural, and political context of persons across the globe. These teachers seek to help persons embody the lifestyle of Christian participation, in striving to right the wrongs of the world. Finally, some teachers see their task as helping learners *make connections* between faith and the events of life, thereby finding meaning in life. Teachers help learners interpret life experiences in the light of the gospel.

While we don't want to pit these attitudes and motivators against each other, it is important to see that our major images create for us an overall attitude about adult Christian learning. Undoubtedly the teacher, whether lay or clergy, is a key figure in shaping the attitudes that adult learners bring into learning. Pastors often operate as teachers of adult learners and teachers. Obviously they play a key role among teachers of adults in the congregation. According to Eugene Roehlkepartain, sixty-two percent of pastors in congregations participating in the *Effective Christian Education* study (Search Institute, 1993) teach adult classes and eighty-three percent say that they like teaching adults. Pastors have the additional responsibility to "equip the saints" and be active in the educating of teachers in the congregation. Teaching has always been among the ministry priorities of the pastor.[7]

All of this puts heavy responsibility on the shoulders of the teacher. The teacher is asked to fill many roles. No single term can cover all the roles filled by the teacher of adults. The teacher is model, leader, guide, challenger, friend, partner, interpreter, host, listener, demonstrator, motivator, midwife, storyteller, learner, planner, class manager, judge—and many more things. These are all functions that matter if teaching is to be effective.

FIVE KEY FUNCTIONS

In the rest of this chapter we will look at five particularly important factors that are keys to good teaching in adult groups. See chapter 8 for additional comments on teacher preparation and planning.

• A solid faith base lies at the foundation of good teaching of adults in the congregation.

• In good teaching of adults there is an openness to life experiences.

• Thorough teacher preparation and planning create maximum adult learning possibilities.

• The ability to know and use diverse kinds of learning experiences helps to ensure that every adult learner is drawn into the learning circle.

• Cooperative teacher and adult learner evaluation helps identify ways in which learning can be more powerful.

A Solid Faith Base

A solid faith base lies at the foundation of good teaching of adults in the congregation. Surely if we were trying to make a list of the things that are important for good teaching of adults, we would have to put the faith foundation of the teacher on top. Faith is not just a matter of content; it is a matter of attitude and action as well. It is the *sine qua non* of the elements that matter. Faith is not only a subject to be taught; it is a value that is made real in the quality of life exhibited by the teacher.

The good teacher is a model for adult learners. Faith must come before the teaching of faith. The teacher is a model not only to learners in the group, but to the entire congregation, including children and youth. Parker Palmer says that it is important for the teacher of adults to be seen as a *professor*.[8] Surprised? Not when we look at the teacher as being someone who professes faith in the life being lived.

Mary Elizabeth Moore adds a significant dimension to professing when she says that teaching involves "sending forth energy."[9] One fine teacher did her teaching on a Friday evening when everybody, including herself, was tired out from a long week of work and ready to coast. Learners invariably left her room renewed because of her contagious excitement and passion; she was sending out her vitality. And the adults in her class were catching it not only in their minds but in their hearts, spirits, and voices. Her genuineness and commitment were so strong that no one could fail to experience learning at its most exciting level.

Teachers as Models. We teach first by modeling. Charles Melchert commented in a recent workshop that what I teach is actually *me*. What gets through to learners is what I am and what I feel is valuable—the things I believe. In the teaching process both learner and teacher enter into each other's lives.

What we model more than anything else should be the sense of God's presence in our lives. Hans-Reudi Weber says it is important that the teacher manifest the presence of God.[10] Teaching to him is a *theophonic* experience because it, like the theophanies of Scripture (Moses and the burning bush, the baptism of Jesus, and the Transfiguration, for example), is the stuff of direct encounter with God. Because of my baptism, God not only presents himself to me and shows himself but he also *dwells* in me. My teaching must be transparent and show the presence of God within. Enthusiasm for the gospel is an important element in the effective teaching of adults. Palmer notes that "students will often say that their favorite teachers are ones who are enthusiastic about their subjects even if they are not masters of teaching technique."[11] Nothing puts adults to sleep like a teacher's halfhearted enthusiasm. If the good news makes a difference in our lives, we will show it!

John Westerhoff talks about the "affiliative faith" of children.[12] Much of the teacher rubs off on the learner, young or old. Children catch faith by associating (usually) with older and more experienced people of faith, through being closely connected with adults who know and confess the tradition. Interestingly, one meaning of the word *affiliate* is "to trace the origin of." Origins such as that of Baptism and the biblical stories of creation, redemption, and the establishment of the church are at the base of our faith that is meant to be shared.

In a certain sense the teacher of adults has more influence on learners than the teacher of children, at least in terms of time. Adulthood lasts so much longer than childhood or youth, whose teachers have an impact on learners only for a comparatively short time.

Teachers as Givers and Receivers. The good teacher takes initiative to share the deeply important things that have been received. One thing is sure: the teacher cannot share something that is not first experienced and owned. The teacher can be giver only after being receiver. The teacher must be both. Alan Jones highlights the importance of this dual blessing:

> What are we going to hand on to the next generation? What do we hand on to our children? Do we hand on a life without commitment? Do we hand on a life which is not marked by the keeping of promises? Do we hand on a life of lost integrity? Or do we hand on a life pregnant with promise because it is God's? . . . Do we hand on fire? There is a great deal at stake in our understanding ourselves as men and women of tradition, in this lively sense. We are those who are called to hand on life. Fire is very dangerous. . . . Our God is a consuming fire. We will be burned up either by the fire of God's love or the fire of our self-centeredness. Which will it be?[13]

Clearly the teacher's growth in faith and in faith energy must not be relegated to the past; they are active elements never given a graduation cap. The teacher both receives (in the past and now) and consistently passes on the good news of God in Christ. Martin Luther reminds us that the church, too, is both constant receiver and mediator of salvation. The teacher is in the dynamic and holy position of both giving and receiving at the same time. We must not make this important position sound too prosaic or ordinary, because it isn't.

What we are given, what we pass on, is alive and hot; it is like handling fire. As one Bible scholar has said, translating the Bible from the original languages into English is like rewiring an old house with the electricity still turned on. The person doing the wiring is bound to get shocked in the process. Because of the powerful message we handle as teachers, we become involved in dealing with a living, even life-shocking gospel—a matter that is not easy and that can and does affect us in an ongoing way as much as it does the learner.

Teachers as Inviters and Exhibitors of Commitment. The good teacher of adults in the congregation views teaching as inviting and exhibiting commitment to God. Herein lies a strong lesson we can learn from the catechumenate of the early church, where the whole, lengthy, demanding process of preparation led toward total commitment to Christ through the community of the church. This means that there must be a lot of evangelical conversation going on in the adult learning group. Such conversation dwells on the promise of the good news and on the Baptism that brought us into a saving relationship with God. Luther did this constantly in his teaching, preaching, and writing, but especially in the catechisms. Spiritual dialogue between faith and life gives shape to his catechisms and should also give shape to adult learning. In his question *"Was ist das?"*—roughly translated "What does this mean for my life every day?"—Luther provides us with an example of the kind of invitation we make in our teaching. As Paul said when he wrote to Timothy, "I remind you to rekindle the gift of God that is within you through the laying on of my hands; for God did not give us a spirit of cowardice, but rather a spirit of power and of love and of self-discipline. Do not be ashamed, then, of testimony about our Lord or of me his prisoner, but join with me in suffering for the gospel, relying on the power of God" (2 Timothy 1:6-8).

Teachers as Keepers of Community Memory. Part of the task of the teacher of adults is to be keeper of the memory of the community. Adult teachers and learners alike not only create important things to be remembered by ages yet to be, but they also must keep the traditions and teachings passed on to them from parents and grandparents and the fathers and mothers of the church of history. This is clearly the task of adults: "Remember today that it was not your children (who have not known or seen the discipline of the Lord your God), but it is you who must acknowledge his greatness, his mighty hands, and his outstretched arm, his signs and his deeds" (Deuteronomy 11:2-3).

One of the important reasons for teaching adults is to aid them in remembering and re-presenting (*anamnesis*). Weber believes that the Bible may have been more what it was intended to be in the days before it was printed and found its way into book form. The oral stories that make up Scripture were first passed on "by heart," or out of memory.[14] He points out that in the Bible *anamnesis* doesn't mean simply remembering in the sense of bringing up on the screen of the mind something from the past: "It means actually to participate in them, to make them present and to re-enact them."[15]

It is the special responsibility of adult learners in the congregation to tend to preserving the memories and traditions of the church. This is done, of course, in the worship and liturgical life of the community. But in adult Christian education there is opportunity to ask questions, respond, and examine in depth the corporate memory and to consider the importance of our response. Human memory is like a camera. It captures an experience from only one particular perspective; it is not an overall picture. Teaching and learning are a matter of putting the various human pictures together so that we can get a more complete picture of truth.

Memory is much more than a matter of gathering facts. Daniel Goleman reminds us that there is such a thing as *emotional* memory and that it is often stronger than intellectual memory: intellectual encounters that lack emotional weight lose their hold.[16] Charles Foster reminds us that memory can never deal only with things past: "The function of memory is not to pull us into the past. It beckons us instead to embrace a future originating in events that called our communities into being."[17]

The importance of community creates a difference between teaching children or youth and teaching adults. Adults are the elders of the community. Just as we have been shaped by those who are elders in our own lives, we in turn become the elders who take part in shaping the next generation.

All people are shaped by their memories. And we, most often not knowing it consciously, pass on what we have received. This is one reason the study of Scripture is so important in adult learning.

Deuteronomy 6 tells us of the importance of keeping the tradition, about rehearsing that memory daily in our living and in our teaching so that we can pass it on to those yet unborn. Luther's Small Catechism is a good preserver of corporate memory. It links our present generation not only with the past but with the future. It points directly to Scripture and is meant to be a summary of the chief truths of the Bible. Luther would probably say, "I have put into my catechism what matters most from the Bible."

A solid faith base is strengthened by learning. The good teacher is a perpetual learner, always growing in faith. This is especially true when it comes to matters of faith. Fowler's research shows that adults, regardless of age, have a still deeper level of faith ahead of them. The catechumenate of the early church provides us with ancient insight that needs to be preserved. Once the catechumens became the elect and were received in Baptism, there followed what was called the period of *mystagogy*, which lasted through and beyond the Easter season. This was the time after incorporation into the Christian community when the baptized and communing new Christians grew in depth of faith while recalling and reflecting upon and affirming the mysteries of the Baptism that brought them into the presence of Christ and that food which strengthened them as children of God. This reflecting, strengthening process lasts as long as life itself. It is a time of growing into what we already are in Christ.

Openness to Life Experiences

In good teaching of adults there is an openness to life experiences. A second matter that is important in the effective teaching of adults is being open to the world in which we live, as contrasted with a closed awareness to what is going on in life beyond the congregation. Psalm 104 speaks strongly of the God who creates and sustains the earth. Psalm 8 is unforgettable: "When I look at your heavens, the work of your fingers, the moon and the stars that you have established; what are human beings that you are mindful of them, mortals that you care for them? . . . You have given them dominion over the works of your hands" (Psalm 8:3-6).

The First Article of the Apostles' Creed is another reminder to us that God is creator of heaven and earth. We are *in* the world but not *of* the world. Luther makes clear in his explanation of the article that "God has created me together with all creatures."[18] Some translations read that God has created me "and all that exists." The Christian lives in the world and is not shut off from the world.

Teaching in a Changing World. Luther gave up the life of monasticism and stepped directly into the risky fire of God's created world. He found, as we find, that the changing world around us teaches us just as much as words teach us. John L. Elias writes, "It is clear that adulthood differs according to the social contexts in which adults live and develop."[19] The term *context* is rich in meaning. It is alive with change. Elias notes a number of dimensions of context and we do not need to reach far to discover more. He notes, for example, changes in demographic context: our population has become more heterogeneous; there is increasing urbanization; geographic mobility is increasing; there is a higher degree of educational attainment; and the number of older adults in society is rapidly changing. These are just aspects of our demographic setting. Religious pluralism is another dimension of our context. "The doctrinal pluralism of modern religions increases the need for more intensive adult education among the members."[20]

Moral pluralism is yet another part of our changing human context. One of the areas in which there has been a shift in adult thinking is in the area of *morality*.[21] Many church members "have begun to look to church leadership not as an authority but as a guide in the moral sphere of life. The principle of individual freedom and responsibility has often been enunciated in moral teachings but it is usually connected with the injunction to submit to the authoritative teachings of the religious bodies."[22] "The attempt of religious bodies to reach those who have '*lost faith*' or *become alienated* has intensified in recent years."[23] "To be truly effective adult religious education must be sensitive to the social context within which education takes place."[24]

Linda Vogel puts it clearly: "To be a person of faith . . . we must be in touch with the world. . . . To be a person of faith one must be in touch with God."[25] Malcolm Knowles reminds us that it is no longer realistic to define the purpose of education as transmitting what is known.[26] We cannot avoid context as we cannot avoid air. Although we are learning more and more about the world we live in, there is still so much to be learned. Christians cannot learn by keeping the world out. If we try, our learning will not correspond with reality.

One of the perennial criticisms of the church is that it is isolated and locked into its own world of concern. Christian education fails when it doesn't take life experiences into account. Christian education must be grounded in life experience. William E. Diehl writes that "laity desperately need help in connecting their Sunday faith to their Monday world."[27]

Adult learning groups that are not open to experiences outside their own rooms are not welcoming to new persons expressing interest in joining. Class visitors will find it impossible to break in. Openness on the part of the congregation and the adult learning group is important. Christians speak not only to themselves but are the bearers of the promise to the world.

Recognizing and dealing squarely with change is a part of good adult teaching and learning. The teacher must be reminded often that we are living in a time that is characterized not only by change but by rapid and wide-reaching change. Some writers have characterized our present situation by saying that we live in an *apathetic* and *distracted* world where change has come so quickly and so often that we no longer see it. Adults—all of us—have more and more things to distract us.

Current Challenges to Teaching. A popular National Public Radio program dealing with computer software ends each weekly episode with the comment, "Remember! Everything you learned here today will be null and void by this time next week." Today the teacher of adults is facing new and difficult challenges that have never come together in quite the same way. Let's look briefly at some of the changes that have descended so quickly on the church and its education programs.

During the last decade or so there has been a reduction in the support for education in congregations from denominational offices. Churchwide fiscal problems and local focus have made it harder for congregations to secure resources, expert outside training for teachers, and motivation from the church beyond the congregation. Congregations have been forced to be more self-dependent.

We are experiencing more short-term teaching at all age levels in the congregation's education program. Where, in the past, a teacher expected to teach every Sunday, teachers today are teaching for limited periods of time, usually for a month or six weeks.

Attendance in learning groups of all ages is more inconsistent and unpredictable. It is difficult for the teacher of adults to expect group members in a gathering to be familiar with what the group did the week before. This makes teaching arduous for the teacher who is met each week by faithful attendees and those who are there once in a while. For one thing, this means that teachers of adults need to think of each gathering as an independent unit of study in which references to immediate past or immediate future gatherings are very limited.

Because of growing pluralism, it is a challenge to identify a common corporate memory in the adult learning group. Learners come from vastly different places, different church traditions, or no tradition at all, and are at different stages in their knowledge of and commitment to the church.

Among many adults, there is a feeling that learning the essential faith concepts of the church is good, but that it really isn't necessary to continue learning once they have reached a "minimum necessary" adult plateau. This usually is defined as the level of youth confirmation. Confirmation has become the ancient exodus experience and the church the Egypt fled.

Bible reading, home devotions, and family conversation around topics of faith are taking place less frequently. Usually the reason given is that the schedules of family members are busy and at cross purposes. What little Bible learning most adults have today comes from that ten-minute period in worship on Sunday when the lessons are read. Occasionally, seasonal reminders like Advent or Lent touch our hearts and inspire us to spend time in Bible reading and reflection. Charles Foster writes that "with each generation over the past fifty years, attrition in knowledge and skills crucial to a corporate Christian witness has relentlessly sapped the strength of the church's identity and mission."[28]

The teacher of adults must be more aware than ever before of how family life is changing. Urie Bronfenbrenner, Cornell University developmental psychologist, writes,

> In the absence of good support systems, external stresses have become so great that even strong families are falling apart. The hecticness, instability, and inconsistency of daily family life are rampant in all segments of our society, including the well-educated and well-to-do. What is at stake is nothing less than the next generation, particularly males, who in growing up are especially vulnerable to such disruptive forces as the devastating effects of divorce, poverty, and unemployment. The status of American children and families is as desperate as ever.[29]

Linda Vogel summarizes our concern: "Religious learning cannot be isolated from faithful living."[30] There can be no doubt that adults are learning more outside the church's teaching session than in it. Learning is a natural function that God has built into humans; we have the capability to learn all the time from all our experiences regardless of where they take place. The teaching session is an important place to clarify, reflect on, and pull together learnings and experiences that daily life gives us little time to process.

If we listen carefully, we can learn an important lesson from life in the changing world outside the learning group. There we spend so much more time listening than we do talking. Listening comes before teaching. Foster makes much of the importance of listening: "The Bible has a lot to say about hearing and about the living grounded in our responses to what we hear."[31] Hans Reudi Weber begins his book *The Book That Reads Me* by reminding us that "hearing has primacy in the Bible over reading and seeing."[32] For one thing, as Foster points out, this means listening to the world's people who are different and who come from a different background: "An education that relies on hearing emphasizes the interdependence, mutuality, and interconnectedness of experience."[33]

Establishing a Climate of Openness. Openness to life experiences must also describe the climate established in the setting of the learning session. Much has been written about the importance of environment or learning space (the need to provide the climate that promotes learning). Malcolm Knowles begins his book *Self-Directed Learning* by noting that establishing a climate that is conducive to learning is perhaps the first and most critical matter in the facilitating of learning.[34] To talk about the teaching environment is to be concerned with things beyond the size of the room in which the group meets and the arrangement of the chairs. It embraces many circles of people and experiences outside the session that affect how we feel and respond in the class.

Henri Nouwen suggests that the second movement in developing spiritual life is the creation of space where students and teachers can enter into a fearless communication with each other and allow their respective life experiences to be their primary and most valuable source of growth and maturation. Space provides hospitality.[35]

Often the teacher has little to say about where the adult learning group meets. We generally give prime space to children's learning groups. The teacher of adults, therefore, must be careful and creative about building an effective teaching space. As Vogel puts it, "The task of adult religious education is to create settings and processes [methods or strategies] that invite people to journey together—exploring, reflecting, experiencing, and acting in and toward faith."[36] And Osmer also notes that "the purpose of our teaching in the church is to create a context in which faith can be awakened, supported and challenged."[37]

The importance of climate for adult learning cannot be overemphasized. *Interpersonal climate* (trust, caring, togetherness) and *physical climate* (comfort, variety, mobility, and sensory accommodation) are both important. Climate is a psychological as well as a physical matter. Leon McKenzie points to the role of the teacher in establishing the learning climate: "As manager of the instructional process the teacher is responsible for initiating the structures that permit the creation of an appropriate climate for learning."[38] Generally, adult educators agree that the best climate for adult learning includes the following:

• *The physical comfort of the learners.* Care must be taken with adult learners because many adults experience deficits in sensory responses. This means that seating arrangements, lighting, and acoustics must be good. We need to do whatever is possible to help adult learners focus their attention. Paul Bergavin has noted, "Trivial things are never trivial in adult education."[39]

• *Freedom of expression.* Something is amiss if adult learners can't feel free to express their genuine questions and concerns. While it is true that there will always be learners (and teachers) who tend to dominate conversation, the teacher is responsible for seeing that ample time is given for response. The teacher who feels compelled to control all that is said must learn that the teacher does not learn *for* the students. Unless there is some kind of physical and verbal response, we'll never know what is happening in the life of the learner.

• *Mutual trust and respect.* Respect between teacher and students and respect among the learners themselves is both verbal and physical. It is shown in communication and in caring response. To respect someone means to value and dignify that person. This is especially important today because of the diversity of persons who make up the church. Such respect can well turn out to be among the most significant of the factors that make up learning experiences for the adult; and this will apply even more to new adults in the group.

• *Shared responsibility for learning activities and outcomes.* Adults are accustomed to making decisions. Why should it be any different in the learning group? The teacher-dominated adult group is probably not the most effective learning group (see figure 1*). The teacher must have confidence that learners can make good decisions about how they learn and what they need to learn. While it may be easier for the teacher to make all the decisions about what happens in the learning session, adults will probably not participate fully unless they have some part in deciding the *what* and *how* of the experience. Adults are masters at knowing ways to check out of full participation—from sitting in the back row to closing their eyes to a "why-don't-you-tell-me" attitude.

How does the teacher set the climate for effective learning? At the beginning of the teaching process, reconcile expectations and articulate the conditions of freedom, trust, respect, and shared responsibility in the learning group. Then, during the course of instruction, support these norms with personal behavior (modeling). Such modeling is of key importance in the building of climate.[40]

* All figures for chapter 4 appear on pages 116 through 120.

Adult Education as Part of Congregational Life. Openness to the whole broad life of the congregation is another important part of adult learning. The congregation, as Vogel reminds us, is the context for adult Christian education: "Teaching must view the total life of the faith community as the agency of educational ministry."[41] The adult learning group is not separate from the many other ministries of the congregation. It is involved in each of them—anywhere learning can and is happening. Too often adult classes become separated from the total ministry of the congregation and become wrapped up in the life of the learning group rather than the mission and ministry of the congregation. There is a proper sense in which the adult learning group can stand apart from the total life of the congregation and look at it objectively; but the movement must always be back into the daily ministry of the congregation, the community of faith. "Faith," C. Ellis Nelson writes, "is communicated by a community of believers and . . . the meaning of faith is developed by its members out of their history, by their interaction with each other, and in relation to the events that take place in their lives."[42]

Maria Harris is recognized as one of the writers in the field of adult education who says that the learning process, especially for adults, is not a cut-off, isolated, or separated ministry of the congregation. She makes the point that adult learning is at its best when it is in touch with the broad dimensions of parish life. In her book *Fashion Me A People*, she uses the Greek terms from Acts to remind us that learning is not something that takes place in the vacuum of a class but is deeply involved with the total ministry of the congregation: proclamation (*kerygma*), worship (*leiturgia*), service (*diakonia*), fellowship (*koinonia*), and teaching (*didache*)[43] are all fair concern for adult learning groups. The members of the learning group are constantly directed to the overall mission of the church of Christ.

Congregations are discovering that what is addressed in adult learning programs in the church is not something we can confine to a "class." It is actually making the entire life and ministry of the congregation come alive. "A fundamental shift takes place in a congregation which moves from a school approach into a community view of Christian education. . . . The purpose shifts from imparting tradition to *traditioning* or using tradition to navigate a change in life."[44] Clark M. Williamson and Ronald J. Allen say it is important that the whole congregation sees itself as a "teaching community." These writers even see congregations as "neighborhood seminaries."[45] Loren Mead also suggests that congregations see themselves as the "new seminaries," the seedbeds of teaching in the contemporary church, where adult education takes on a new priority.[46]

Teacher Preparation and Planning

Thorough teacher preparation and planning create maximum adult learning possibilities. A look at the task of teaching identifies for us the importance of preparation and planning as our strongest tools of intention. Vogel sees adult education as "the lifelong process of intentional engagement with the faith story of our particular faith community, with our own stories, and with those of all people and communities."[47] *Intentional engagement* means preparation and planning. Intentionality suggests that we carefully think ahead about the situation we are to face and construct it, as far as is possible, to achieve our hoped-for outcomes. Purpose, preparation, and planning are the tools of intentionality.

One of the first factors brought to our attention by intentionality is that good teaching is more than telling. "There was a time, before the Gutenberg revolution and the large-scale availability of printed materials, when teaching consisted largely in telling things to learners. . . . The duty of the teacher was to tell something in a form that helped learners remember; the chief duty of the learners was to remember . . . and be able to transmit the myth to the next generation."[48] Paulo Freire's *Pedagogy of the Oppressed* is a devastating attack on the concept of teaching as telling.[49]

Create a Teaching Plan. Leon McKenzie discusses the planning role of the teacher:

> Education, in the instructional sense, involves the agency of a teacher who, ideally, helps others learn. This learning takes place in a systematic rather than random fashion. What imposes order or system on the learning is an *instructional plan* that identifies specific learning objectives, human and material resources for learning, teaching-learning techniques, and a particular sequence of events gauged to assist the learners in the attainment of the objectives. The instructional plan is implemented in a desired . . . climate conducive to learning. The teacher is responsible for initiating this climate, and for supporting adult learners in the maintenance of the climate.[50]

Much of what happens in teaching is hidden from view (see figure 2).[51] Much more substance is found beneath the surface than is visible to the eye. Effectiveness is directly related to the time spent in planning beforehand. When Osmer talks about how the terms *systematic* and *intentional* distinguish education from socialization and enculturation, he is also describing the kind of planning that makes adult learning effective.[52]

Effective teaching usually begins with the use of a brief written planning form, perhaps no more than an outline on a single sheet of paper. The teacher needs to know what is going to happen next and why. The steps of the process must be in the mind of the teacher and, because of this, the particular planning form may not be referred to once a learning session is underway. Although such forms may be used for only a few sessions in their written detail, the structure they provide stays with and governs the teacher's approach for the future.

Good teaching involves being able to make good teaching plans. The plan is not just an outline of what is to be presented to the learners, but includes the key elements around which the teaching session revolves: identifying or forming objectives, deciding on what methods or strategies will achieve the objectives, selecting resources that relate directly and specifically to the purpose, and evaluating what has happened with the learners.

It would be correct to say that good teaching is actually managing learning. James Michael Lee describes teaching in this way. It is "that orchestrated process whereby one person deliberately, purposively, and efficaciously structures the learning situation in such a manner that specified desired learning outcomes are thereby acquired by another person."[53]

The teacher is the manager of the instructional situation. Clearly not all teachers manage in the same way. There are different kinds of managers. McKenzie identifies four styles: domination management, consultative management, consensual management, and compliant management. He concludes, "The most sophisticated research to date suggests that both ends of the continuum of decision style, the dominative and the compliant styles, are not facilitative of learning."[54] Figure 1 illustrates an expanded continuum of teaching styles from teacher dominated to learner dependent.[55]

Probably the best known and most widely used approach to planning for adult education is presented by Knowles, who sees these as the important elements in the process:

    a) the assessment of *needs* and interests of individuals, organizations, and communities;

    b) the translating of needs into program *objectives* by screening them through the criteria of institutional purposes, feasibility, and the interests of the persons involved;

c) the design of programs for learning *methods* or learning *experiences*;

d) the *implementation* of the programs (management of facilities, procedures, promotion, budgeting, and financial support);

e) the *evaluation* of program objectives through standard methods.[56]

Teach to Achieve Objectives. Good teaching moves toward specific objectives. While planning includes a number of parts, no part is more important than developing or using *learning objectives* that are clear and strong. Objectives (purposes, aims, goals) give direction to adult learning. Osmer affirms that "we need a clear idea of what we are trying to accomplish."[57] With adults it is important that "the development of objectives in adult religious education [should] be a cooperative effort"[58] (refer again to figure 1).

One helpful approach to the design of effective experiential learning for adults is the group of strategies called *participative learning* (see figure 3 for a simple analysis of the steps included in one approach).

Good teaching also involves personal relationship building. Relationship building among members of the learning group must be part of the plan. The building of community within the learning group is important. Current study of active, exciting congregations points to the importance of belonging to small groups in which there is opportunity for adequate and manageable personal interrelationship. Adult learning in many congregations has already demonstrated the effectiveness and importance of having primary anchor groups of limited size in which each individual has the time and opportunity to "fit," to listen, to speak, and to interrelate on a one-to-one basis with a few persons.

It is critical to think of teaching as an activity in which adults aid each other.[59] All the members of the group help each other learn and achieve objectives. There are four different kinds of helping attitudes that are commonly identified in adult learning groups: I'll help you by doing it for you; just watch me do it and you'll learn; we've got to experiment together and we'll both learn; and I don't have all the answers. The first of these is another way of making learners depend on the teacher. The other three, however, can provide handles by which to grab "teachable moments." The question "Am I being as helpful to my learners as I can?" is important for teachers.

Being prepared means that the good teacher is always learning. One important kind of learning is *improving personal teaching skills*. Teacher training is important for the teacher of adults. The *Effective Christian Education* study concludes that it is a myth that good teaching can occur without training.[60] Effective teaching is a result of adequate and persistent teacher training. Roehlkepartain suggests that teachers of adults can profit from three types of training: in-service training, instruction in teaching methods or strategies, and instruction in theology and tradition.[61] In-service training (with the use of coteachers, for instance) can be managed whenever a teacher recognizes the need to develop more teaching skills. Instruction in theology and tradition is available in reading, conversation with the pastor, and reading to increase knowledge and skills. Read more about training in chapter 8.

Variety of Learning Experiences

The ability to know and use diverse kinds of learning experiences helps to ensure that every adult learner is drawn into the learning circle. We have seen Jack Seymour and Donald Miller's description of five basic attitudes of the teacher. There are also different models or styles of teaching to be used once learners' needs and objectives have been determined.

The standard teacher text by Bruce Joyce and Marsha Weil, *Models of Teaching*, identifies twenty-one different models under the following general categories: information processing models, personal learning models, social models, and behavior modification models.[62]

John Elias sees the following commonly recognized approaches in teaching adults:

• *Individual/independent study.* The learner works alone to determine what should be learned and how.

• *Tutoring.* The learner is in the hands of an instructor and the two work privately on goals and methods.

• *Learning groups.* Learners work together in small groups where they help each other determine the best learning process for the group as a whole.

• *Teacher-directed group instruction.* The instructor decides what is best for the group and how to achieve it.

• *Committee-guided learning.* The ends and processes of learning are set by a number of experts who work through a teacher.

• *Collaboration.* Learners and teachers work together on goals and methods of instruction.

• *Institutional design.* The school and the power behind the school have complete say regarding ends and means in learning.

In another place he addresses common types of teaching: lecture, lecture-with-audience-reaction, buzz groups, observing groups, idea inventory, question period, group discussion, simulation (role playing, case study, demonstration), and extended educational experiences (clinic, institute, workshop, conference, etc.).[63]

Teaching Strategies and Learning Experiences. The means a teacher uses to bring the learning plan to life are commonly called *methods, strategies,* or *learning experiences.* While these terms are commonly used interchangeably, the term *strategy* implies a carefully crafted and consistently applied plan. These strategies put in motion and activate the process of learning in the life of the learner. They provide a way to explore the purpose at hand. Clearly, the strategy used is important because it can either turn on or turn off the learner. Marshall McCluhan is remembered for telling us that the medium *is* the message, that people usually remember the *how* more than the *what.* Some teachers think that the *how* isn't as important as the *what* and give all their attention to cognitive things. Michael Harton warns us of the false assumption that "because adults are more mature, teaching them does not require attention to *process* as does teaching children and adolescents" and that "adults are only interested in content."[64]

The good teacher will not confine teaching to meeting cognitive objectives, but will remember that much of Christian learning has to do with longings of the heart and mysteries beyond the mind. The instruments by which we know the world outside include heart, mind, soul, and body—all we have. We actually learn through a single instrument (our total being) that includes all these in connection with each other. John Westerhoff and Gwen Kennedy Neville tell us that a seventeenth-century debate over the emotions in human personality took place between Johann Sebastian Bach and Johann August Ernesti. Ernesti, who was a pioneer in the critical study of Scripture, insisted that learners should study more and sing less. Bach responded that the biblical text is designed to release within the reader a deep sort of spiritual activity in faith. Where Ernesti chose religion (a rational, analytical, and intellectual perspective), Bach chose faith (the intuitive, experiential, attitudinal perspective).[65]

The 1995 study on confirmation ministry by the Lutheran World Federation points out that a shift in education is taking place across the worldwide church:

> Pedagogy is no longer only an instrument of theology attempting to transmit eternal truths. Instead, theology and pedagogy are becoming full partners as people come together, aware of their situation, use the Bible and the Small Catechism to reflect on their lives, and build new ways to act together as community . . . .

While in the past, many may have viewed education, learning, and pedagogy as a collection of techniques used to transmit theological understanding, a current movement is the growing equal partnership of theology and pedagogy. A new method emerges as theology and the learning process interact with each other. God is no longer something learned about, but is actively involved in the world, life and history of the learner. Increasingly, the church is challenged to reconsider its way of teaching.[66]

One of the exciting conclusions reached by Daniel Goleman, in his book *Emotional Intelligence,* is that effective teaching touches and shapes not only our cognitive, understanding skills; it also reaches our emotional and action skills. The Latin term for emotion is *motere,* which actually means "to move" or "to move away." Goleman writes that "intelligence can come to nothing when the emotions hold sway."[67]

Although there are many teaching methods or strategy models that can be helpful to the teacher of adults, three are especially promising:

• the TIC TAC TOE model;

• the Mosston continuum model (figure 1);

• "bread and butter" strategies, summarized by Richard Osmer.

TIC TAC TOE. One very simple way to understand teaching methods is to focus on the physical position of the teacher. The "teacher-in-center" approach has the teacher in charge in front of the class. The teacher plays the major role and provides answers for learners. What happens in the class is determined by the teacher.

The "teacher-among-class" style has the teacher working with students in a give-and-take manner. Learning and teaching are seen as joint responsibilities. The teacher does the basic planning, but the learners are involved in determining many of the details of the session.

The "teacher-on-edge" approach has the teacher planning learning experiences, often cooperatively. Once students understand the task to be done, the teacher stands back and lets the learners go about their learning. The teacher intervenes from the edge of the room to give guidance.

The acronyms for the three are TIC, TAC, and TOE.[68] In the classic styles of leadership we might call these styles authoritarian, democratic, and laissez-faire. The beauty of this overly simple analysis is that a single three-letter word spoken or thought can move a failing learning experience into an effective learning experience.

The Mosston Continuum. On the other hand, Muska Mosston outlines a detailed model of teaching methods that focuses on who makes the decisions about what happens in the adult learning group (see figure 1). It is helpful to see these styles on a continuum. There are many choices to be made in three essential time frames: pre-impact (what happens before the session actually begins), impact (the session itself), and post-impact (after the session ends).[69] The more they are allowed to cooperate, the more adult learners buy into the process.

Bread and Butter Strategies. Between these two extremes we find the more common "bread and butter" strategies of teaching. Osmer has a helpful summary list in his book *A Teachable Spirit.* He looks to H. R. Niebuhr, who describes faith as having four sides: belief, relationship, commitment, and mystery. Four teaching strategies come to mind as being the most common.

• *The lecture method* addresses the belief side of faith and is usually the first strategy mentioned when we list methodologies. This approach sees teaching as primarily the transmitting of information. Osmer points out the appropriateness of this approach for meeting some objectives and has over twenty pages of helpful commentary on planning good lectures.

• *Discussion* is the method that helps people to relate to each other. The art of teaching by discussion is one of knowing how to ask and answer questions. Osmer even mentions the creative use of silence as teacher.

Hans-Reudi Weber is a Christian educator who ordinarily works directly with the Bible in teaching large groups of learners, most often in third-world countries. He has developed a discussion method that relates not just to a small handful of learners, but to hundreds meeting together in convention fashion. His approach emphasizes *oral transmission,* which he sees as a method teacher and learner follow together.[70] Weber sees five different ways in which biblical truths may be taught: the oral approach (listening to the Bible being read aloud, telling stories from the Bible, and singing); reading the texts (detailed reading by learners, studying and memorizing words, summarizing, and looking at different literary styles); drama (celebration, worship, symbolic acts and gestures, and the reenactment of Bible stories); making the Bible visible in action and art; meditation (use of mime, rumination, icons and the *lectio divina*).

• *Storytelling* strategies help us arrive at commitment. This method of Bible study is actually a revision of oral tradition. Already in Bible times there were a variety of methods of teaching being used.[71] The telling and interpreting of stories includes narrative, reflection, and encountering. Osmer suggests that this is the best strategy to use when remembering is important to us.

• With *parable and paradox* we are able to touch the aspects of mystery we associate with Christian faith.[72]

Choosing a Teaching Strategy. It is true that teachers develop what Osmer calls "bread and butter" teaching strategies or methods. But the good teacher knows that adults get tired of the same kind of bread and like to have a variety.

We often hear that the teacher is free to choose among many different styles of teaching. Although this is technically true, there are things that limit our choice of methodologies. First, the strategy we choose should be linked with the objective with which we are dealing. Another is that using new learning activities always takes more planning and implementing time. Third, it is also true that certain learning groups have "hardened" to the point where a particular style of teaching has come to be accepted as the *only* way teaching happens in this group. A fourth is that while teachers will hopefully venture into trying new and more effective methods and strategies, they invariably revert to teaching in the way they themselves were taught. Memories—conscious or unconscious—of teachers past lead us to teach as we have been taught. While it is good to honor those who taught us well, we must be conscious of and in control of the teaching methods we select.

Just as the content of what is taught must be well known to the teacher, so must the *how*, the strategy for getting the objectives across. Using different teaching methods is not simply a matter of reading teacher-guide comments on teaching techniques. Although the approaches we have noted are helpful and tested, each must be personalized and improved by the teacher, keeping specific learners in mind. Every teacher has natural abilities and unique teaching gifts; however, we don't choose strategies because they are easy for us or simple; we choose methods that have the greatest potential to help learners achieve the objectives at hand.

It is probably true that most adults approach adult learning groups in the traditional fashion, expecting to have a teacher who is something of an expert and who can tell them what they ought to know. But *knowing* (cognitive learning) is only a part of effective adult education. If learning is to go beyond mere knowing, the teacher of adults must be able to utilize different teaching methods.

Good teaching stimulates interest. Good teaching is lively teaching. Teaching is more effective when it involves the whole being of the learner. Weber suggests that the good teacher is an *animator*, one who makes learning come alive and engage the whole being.[73] Personal interest is related to the emotions. Interest lies at the base of mental development; it is the doorway to attention, comprehension, and apprehension.

The good teacher knows that adults learn in different ways. Some learn best by listening and reading. Others learn when their feelings and emotions are stirred. Still others need an active learning environment in which all three—mind, feelings, and body—are stimulated.

One way for the teacher of adults to be assured that all types of learners are touched in a given teaching session is to build into the session objectives that relate to each domain of learning—cognitive, affective, and active. This means that we will also use different kinds of learning experiences to stimulate different kinds of learning. For instance, we cannot usually expect adults who see each other only once a week to open up easily concerning deeply felt matters. Goleman notes that "people's emotions are rarely put into words."[74] However, when the whole person of the learner is involved, then learning is more likely to happen, even in areas like the cognitive and affective. As Knowles states, "The learner should be an active participant, discovering for himself those things he is ready to discover at a particular phase of his personal development."[75]

Weber bases his strong support of active adult learning experiences partly on the fact that in the Bible verbs predominate over nouns.[76] In *A Simple Way to Pray*, his 1535 letter to his barber, Peter Besskendorf, Luther says that the parts of the catechism are "flint and steel to kindle a flame in the heart."[77] He means that the heart must be on fire for Christ and that the body had better get going.

Cooperative Evaluation

Cooperative teacher and adult learner evaluation identifies ways in which learning can be more powerful. Evaluation is used whenever there is concern for improving the quality of teaching. The term "evaluation" includes in it the idea of *value*. It addresses the things we hold to be important and reminds us to see that they are included in the teaching-learning process. Obviously, if we are going to appraise, we must have a clear idea of what it is we value most. "The quality of the learning experiences which are provided for learners will depend, in part, on the evaluative information which is gathered to support quality planning and development."[78]

In its most simple form the evaluation question is, Are the adults in this learning group learning what we hoped they would? The question is not easy to answer because there are many reasons (noted earlier) why adults participate in adult learning.

Evaluation is one of the teacher's most effective learning tools. Measuring is for the sake of both learner and teacher. Roehlkepartain points out that teacher satisfaction actually increases when evaluation is "constructive and regular."[79] McKenzie adds that "evaluation is necessary to minimize the possibility of instructor illusion regarding outcomes of an educational activity and to provide the instructor with information that may be used for instructional improvement."[80]

Often we hear that evaluating learning in the church is next to impossible because faith is an internal attribute and coming to faith is the work of the Holy Spirit. Yes, the Spirit is actively involved in the class. But it would be silly not to look at the effectiveness of what is going on in the learning situation. Thomas Aquinas pointed out that it is presumptuous to leave everything up to the Holy Spirit.[81]

Assessment in Christian education can take place at different times, in different ways, and in various places. Informal appraisal should take place constantly in conversation and indirect questions. The teaching process can be evaluated by different persons, either inside our outside the adult group. The process usually begins with a clarification of why the group is gathered and what was hoped would be the results of the gathering (objectives). There are other basic concerns addressed in evaluation: program purposes, organizational structure and climate, accuracy of the assessment of needs and interests, program design, operation, and evaluation (are we evaluating the right things in the right ways?).

Two types of evaluation are most common. Final or end evaluation is also called *summative* evaluation. Benjamin Bloom, the educator who helped us understand the different kinds of objectives and the three domains of learning (cognitive, affective, and active) is helpful in describing the role of evaluation in adult education. Summative evaluation refers to the focus of evaluations performed at the completion of a learning activity, course, or a program. It is intended to provide judgments about the program's, not the learner's, merit.[82]

In-process evaluation is sometimes called *formative* evaluation. Formative evaluation provides an indication of future directions for sessions, parts or all of the specific program that is in progress.[83]

It is important in evaluation that we don't frighten learners. Don't judge people, but rather the effectiveness of the learning process. It is important to evaluate not the achievements or shortcomings of learners or even teachers, but to evaluate needs, programs, and plans. We do not award grades or hand out crown stars. Fortunately, the *Effective Christian Education* study discovered that congregations "are much more likely to evaluate programs than people. . . . Each program should be evaluated in light of the established purpose, goals, and objectives."[84]

Most of the evaluation in adult education is informal, and done through conversations of group members either during or after sessions. At its simplest, evaluation includes four questions: Have we met the needs of group members? Have our objectives been clear and on target? Have we reached our goals? How has our learning related to the total community of faith and the mission of the congregation?[85]

Evaluation will happen whether or not we plan it. Adults will talk informally around the edges of the group or beyond the ears of the group and the teacher. Intentional cooperative evaluation will help the learning program become more effective, both for learners and teacher. (See further discussion of this in chapter 8.)

CONCLUSION

However we look at the teaching of adults, the teacher plays a vital role in guiding the process. The power and importance of teaching cannot be overstated; it has tremendous potential for shaping adult lives.

Teachers have the privilege of being the persons in the adult learning group who learn most. The teacher of adults usually ends up learning more than other group members if only because of the hours of planning that have preceded the learning session. Harry Overstreet has written that "a mature person is not one who has come to a certain level of achievement and stopped there. He is rather a *maturing* person, one whose linkages with life are constantly becoming stronger and richer because his attitudes are such as to encourage their growth."[86]

Look at the difference good teachers have made in your life. Their contributions were probably due not so much to the content they covered, but to the way in which they modeled the importance of learning in a personal way.

Teaching is an important office. Where there is little good teaching the church is in danger. "Without this function, the church would not be the church."[87] Teaching is a special calling. The teaching office is an office of honor, trust,and respect. Teaching is a privilege—and a deep responsibility.

The teacher has the opportunity to be part of the shaping of the ongoing gospel message. In his book *Biblical Interpretation in Ancient Israel*, Michael Fishbane writes, "The texts and traditions . . . of ancient Israel, were not simply copied, studied, transmitted, or recited. They were . . . subject to redaction, elucidation, reformulation, and outright transformation. Accordingly, our received traditions are complex blends of *traditum* [the content of tradition] and *traditio* [the process of trans-mission] in dynamic interaction. . . . They are, in sum, the exegetical voices of many teachers . . . from different circles and times, responding to real and theoretical considerations as perceived and as anticipated."[88]

Teachers are servants of the message, a message with ageless dimen-sions. Teaching is important, but "all this is mere striving and childish stammering if one compares it to the overwhelming grandeur of the subject."[89]

While it cannot be denied that some people are "born teachers," most who teach strive constantly to become better teachers. To review, the keys to good teaching of adults are reflected in these statements:

• We must begin with an awareness that teaching is vital to the mis-sion of the church.

• A solid faith base lies at the foundation of good teaching of adults in the congregation.

• In good teaching of adults, there is an openness to life experiences.

• Thorough teacher preparation and planning create maximum adult learning possibilities

• The ability to know and use diverse kinds of learning experiences helps to ensure that every adult learner is drawn into the learning circle.

• Cooperative teacher and adult learner evaluation helps identify ways in which learning can be more powerful.

116

Figure 1
Teaching Styles in Adult Classes: A Continuum Model

COMMAND STYLE	TASK STYLE	RECIPROCAL STYLE	INDIVIDUAL PROGRAM
Theoretically the teacher makes all the decisions re: • preparation • execution • evaluation Teacher is sole decision maker There is only one set of objectives; the teacher's Denies differences in individual: • skills • interests • aspirations Value system is that of the teacher Most used method is demonstration by an expert who provides the standard performance Implies hierarchy of knowledge and power	Learner not involved in most decisions Learner accepts teacher's decisions in the Impact Area Learner can choose where to work or sit (e.g. at a particular learning center or using a particular medium) Studying, learning can happen in different places Learner makes decisions about when and how to study Introduces element of trust Communication becomes more important Introduces idea of individualized response	Learner allowed to make some decisions in Impact Area Learners divided into pairs; one is teacher and one is learner (doer) —roles are alternated Teacher communicates only with teaching partner Immediate feedback from learning partner Introduces element of trust Some decisions are left up to teaching partner Introduces personal relationship Means adjusting larger class organization	(Teacher designed) Teacher lays out cafeteria of topics and tasks Learner selects tasks and level of performance Teacher lays out the frame Objectives set by teacher Objectives are limited, specific and often behavioral Tasks require independent performance Design recognizes differences in individual interests and abilities Learner active in self-evaluation Requires learner self-discipline

GUIDED DISCOVERY	PROBLEM SOLVING	CREATIVE TENSION	INDIVIDUAL PROGRAM
Learners recognized as having different interests and skills	Learner seen as able to solve problems	One learns when one needs to learn	(Learner designed)
Significant change in Impact Area where learner can select subject matter	Teacher sets up open-ended problems for learners to resolve	Learner experiences a need to learn and creates a way to learn	Whether there is learning or not depends completely on the learner
Certain matters disturb the minds of some learners and set up disequilibrium	Learners encouraged to use cognitive powers	Teacher makes suggestions but does not control the learning process	Design is open-ended
Goal of learning is to create equilibrium by removing cause of irritation	Learners can decide in any matter so long as problem at hand is solved	Learner judges when learning is completed and adequate	Learner has complete decision-making freedom in all areas: • Pre-Impact • Impact • Post-Impact
Teacher deliberately sets up irritations for learners	Learner involved in more quantity and quality decisions	Teacher moves to give learner confidence and resources	Teacher stands on edge or further away from the learning situation
Learners encouraged to make/discover solutions		Teacher intervenes only when asked by learner	Program encourages independent creative behavior
Teacher usually knows the answer but never tells		Learner responsible for putting learning into practice	Program requires additional planning and time on the part of the learner
Teacher accepts and reinforces learner solutions			
Teacher helps to direct: • nature of learner steps • initial steps • further steps • size of steps			

An analysis based on the question, "Who makes the decisions about learning?"

These decisions relate to three areas:
  A. Pre-Impact (preparation)
  B. Impact (execution)
  C. Post-Impact (evaluation)

Figure 2
An Overview of the Teaching/Learning Session

Much of teaching effectiveness is determined by what happens before and after the teaching session.

A. Teaching is like an iceberg. What is experienced by the learner is only part of what goes into the learning session.

B. What happens in the group learning (2. Impact Area) is preceded by planning (1. Pre-Impact Area) and is followed by evaluation (3. Post-Impact Area).

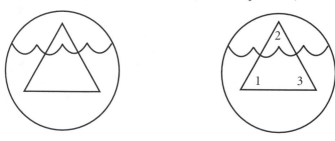

C. The teaching/learning process includes a number of more or less sequential steps.

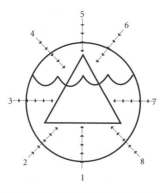

1. Start or restart (determine content and direction)
2. Early planning (get objectives in mind)
3. Final preparation (determine objects and complete session plan)
4. Opening experience (plan strong initial learning experience)
5. Learning experiences (choose active involvement experiences)
6. Closing experience (plan closure for impact)
7. Teacher evaluation (put session in context of unit or course)
8. Thinking ahead (restart the cycle)

Figure 3
Experiential Learning Theory

Most of us have said at one time or another that we learn most from experience. This is only partly true because, even though we have "experienced" new learnings, we seldom take time to stop to process and internalize the experience to make the learnings stick.

Most teaching today is deductive in nature (i.e. it begins with a conclusion or generalization, something that is true in most cases.) The facts related then are illustrated with examples and end up with the learner to be applied. Facts are presented by teachers to be either accepted or discussed by learners. The facts are considered to be more important than the students; facts are objective. Study becomes content centered. Learners learn to depend on teachers to be authority figures or experts. Students are expected to move from the abstract to the concrete.

Experiential learning is much more than simply being thrown into a group action. In it, the learner is encouraged to take a disciplined look at experience, especially a common experience that belongs to the group, and then reflect on its full implications. In this theory the learner moves from the known to the unknown (i.e. from something actually experienced to applying it to situations yet unknown). The idea is that basic learnings, beliefs and commitments are better internalized when they are thought out rather than handed out. The Latin verb *educare* means "to lead forth" or "to draw out": it does *not* mean "to feed in." In this approach persons and experiences become more important than materials or facts known by the teacher. Adults often have difficulty in moving into this type of learning because they are more limited than children—not in abilities or understanding, but in freedom and openness.

The theory can be summarized with the acronym "D-R-A-P-E" because it falls into five more ore less sequential parts, which are described on the following page. Learning is like draping yourself around an experience, either alone or in a group.

D is for "do" or "experience." Most learning begins with participation in experience or with the actual practicing of a skill. In a good lesson plan the skill or experience will be described by an objective, and a common group experience will be developed at the beginning of the learning session. Adding to the element of "doing" activities like "thinking about" and "talking about" gives the learner an actual, objective frame of reference that is more or less common to the learning group. "Doing" involves the entire learner—mind, heart, and body.

R is for "reflect" or "replay" or "describe" the experience. Once the experience has been completed, it is time to take a close look at what happened. The teacher may help the group zero in on a particular part of the common experience for the purpose of review. This is the "becoming aware of what happened" step. What exactly did we do? How did we do it? Who did what? What prompted what? What was communicated? What feelings were expressed?

A is for "analyze" or "probe" or "think deeply about." In this third step, we attempt to look at the forces that were moving behind the actual things that happened. What does this mean? What causes what? What insights did we gather? How were you personally affected by the experience? What did you discover—about yourself, about others, about truth?

P is for "put into use" or "apply" or "generalize." Here we work to ask about the relationship between the experience and what lies ahead of us. We attempt to apply learnings to life through such questions as: What does this mean for daily life? What will I do with what I have learned? This amounts to a concept or generalization where learning is applied to other parts of life. Here is where we work on transferring learning to life outside the learning group.

E is for "evaluate" or improve the efficiency and effectiveness of the whole experiential learning process. This is done when the teacher and learners work cooperatively and anticipate making future experiences more helpful.

chapter five

Content Areas
of Adult Education

Donald R. Just
Eugene C. Krieder

"Therefore, since we are surrounded by so great a cloud of witnesses, let us also lay aside every weight and the sin that clings so closely, and let us run with perseverance the race that is set before us" (Hebrews 12:1).

No one runs alone, or the whole race in one moment in time. The essential challenge of lifelong learning is to find oneself, as an individual or as a congregation, within the sweep and gift of our biblical and denominational tradition and heritage, claiming it for now and for what lies ahead. Our challenge is to discover the focus of learning for the particular Christian life each of us faces. We cannot be all of history; we can only be who we are in it.

Lifelong learning not only looks to the future. It also looks to the past, for the sake of the future, with an emphasis on who we will become, attending to the creative urges and impulses of the Spirit in order to know more fully the call of God to be faithful in the joy, responsibility, and trust of living. The ambience of such a posture is alive both with things to know and ways to live. This chapter calls adult education leaders and teachers to explore these urgings and impulses through the four traditional content focus areas of Christian education:

- the Bible;
- church history;
- theology;
- ethics.

THE BIBLE

Holy Scripture

Important things are often held in high esteem, yet not honored by the use for which they were intended. Christians have experienced the Bible this way. The Bible is Holy Scripture. They study it to know it better with that thought in mind, but they do not always give equal attention to applying what it teaches in daily life. The Bible is the foundation of Christian knowledge. It is also the soil in which the roots of faith are nourished and grown. The Bible needs to be studied and used in lifelong learning.

As the story of people's experiences with God, the Bible came about through a long process. It was first part of the community's oral tradition. Later this tradition was written. That record gained significance beyond the concrete human situations out of which it emerged. People began to place high value on it because of the claim that it was inspired by God's Spirit. The community eventually called it Holy Scripture.

The Bible is a story about how God and people work things out in the world. It is like a dialogue between God and people that draws readers into the conversation in order that they, too, might find God's living word as they interpret, understand, and believe what they discover in Scripture. In the human words of Scripture, God calls people to faith through wonder and imagination. The Bible is the written record that keeps the conversation between God and people going from generation to generation, revealing God's will for all creation.

That conversation is sustained by the confidence and hope it engenders in each generation, as people learn about God's will and promises for them. The Bible is authoritative because it reveals God's love in Christ to us. It becomes authoritative for a Christian community, not because it is capable of revealing once and for all everything about God, but because it provides the vehicle of conversation through which God is made known to each particular person, generation, and age.

Thus, the Bible is a living record, constantly moving through the lives of people with a message that takes shape out of the particularities of each conversation. It is not a collection of definitive answers but the authoritative source and norm through which the Spirit leads people to faith and life. The Bible is the point of contact that continues to spark the conversation between God and people in ever new and fresh ways.

This does not mean that God's Word is tentative. It does mean, however, that God's Word is always mediated. God's living Word comes through what God has created. God's Word uses the "language" of creation. The Bible brooks no virtual-reality seekers who want to claim as actual and real some fantasies about a never-never land where life is goodness beyond imagination. The Bible is a testimony about what we can come to know about life in the presence of God—with all its ups and downs, its contradictions and assurances.

God's presence and Word are gifts. The gift of Scripture is a concrete sign that God's people need to listen always with anticipation to the conversation going on between God and people, regardless of who the principle speakers and listeners might be at any given moment. What, for example, can be heard in the conversation between God and the patriarchs, between God and the people to whom the prophets spoke? What is in the conversation to be heard in the surges of history from the time of Solomon through the life, death, and resurrection of Jesus and into the struggles of the early Christians? In each facet of the conversation, Scripture can signal the continual, revealing presence of God in the community of believers. As God's Spirit inspired the biblical writers, and later the interpreters of Scripture, so that same Spirit inspires Bible users in every age to find in Scripture an entrance into God's conversation with people.

The Bible for Lutherans

What has been said above more generally about the Bible and the people of God can certainly be said about Lutherans specifically. But as Lutherans befriend Scripture as the authoritative source and norm for their faith and life, they generate a particular way of using the Bible. For Lutherans, the authoritative character of Scripture requires careful listening to what it says and means. History has taught us that the vitality and significance of the Bible does not depend so much upon its visibility and availability in the church as upon the way people interpret it and understand it for their lives. Yet, interpreting and understanding are not simple or even obvious tasks. The history of Lutheranism reveals a strong conviction that Scripture does not just stand as words and, therefore, a deep commitment to the *interpretive* use of Scripture.

Though Lutherans do not claim a special entrée into Scripture or concede such a claim to other Christians, Lutherans hold that using the Bible as a norm for faith and life means discovering its message from the perspective of the gospel, the good news that we are forgiven sinners justified by Christ through faith. Christ and his message are the norm for understanding the Bible. Luther spoke of the Bible as the cradle that bears Christ. We listen in on the God-people conversation, as far back as it goes, through what is revealed in Christ. Christ is the point of contact through which we enter that conversation and discover its meaning. This perspective is sometimes called the "Lutheran hermeneutic," the way Lutherans go about interpreting what the Bible says.

All Lutherans, however, are not agreed about how this principle of interpretation works. Different opinions exist about what the gospel is as the norm for faith and life. Nevertheless, it is ultimately the community of the church as the fellowship of believers that interprets the Bible, however large or small that fellowship might be. Lutherans are part of the church catholic and, as such, add their perspective to the larger conversation.

Given the diversity within Lutheranism and the Lutheran voice as just one among many in the Christian church throughout the world, Lutherans have pressed hard in holding that the inspiration of the Holy Spirit comes to all people as their settings and situations change over times and places. One interpretation about something the Bible says for life, at one point in history, cannot preclude a different interpretation for people at another time. So, when Lutherans confess that the Bible is the *inspired* Word of God, they do not refer just to the text of Scripture. They also mean that the Holy Spirit inspires those who interpret the Bible.

Such a point of view, however, does not mean that the Bible is any less worthy of being called the Word of God or that its power over life is diminished as people in different times and places listen to it to discover together what it is saying for their lives. The Bible is at the center of things for Lutherans. It is at the heart of the Lutheran confessions. But each person and community of faith must listen carefully to hear the heartbeat in order to gain an answer to the question, What does the Bible mean for us? The key to the Lutheran perspective on the Bible is in the claim that the Word of God is supremely manifested in Jesus Christ and incomparably testified to in Holy Scripture. This perspective helps people find their way into the Bible story and lets the Bible story get into them. All this readies the Bible for use in the community of faith, whatever its circumstances, through a wide range of study interests, tools, and resources.

Using the Bible

Most adults are acquainted with the Bible through its use as devotional literature, as a source of guidance and answers for life's questions, and as the history and literature of the religious community. Each of these uses may involve both individual and community activities that vary greatly according to the needs of people and result in quite different experiences of learning. But the important thing about such differences is that they can open new, and perhaps unexpected, doors to Bible study and learning. We all have limited perspectives on the Bible and selective uses for it. Consequently, our learning is limited. Our lives can be enriched as more doors are opened to Bible study and learning in our churches.

For adults who are active in Christian education, Bible study often means a Sunday morning or weekday evening class. Those experiences are connected to a wide network of occasions in community and personal living that are doors to Scripture. The liturgy of public worship is rich in biblical material: lectionary, Psalms, sermons, hymns, and prayers. Formal Bible study can grow out of what we experience in worship. Small groups—family, youth, women's, men's, friendship groups—can be encouraged to discuss what was learned in those settings from and about the Bible.

The events in participants' personal lives can lead to passages in the Bible, to questions about God, or to some reflections that help them probe deeper into the meaning of a life in faith. Faith partner groups of two or three people are additional places to share Scripture in this way so that people can expand their understanding of Scripture together. The Bible is open to many approaches for study outside its connection with liturgy. These include:

• *Questioning the text.* After reading a selected a Bible passage, each person writes questions that they have about the text. These questions are shared in the whole group, followed by comments about the questions or a discussion on this approach as contributing to the life of faith.

• *Faith story/our story.* Ask each person to read a selected Bible text with this question in mind: Where am I in the text? As individuals share their awareness, point out that the canon of Scripture does not change when we do this, but our understanding of the text will be changed.

• *The Bible from Bible helpers.* Select a Bible passage or a topic such as sacrifice, parable, passover, or eschatology. Ask individuals or groups to find out as much as they can about the selection by using Bible commentaries, dictionaries, concordances, and other helpers such as Bible word books and different Bible versions. Share the findings and discuss how these resources help one understand the text.

• *The whole Bible.* Point out that although we think of the Bible in unity, there is much in it that cannot be taken in all at once or understood from one perspective. Bible study must include the scope of the whole biblical message to do justice to the particularities of its story. Two whole-Bible study approaches are (a) daily lectionary or Sunday lectionary[1] and (b) continuous reading of the Bible, reading one or two chapters per day. In each approach consider three things:

   a) what the texts say about our daily and seasonal life;
   b) what the texts say about the biblical story in general;
   c) how Bible study affects one's view of Scripture as the
       Word of God and one's use of the Bible in daily life.

• *Shared Praxis.* Shared praxis, as described by Thomas Groome,[2] is another approach to Bible study. It weaves together the life experiences of adult learners with the story of the Bible and the Christian faith community, and leads to a shared vision and action. This takes place in five movements:

1) A specific topic or focus for the session is announced. Participants are invited to create and name their personal response to the focus for the session.

2) Participants tell the story that is behind their response in the first movement ("Let me tell you why I said that . . . ").

3) The stories of the faith community (biblical, historical, theological, ethical) that relate to the session focus are told.

4) Participants engage in a dialog between their stories and the stories of the faith community in order to gain a richer understanding of both.

5) Participants discuss their vision and the vision of their faith community and decide on a course of action.

• *Published Bible study resources.* Denominational publishers and independent publishers offer a wide variety of prepared Bible study curriculum with study helps for participants and leaders. Look for the methods above within these resources.[3]

Living in Stories

The Bible is a life-giving story of God's relationship with God's creation. In our teaching, the use of stories—biblical stories and life stories—is also life-giving. A story is as big as life. Its meaning is in the telling and hearing. Here are two stories:

The Little Apple Girl

Several years ago, I set out on my fall trip to make applesauce at the preschool. The children were always prepared for my visit. We peeled the apples, cut them into pieces, and made applesauce for our snack.

That day, three-year-old Sandy arrived dressed like an apple. A red jumper, a green ribbon in her hair, and a small apple pin on her blouse. She and the other children took turns helping me get the applesauce ready, then were off to other activities. I was by myself spooning applesauce into small dishes. That was Sandy's moment. She made a beeline for me, braced herself stiff, and blurted out, "I don't like applesauce."

"That's okay. Just take a taste," I assured her. She knew that. With her confession out, she skipped away. Then a quick dash back to me.

"Do you know who I am?" she asked, doing a pirouette.

"Cookie Monster?" I tried.

"No." She looked a bit bewildered.

"A fairy godmother?" I hoped.

"Noooo." She was very disappointed with me.

"Superwoman?" My desperate and final attempt.

"No! I'm an apple!"

"An apple?" I said with a big question mark in my voice. "Last week you were a cowgirl. Can you be anything you want to be?"

"Sure!" Her voice said my last question was a bit stupid.

"But then how will I know who you are?" I tried again.

She tugged at the apple pin on her blouse, pushed it toward my face, and said, "If you want to know who I am, you gotta look close!"

A Land of Stories but No Storytellers

Once there was a land called The Land of Stories. People came from far and near to share stories. This land was a lively place. Sounds and movements of stories filled the air day and night. Stories delighted the heart, lifted the spirit, and whetted the imagination with magic and wonder. Everyone had a place and a time.

But things changed. Stories began to crowd the air. There wasn't time to savor them anymore. Someone suggested that stories be numbered. They would not have to be told. They could be remembered by calling out their numbers.

But the cure was worse than the ailment. The sounds and movements of stories that once birthed magic and wonder disappeared. People became a dull, grayish folk. Liveliness was reduced to a hollow echo of what had been. The Land of Stories was now a place of no storytellers.

What's in a Story? One could say that the story "The Little Apple Girl" is about Sandy. But it is really not *about* her; it *is* her. You can know the meaning of the story only when the little girl comes alive in its telling and hearing. That's why, too, the people in the land without storytellers languished and became reminiscent of Jeremiah's words, "The harvest is past, the summer is ended, and we are not saved" (Jeremiah 8:20). Stories had evaporated as fugitive emotions. Life was at a low ebb with no real connections; it was less than it was meant to be.

Two fundamental characteristics of stories, especially important for a community of faith, are that stories are incarnations of what they say and that they work as bridges connecting individual journeys in faith.

Stories are more than illustrations of people, places, and things that happen to interest the storyteller or the listener. Rather, they put those realities in front of us anew every time they are told and heard. They make tradition come alive as they bring to mind customs, beliefs, and celebrations coming out of our past and present. Stories let a person into other people's lives and events. They excite the imagination to reach for feelings and thoughts other than one's own. They invite the spectator in us to be a participant through the subtleties and nuances of telling and hearing. Stories themselves are the venue of meaning, only to be fully grasped when the story line finds itself in our lifeline.

The Christian faith tradition is full of stories of the great and near-great that can help keep the parts of life together. These stories also offer possibilities for reconstructing life in the present. As we enter stories, they offer value, direction, and cohesion for the deep realities with which we live daily. In the intersection of our life and stories, we can discover the lost vitalities of faith. Stories help us regain a living sense of the faithful lives that once embodied beliefs and words so that we might come to live such faithfulness ourselves.

As such, stories are bridges between teller and listener. In the way they are told and heard, stories establish a relationship between people so that the meaning gleaned is always shaped both by both teller and listener. Whenever a story is transmitted, it is transformed. That is why stories are never told or heard exactly the same way twice. Moreover, that is why stories need to be told and retold. There is a living world in every story that comes to life anew every time it is experienced as a bridge linking teller and hearer.

Stories at their best are not so much about answers as they are about questions. They prod the imagination to wrestle with both ambiguity and clarity. They let us see faithful living in joys and in sorrows, in moments of doubt and of certainty, in brokenness and reconciliation. Stories are bridges connecting—in the presence of God—the journey in faith that we live with such journeys of others.

Teaching and Learning with Stories. A good story has to be shared. It will find words for ready ears to embody meaning and become a bridge for discovery.

Congregations can encourage storytelling by organizing those interested. A storyteller with some experience can be helpful in getting started with the group, but experts are not needed. More importantly, fan the flames of interest and people will gather to trust each other and share their journeys of faith and life in story. Plan a comfortable schedule and meet regularly. A designated leader should get the group started. But then let the leadership rotate among those willing.

Four steps can help tell almost any kind of story:

1) *Choose the story*, a story that you like and want to tell.

2) *Learn* the story. Get to know its essence, its focus, its key lines and connecting words. Let yourself "enter" the story, but *do not* memorize it for the sake of telling.

3) *Tell* the story. Experiment with voice and gestures; use the appeal of all the senses; practice it with a story partner; begin and find out where the story will go.

4) *Live* the story. Let the telling make you aware of who you are as a storyteller and build on that, knowing there is magic in storytelling —the moment of the story that suddenly comes to you. Honor the bridge between you and the audience.

Start with your favorite Bible stories, or the Bible stories that puzzle you. Read them. Tell and listen to them with others. Fill your life with the stuff of the story by the internal or external dialogue that always takes place between teller and listener. Let the story be told and allow your imagination to raise questions and wonder about what it says.

Let Scripture, then, lead you to stories from church history. Reach back as far as you wish, or stay close to the present. What are the lives and events and places that you find there all about? Inevitably, you will find yourself in the story, breathing right along with the people and living through the same kind of events as they.

The beginning of the bridge of story is there, in the real connections it makes with your life. Sharing the story with others will help you and and your listeners discover ways to make the story your own. Stories are entry points for human experience.

It should not take long to realize that the stories of faith and faithfulness are all around, waiting to be told and heard. Their value comes to the surface in the lives of the people they are about—the faithful wherever they are.

As you explore and discover the story bridge with others, be teachers and learners for each other. Value each other's understanding of the story. In this way you can be resources for each other's journey in faith.

Recognize that stories—biblical stories, stories out of the church tradition, and personal stories—come from somewhere and go somewhere.

They represent a journey. Honor that journey and how each person discovers its meaning. The teller of the story creates the form of the story. The listener creates the response. The roles are reversed again and again as the ripple of meaning emerges in the shared life of the community of faith. Plan with your pastor and other education leaders in the congregation to offer the stories of your group to the congregation.

Join the Conversation

Bible study is the conversation with God that we join throughout our journey in faith. It begins with listening to what has been said between God and people in the past and then invites us to join the conversation. The conversation is many-sided and goes in many directions, and its goal is to help people grow in faith and faithfulness together in the presence of God's Spirit.

CHURCH HISTORY

One reason for studying church history is to gain knowledge of the past that can enrich our lives today. The past always needs to be interpreted. Its records are bare-bones accounts. They can describe what happened as any observer might, but those records can never preserve the "life moments" of the people whose lives were the warp and woof of the tapestry of history.

The study of history invites us to live into the past to discover the fabric in that tapestry and to allow its color and texture to influence the fabric of our lives. We learn the faith and what it means to be faithful by looking at the faithful, however far into history the faithful lead us.

Growing in the Soil of the Past

Some Lutherans today claim the Reformation as part of their family heritage. Others find the Reformation teachings for the first time in Lutherans they have as friends or meet in church. In any case, it is clear that people who claim the Reformation as the foundation for their religious beliefs today do not live as sixteenth-century German folk.

The choices in our world dwarf anything Martin Luther could have imagined. Even things that mattered most to Luther in religion were shadowed by a system of church life and personal piety that do not easily fit our lives. The religious impulses and intuitions Luther gave to the world were shaped by his times. And yet, developments in theology and religious life spawned by the leaders of the Reformation are the tradition and heritage that shape contemporary Lutheran experience.

That link between past and present characterizing Lutheranism today is like the experience Luther had. The roots of his reforming work reached back through the centuries of Christian faith and life that preceded him. The soil that gave life to those roots was the early church and ultimately Scripture.

So too for us. Our tradition and heritage as Lutherans go back to the moment in history we know as the Reformation. Our roots are there. But as with Luther, our roots find the source of their strength and life in the soil of early Christian faith and life that were based on Scripture. To say we are Lutherans today and to study our tradition and heritage means, first, to find our place with Luther. Through the Reformation we are led to the deep, rich soil of the past that preceded Luther. There we look for clues that will keep our heritage as invigorating and forward-looking for us as Luther's was for him.

Martin Luther's Legacy: Model for Our Heritage

Luther did not want to overturn faith and church practice just to be more contemporary or relevant. He was very much concerned about what was going on in the church of his day, but he was not led to give up the past and give in to new spiritual experiences. He wanted to recover the value of the past and interpret it for the present. Luther went to the foundations of the Christian faith in the New Testament, in the creeds of Christendom, and in the early Christian practices. He recovered that legacy of Christianity.

Luther discovered the fabric of history in the ancient tapestry of the church's faith and life. In doing so, he gave us a living heritage and a model for studying and using it today. Luther took Scripture, the Apostles' Creed, Nicene Creed, and the decisions of some early ecumenical councils such as Nicea (A.D. 325), Chalcedon (A.D. 451), Constantinople (A.D. 553), and made them the basis of confessional writings that defined Reformation beliefs and practices. These writings included the important educational document, Luther's Catechism, which is the basis for Reformation education today.

Luther's model for studying history is a valuable one. Luther moved from Scripture to education through the interpretation of history. This model can provide a focus for adult education in the church today. Get to know the past in Scripture and creeds as Luther did. Then think and study about how this knowledge can be applied to faith today. The church of the Reformation is *semper reformanda,* "always reforming."

Luther's legacy was not just another look at life in sixteenth-century Germany to see what was new and interesting and vital for Christian

faith. Luther's legacy, rather, provided sixteenth- century clues for opening the doors on theology and piety. He helped people travel backward
and forward, so that the gospel could be heard in the present.

Lutheran Beliefs and Practices

The Reformation was inspired and defined by the Bible, and the
Reformation's cultural and intellectual life reshaped the understanding
and use of the Bible. This is the dialogical challenge that Lutheran learners face if the Lutheran church is going to be *semper reformanda*.
Scripture is part of the tapestry of history, whose fabric makes interpretation possible. When he was before the Diet of Worms, accused of
going against the teachings of the church, Luther rested his case on the
Word of God. The Bible is authoritative. It is the norm for faith and life
for Lutherans.

Lutherans believe that what matters most in the Christian life is
God's unconditional love for people in Christ. Such love is there in spite
of sin and the brokenness of people's lives. God makes people fit for the
relationship God wants with them. That fitness is justification. There is
nothing we can do or should do for our salvation. Because of Christ,
God declares our justification once and for all. This means that we are
not made right with God over a period of testing by trial and error until
God finally works out all the wrinkles. And it certainly doesn't mean
people need to cooperate in a process like this. God *declares* our justification to be so.

And yet, sinners we are just the same. But God declares us to be forgiven sinners. Luther put that paradox this way: we are at the same time
and always both justified and sinners—*simul justus et peccator*. The
paradox doesn't stop there. It grows into life. Though we cannot do
anything to save ourselves, as forgiven sinners we are free to live for
others. Our lives should serve the well-being of all people and give
praise to God.

Lutherans, like all baptized people, begin their Christian life in the
Sacrament of Baptism and live through baptism in a journey in faith,
sustained by the Sacrament of Holy Communion. Those two sacraments are the means of grace for Lutherans. They have been instituted
by Christ, contain the earthly elements of water, wine, and bread, and
are sealed by God's promise of blessing.

For Lutherans, life in the presence of God means living the promise
of God on the way to fulfillment. We live in the world by law and
gospel. We live under the law for everyone's good. It sets limits for
human well-being and drives us to the mercy of Christ where we know
the good news, the gospel, of our unconditional forgiveness.

Luther insisted that the church is the fellowship of the priesthood of all believers. He believed that the church is the recipient of the benefits of divine grace through the work of the Holy Spirit in preaching, in hearing the Word, and in the sacraments. The metaphor of justified and sinner at the same time can be used of the church, too. The church is a gathering of all the baptized, in which only God knows the true believers. When Lutherans worship, that act is their witness to what God's Spirit is doing in the world. Public worship is also the gathering from which they go forth, using the gifts of the Spirit, in ministry to the world.

Lutherans believe the best vantage point for coming to know God is at the foot of Jesus' cross. There, in it stark reality, is the mystery of love. The cross is not a place of glory or a place to see God in majesty. It is a place of suffering. It is like a mirror. In it we can see ourselves in the one who alone can save us through suffering, death, and the power of his resurrection.

The Ongoing Challenge of Learning

Our heritage embodies a call to ongoing learning that goes beyond gaining more knowledge about what we already know. In studying church history, our task is to find a way into these beliefs and practices to make them truly our own.

The challenge is fourfold:

• *To trace* our roots back through the rich soil of Scripture, the early church creeds, and the legacy of Luther's Small Catechism. This means intentional study of Scripture, reflection on what the creeds tell us about our life in the presence of God, and use of the catechism as a guide for interpreting Scripture and the creeds.

• *To discover* entry points into that legacy through concrete situations in daily life.

• *To probe* these entry points individually and in congregational study and life, and in dialogue with those beyond the immediate faith community.

• *To apply* what we learn to daily living through the guidance of the Holy Spirit and the support of the community of faith.

What we learn and apply will never be simply taken over from the past. It will be what we discover about God's Word *for us* in all walks of life: economics, education, politics, environmental concerns, social issues, questions of piety, to mention a few. There will be no easy answers to any of the questions we encounter, because we are always justified and sinners at the same time. It is also because the law and the gospel will always be part of our struggle to be faithful, and because we see and know God best from the vantage point of the cross.

Luther taught people to live boldly in the presence of God. That teaching is also for us as we study our church history, living our tradition and heritage into the present and the future.

THEOLOGY

The mission statement of one college reads, "The purpose of Concordia College is to influence the affairs of the world by sending into society thoughtful and informed men and women dedicated to the Christian life."[5] Such a statement might well serve as the mission of adult Christian education—providing learning settings and instructional programs to help prepare "thoughtful and informed men and women dedicated to the Christian Life." The mission of Christian adult education is at least twofold: (1) to accurately convey to participants the truth of the Christian faith tradition, and (2) to assist hearers in the development of a capacity for deliberate action. Or, as Stanley Hauerwas urges, to foster a "community capable of hearing the story of God we find in the Scripture and living in a manner that is faithful to that story."[6]

Our theology and our truth is the story of God's gracious action on our behalf "that while we were yet sinners Christ died for us" (Romans 5:6). George Forell has observed that one particular verse in the New Testament is axiomatic for Christian faith: "God was in Christ reconciling the world unto himself" (2 Corinthians 5:19).[7] Christian theology is the knowledge base; through it we interpret the world in light of our particular religious tradition. It is the process of viewing the world though the particular prism of our vision. To be sure, we are also informed by a whole range of disciplines and points of view besides theology, but as John Cobb states, "Christian theology works from an intentionally Christian point of view."[8]

A second aspect of the educational task goes beyond knowledge to action. Action is faith lived out in the realms of family, work, and society. Individual Christians, informed by their faith, are called to work and live as active agents of the values of their tradition. These "ordinary saints" bring their religious understandings to bear on their day-to-day roles.[9] While some may not live out the faith as fully as they might like, due to civil and occupational limitations placed on their various roles, they bring some part of their theology and faith to bear on their homes, communities, and places of work. They are important witnesses to the Christian tradition.

As all believers are understood to be priests, perhaps it is not difficult to see all believers as theologians—highly "practical" theologians, reflecting on the meaning of the gospel for their daily lives. Adult Christian education needs to understand and define, or perhaps redefine, the congregation or faith community as a theologically reflecting body.[10] A high priority must be placed on providing educational opportunities that foster reflection on the meaning of the gospel for daily living.

Early Forms of Theological Education

The church, from its earliest times, has fostered opportunity for reflection on the meaning of the gospel for daily life. The Acts of the Apostles offers us one meaningful glimpse of Christianity's earliest efforts. The second chapter of Acts notes that the early Christians "devoted themselves to the apostles' teachings and fellowship, to the breaking of the bread and the prayers"(2:42). As time passed, a more structured curriculum emerged, which consisted of five forms:[11]

- *Kerygma.* Proclaiming the news of Christ's resurrection.
- *Didache.* Teaching and learning the faith.
- *Leitourgia.* Gathering to pray and share in the eucharistic feast.
- *Koinonia.* Gathering for mutual support and fellowship.
- *Diakonia.* Service and outreach to the community.

Education, as understood by the early church, incorporated many facets of ministry—taking those forms which ecclesial life presented to it and using them to edify the members of the faith community. According to Maria Harris, "Education is the work of lifting up and lifting out those forms through which we might refashion ourselves into a pastoral people."[12] The curriculum is the entire course of the church's life found in all its forms. When this is the case, Harris argues, the church does not have an education program but rather it *is* an education program.

The five historic forms noted above constitute both the purpose and work of the community of faith. When the five forms are all present—and it would seem that they need to be—there exists in the congregation a meaningful and comprehensive theological education program. These forms of ministry connect with each other in the mission of being the people of God in that place. For example, while *didache* may be seen as the most formal instructional form, there is teaching and instruction taking place as the Word is proclaimed (*kerygma*) and as believers render service to those in need (*diakonia*). The gathered people as *koinonia* make up a powerful and persuasive educational mechanism for theological reflection and for forming character and behavior in participants.

Learning and Leadership

Gathering for worship (*leitourgia*) offers a particularly rich menu for theological reflection and instruction. Eucharistic worship especially touches on the whole Christian experience—giving thanks and commemorating what God has already done and experiencing anew God's saving power. Creation, redemption, and the working of the Spirit are all recalled and celebrated. The very presence of Christ is acknowledged in the breaking of the bread.The challenge to planners and leaders of adult education is to be more intentional in optimizing the instructional aspect implicit in each of the five forms. When the liturgy is properly taught and presented in creative ways it can take on even deeper meaning for participants.

The cycles of the church calendar, particularly Advent/Christmas and Lent/Easter, proclaim in considerable detail the key events of Christ's life. Worship leaders need to find occasion to explain liturgy. Plan a narrative communion service to narrate the various movements of the liturgy in a regular worship setting. Worship temple talks or explanations in worship bulletins can be utilized to describe features in the worship, especially aspects that may be new or appointed for the day. There are a variety of meaningful roles for worship assistants. The training of assisting ministers, lectors, communion helpers, cantors, musicians, and ushers, to name a few, create opportunities for instruction on the meaning of worship. Chancel drama, dialogue sermons, and role playing one or more of the readings for the day offer opportunities for deeper learning.

Teach Us to Pray

Prayer is one of the most important practices developed in the worshiping community. It is an important component in any education program. Most of us probably remember from earliest childhood the important prayers prayed in worship. We heard early on that praying was a discipline to be practiced daily. Yet many of us are hard pressed to recall any instruction in how to pray, other than perhaps an assignment to write a prayer for a public occasion or the catechetical study of the Lord's Prayer. It is indeed noteworthy that Jesus took time to teach the disciples how to pray and in the process offered them a model prayer.

Jesus' practice of spending time alone in prayer set the pattern for the early Desert Fathers. Henri Nouwen has observed that, contrary to popular belief, the early Desert Fathers did not go to the desert to escape from public life, but rather so that they might receive, through prayer, refreshment and instruction for the journey.[13]

The tradition of daily prayer is a spiritual discipline and practice available to us in our time. Whether we pray the daily prayer of the church alone or with others in a worship setting, we never pray alone. Prayers express the communal life of the church. As Baptism has given us the Spirit of God as a constant companion, our prayers join us with all the faithful. The adult education program must convey to all hearers the promises, comfort, and direction that are ours in prayer. Proper instruction can open to all believers the treasury of evening and morning prayer. Through the regular discipline of daily prayer we are further nurtured by the psalms, appointed lectionary readings, canticles, and prayers appropriate to the occasion.

There is renewed interest in spirituality both inside and outside the church. Congregations would do well to make available spiritual direction for those desiring it. Retreats devoted to prayer and spirituality can provide powerful settings for growth in those areas.

Living Out the Baptismal Covenant

With each baptism, congregations recommit themselves to an educational ministry. Most often that commitment is seen as the sponsorship of an education program designed to assist parents in the task of nurturing their children in the faith. However, the educational commitment is to "lifelong learning." One purpose of the church's educational ministry is the preparation of candidates for public profession of their faith at confirmation or Affirmation of Baptism. Besides asking for a profession such as the Apostles' Creed, the examination at Affirmation of Baptism asks the following question of the candidate(s):

> You have made public profession of your faith. Do you intend to continue in the covenant God made with you in Holy Baptism:
>
> to live among God's faithful people,
> to hear his Word and share in his supper,
> to proclaim the good news of God in Christ through word and deed,
> to serve all people, following the example of our Lord Jesus,
> and to strive for justice and peace in all the earth?[14]

It is interesting to note that the public profession called for at Affirmation of Baptism contains elements of the five historic forms of ministry described earlier.

In most churches, there are adult education programs to prepare candidates for Affirmation of Baptism or church membership. Some are highly structured catechumenate programs; others are a single "get-acquainted meeting" on the day of reception into congregational membership. Courses generally include some form of instruction on such topics as Scripture, church doctrine, the church, worship, and the meaning of congregational membership.

The notion of "membership classes" probably understates the nature of the educational task. The term *inquiry* may express the task more accurately, while a more appropriate idea is that of *discipleship*. If the community of faith is going to be something more than a club, the curriculum must offer a process by which the nature of discipleship in the faith community is made clear. Candidates need to become acquainted with the congregation, its programs, and the theology that informs its congregational life. Even more importantly, candidates are invited into a deeper personal relationship with the Lord of the church as Jesus' disciples in the context of a faith community.

"People of the Way" was the name given members of the movement around Jesus (Acts 18:25). Followers of "the Way" received instruction and training in a pattern of living appropriate to Christian discipleship. Frequent reference was made to "the Way of the Lord," which included many ethical components requiring instruction. The image of "the Way" is that of "a goal-oriented journey in which the manner of the journeying is itself a constituent part of the pilgrimage."[15] The context for instruction was the community of faith. The content was instruction in the way of life in the community.

The instructional model of the early church continues to offer important clues as to the content and method of discipleship classes in our time. According to James Childs, "In the tradition of biblical faith, the life and worship of the congregation provide the occasion for the development of faith, formation, and decision."[16] Faith, formation, and decision are the key components in adult catechetical instruction:

• *Faith*: our understanding of God's gracious act on our behalf though Jesus Christ.

• *Formation*: the process through which Christian character is formed.

• *Decision*: our choices and the process by which we make choices.

Adult membership programs need to address all three components in order to effectively prepare candidates for a life of theological reflection and discipleship within the Christian congregation.[17]

ETHICS

It is the assumption of biblical writers and Christian theologians alike that we are morally responsible for the ways in which we conduct our lives and that this responsibility is learned in the communities to which we belong. The Beatitudes, the parable of the good Samaritan, the feeding and healing stories of Jesus, as well as many Old Testament narratives, offer models for responsible moral action.

Adults bring to programs of adult Christian education perspectives on moral responsibility based on their experiences. Many of these perspectives have been tried and found useful. In addition, Scripture and the "clouds of witnesses" that have gone before offer important insights into the will of God in matters of moral conduct. Finally, Christians believe that we are moral agents who, under the guidance of the Holy Spirit and with the help of the biblical witness and the community of faith, can make ethical, God-pleasing choices.

Moral Discourse

The notion of moral responsibility assumes that there are better or worse choices to make in given situations. Use of terms such as *good*, *right*, and *ought* assumes that levels of conduct exist that are more or less appropriate as one's response to ethical situations.

Theologians and ethicists have identified different levels of moral discourse present in adult life. According to Henry D. Aiken, it is possible to distinguish four levels of moral discourse:

- expressive-evocative;
- moral;
- ethical;
- post-ethical.[18]

Aiken's grid is helpful for understanding the processes by which we make moral decisions. For the purposes of planning content for adult Christian education, a simpler grid can be constructed using Aiken's design.

Four Levels of Moral Discourse for Christians

1) *Moral action-based consequence.* At the most basic level, action is determined by one's perception of the possible consequence of such action: If I drive too fast, I may get caught; therefore, I will drive within the speed limit. If I strike out in anger, someone may strike me back; therefore, I will not risk striking out.

2) *Moral action prompted by custom and norm.* At this level, moral action is acting according to accepted norms. A good citizen obeys the laws. Reflection about action at this level focuses on the value of established custom and meeting expectations.

3) *Moral action taken on the basis of some principle.* We may be moved to act and respond to a certain situation out of compassion or love. Principles of benevolence and loyalty often operate here: I help because I care about the environment. I give because there is need and I can help.

4) *Moral action prompted by post-ethical considerations.* This is the highest level of moral discourse. It is also the most personal. Action at this level may indeed be rare. The stimulus for action here is beyond that of principle. We are moved to act by something beyond us. It is an action about which we might say, "I could not do otherwise."

The moral discourse grid provides a tool for discussing levels of moral action. At the lowest level, we see that much of our moral action is mere reflex prompted by what we fear might be the consequences of a given action. The higher levels call for more and more thought about why we acted as we did. Always there is the question, Why be moral at all?

Much of our knowledge of the biblical witness regarding moral action has come to us by way of Sunday-morning worship. The common lectionary and sermons have unpacked for us important meanings. Additionally, our own reading of the Scriptures may account for further knowledge and familiarity with the biblical witness. However, still needed in addition to our hearing and reading of biblical texts is conversation and interaction with fellow searchers regarding the meaning of the texts in our daily lives. The community of faith becomes an invaluable reference group for application of theology to everyday life. The congregation—by definition the gathered people of God—offers a unique forum for dialogue and deliberation about ethics—faith in action. Deliberation over moral issues and spiritual formation are tied into our shared stories and the continuing life of the faith community.

A Climate for Dialogue

How do communities of faith take full advantage of opportunities to address ethical matters, reflecting about moral beliefs at work in the activities of daily life? Perhaps congregations do this best by fostering a spiritual community that is clear about its central mission, proclamation of the gospel. Clarity about the meaning of the church's historic confessions guard against human distortions of the core vision. Clarity about the core vision, key doctrines, and the role of the biblical witness allows for a variety of perspectives concerning more speculative matters, including the church's social teachings. Indeed, the congregation must be equally clear about inviting discussion of these matters.

The Adult Forum. Moral issues and ethical challenges abound in every faith community. Resources to engage these include mature, gifted, and able members of the congregations. Their witness needs to be drawn out and affirmed. What accounts for their level of faith? How is this faith manifested in character and virtue? What guides and empowers their decision making? If such individuals are unwilling to give testimony in the larger adult forum, they might be encouraged to participate in small groups or in one-to-one settings. These sisters and brothers are the mentors every community needs for leadership.

Find opportunity to examine the biblical stories of Abraham, Daniel, Joseph (son of Jacob) Nathan (especially his witness to David), Sarah, Ruth, Mary, Stephen, and others. Examine the moral issues they faced and their ethical deliberations. What levels of moral discourse are at operation in the story? Discussion leaders might utilize the socratic method used by the Great Books Foundation, whereby the discussion focuses on the key questions in the story.[19] Such questions include: What was at stake? What are the character issues? When is an action deemed courageous? How was the character's faith in action? What is virtue? What is the good? What does it mean to be moral? Why be moral at all?

There are current issues as taxing as those faced by persons in the biblical accounts: capital punishment, euthanasia, abortion, human sexuality, racism, ecology, and many others. Plan the discussion format and leadership carefully. The purpose of the discussion and the format by which it is to be done must be clear to all involved. Good leadership is needed to ensure that the purpose and format are honored.[20]

It may be helpful to adults to consider current issues and the persons involved in them through the lenses of four approaches to moral decision making described by Marc Kolden.[21] It is also helpful to discuss the strengths and weaknesses, as well as the theological implications, of each of these models.

1) *Character ethics.* Concerned with character traits of individuals, particularly those having to do with virtue or excellence. The focus in this model would be on becoming and being a virtuous or excellent person. Actions would not only be consistent with these virtues, but they would, in turn, develop and reinforce such attitudes.

2) *Consequence ethics.* Always asks whether the result of an action is good or useful. If it is, then the action is considered to be moral; if not, it is immoral. Sometimes, it has been seen as "the greatest good for the greatest number."

3) *Obligation ethics.* The main emphasis in obligation ethics is on doing one's duty, doing what is right or lawful—that is, what one is obligated to do whether or not it fits with one's character or achieves a desirable result.

4) *Contextual ethics.* The focus is on doing what is appropriate to the context or what is responsible in a particular situation. This model was formulated primarily to find a better way between the consequence and obligation models. It is an attempt to retain their strengths and avoid their weaknesses.

CONCLUSION

The four traditional content focus areas of Christian education—the Bible, church history, theology, and ethics—provide a rich foundation for addressing the issues and concerns of adults in our churches today. In planning learning opportunities for adults, it is important to seek a balance among these four areas that will help participants meet the goals that you have set together. But don't stop there. Let these four areas expand to include additional spheres of investigation and exploration. Through these four areas and in new ways, seek the wisdom and insight that will nourish faith and spur mission and growth.

chapter six

Exploring Opportunities for Adult Learning

Mary E. Hughes
Diane J. Hymans

It's Sunday morning and the fellowship class at Peace Church is gathered in a circle, as they do every week during the Sunday school hour, to study the Scriptures together.

On Wednesday morning, Martha, who lives in a retirement home, has just received her monthly copy of her denomination's magazine. As is her custom, Martha first searches for the Bible quiz to test her knowledge of Scripture and to look up the answers to those questions that she got wrong.

Late Wednesday afternoon, Robert starts out on his daily, half-hour commute home from work. He slips a cassette tape into his car's tape player to help make the journey go faster—a tape he checked out from the excellent selection in his church's library. By using his daily travel time in this way, Robert has "read" a number of books relating to matters of faith and life.

On Wednesday evening, Grace Church's choir members gather for their weekly rehearsal. For the first twenty minutes, Jane, one of the members, leads the group in an in-depth study of the Scripture text related to Sunday's anthem.

Though it may not look like it immediately, all these individuals are engaged in Christian education. For many people, something resembling the fellowship class meeting during the Sunday school hour may be what first comes to mind when we think of adult education in the church. But that traditional model, while still present in most congregations, is far from the only way in which adults in the church are engaged in teaching and learning these days. People are meeting in all kinds of places at many different times during the week to study and to learn. They gather in large groups and small groups. Some, like Robert, are learning on their own. Many new opportunities for adult education are the result of the church's response to the changing lifestyles and needs of adults.

In this chapter we will examine what needs to be considered as we plan educational opportunities for adults in our churches. We will expand our concept of adult education to include all of the intentional, planned, purposeful teaching and learning experiences that the church provides for adults, whether or not they occur in a traditional class-room. We will consider a range of options for adult education that are being used in many churches around the country, and we will look more closely at four congregations to see how they are putting together a comprehensive program for adult education.

THE WEB OF ADULT EDUCATION

When we begin to think about designing educational opportunities for adults in the church, there are a number of concerns that we must keep in mind. The adults who come to our churches today bring with them a range of needs and interests that grow out of their own life experiences. They are hoping to discover what their faith has to do with the questions they wrestle with every day. In addition, adults today possess a variety of levels of knowledge of the faith tradition, as well as different degrees of commitment to the church and to the Christian education opportunities it offers.

There are still significant numbers of adults who are lifelong members of the church and who have developed a regular habit of attendance at Sunday school, women's Bible study groups, or other educational programs. We can count on their loyalty to bring them to the church whenever something is happening there. Many of these individuals have spent years studying the Bible and the Christian faith and are able to draw deeply from these resources to make sense out of their lives and the world around them.

But these individuals may no longer be the norm. The Search Institute study *Effective Christian Education: A National Study of Protestant Congregations* has been mentioned in earlier chapters. One of the findings of that study was that only twenty-eight percent of adults in five mainline denominations are active participants in Christian education in their congregations.[1] The vast majority of adults in our churches do not participate at all, or do so only occasionally. What is more, these numbers refer to all Christian education programs being offered in churches—Sunday school classes for adults, Bible studies, retreats, workshops, support groups, plays, and musical programs. Although there is no exact data to draw on, too many congregations report that few adults are showing up for Sunday school.

The reasons for this decline in attendance are complex. The changing life experience of many adults and families today surely plays a role. The demands of work and family for many people are affecting the way in which they use their time. In families where both spouses are employed, weekends are often the only time available for family activities, and these must be scheduled in between errands and chores that cannot be completed during the week. Weekends are also being used more for leisure activities that may compete with Sunday mornings at church. While we may not always be happy with this reality, we cannot ignore it. When we plan for adult education in the church, we must pay attention to the demands already being made on the time of the adults who may participate.

This means that scheduling adult learning opportunities calls for some creative thinking. Although most congregations will probably continue some type of adult education on Sunday mornings, adult learning opportunities cannot be restricted to Sunday mornings. Educational experiences, both formal and informal, can occur almost any time. Many churches today offer classes and study groups at a variety of times during the week. There are any number of alternatives—listening to books-on-tape in the car, meeting with a group over breakfast or lunch to discuss the relationship between faith and work, one-on-one meetings between a pastor and a parishioner to talk about a book both are reading. One possibility that is often forgotten is to claim those opportunities that are present when groups of adults are already gathered. Many congregations are using a portion of their time at council and committee meetings or choir rehearsals for study of some sort. Each congregation, even each group within a congregation, will have to wrestle with matters of scheduling to find what works best for persons in their particular setting.

Another factor that requires attention when designing educational opportunities is the reality that adults in our congregations come with different levels of knowledge about the Bible and the Christian faith. Some are familiar with the stories and language that form the Christian tradition and are able to draw on this resource to make sense of their lives. But many others are in a different place. We find more and more people in our churches who come without basic knowledge of the faith tradition. They do not know the great heroes and heroines of the Bible. They are not sure where to find the book of Matthew in the Bible, much less Habakkuk. They are uncertain about what it is that makes Lutherans, or Methodists, or Presbyterians distinct from other denominations. And they have no idea why worship is ordered the way it is or how their church is governed. We can no longer assume that adult learners come to Christian education offerings with some basic information about the faith on which to build.

C. Jeff Woods, in his book *Congregational Megatrends*, suggests that these individuals need what he calls "immigrant education."[2] Just as immigrants who arrive in a new country must learn the language of their new home in order to be able to function there, many newer members of our churches need to learn to speak the basic language of the Christian faith in order to be able to contribute to the life of the church and live faithful lives. These individuals may be new to the Christian faith itself. Or they may have returned to the church after being away for a while or come from a different denomination. We must provide some educational opportunities that assume nothing on the part of the learners and that provide basic introductory information on the Bible (where it came from and what's in it), on the elements of worship and the sacraments, on how the church governs itself, and on the basic tenets of the faith. And these educational opportunities must be provided in an atmosphere in which there are no questions that are off limits and in which it feels safe to say "I don't know."

At the same time, there are other adults who have been in the church for most of their lives and are ready for something that will be more intellectually challenging. Just as we may not pay sufficient attention to those learners who need basic knowledge of the faith, these adults are often ignored also. Many of these individuals are drawn to in-depth Bible studies like *Inspire*, *Crossways*, or *Kerygma*. Some of them may be ready to read and discuss the works of the great theologians of the church in a group led by a pastor. These are persons who want something they can really chew on, something that will make them think about their faith at a deeper level. Sara Little has wondered whether the church has lost some of its more sophisticated thinkers because we haven't been willing to provide them with the intellectual challenges they seek.[3] A pastor in Ohio reported that he recently offered a two-Sunday introduction to New Testament Greek to members of the congregation. Enough people responded so that he is starting a class in Greek that will last most of the school year.

Another important consideration when planning adult education is the question of meaningfulness. Chapter 3 discussed the question of motivation for adult education. The issues raised in that chapter cannot be ignored. One thing that seems certain is that adults, unlike children, have more personal authority to choose to attend or not to attend Christian education opportunities. That choice is often based on whether or not the experience appears to have any personal significance for their lives.

Adults come to Christian education opportunities for different reasons. Some adults are what Nancy Foltz calls *learning oriented*.[4] They seek knowledge for its own sake and find deep satisfaction in studying the Christian tradition. They want to know more about their faith, to understand it at a deeper level. They look for classes that satisfy that need. Other adults are goal-oriented learners. They use educational experiences to accomplish an objective, to help them solve a problem that grows out of their life experience, or to address an issue facing the community. While learning-oriented adults may enjoy classes on the Bible or theological matters simply in themselves, goal-oriented adults want classes that have something to do with what is happening in their lives. They look for courses the church may offer on topics such as parenting questions, significant questions of faith, or personal spiritual growth.

Another consideration in planning adult education opportunities is taking into account how the needs and interests of adult learners change throughout their lives (see chapter 2). The questions that are most relevant to adults in their twenties and thirties are not the same as those being faced by midlife learners or by older adults. Where we are in our life span affects what is most meaningful for us. Developmental matters call for some attention when designing learning experiences for adults.

One final concern deserves consideration when planning adult education opportunities. Just as adults come with different needs and interests, they possess different learning styles as well. Chapter 3 introduced four ways of conceptualizing adult learning styles: concrete experience, reflective observation, abstract conceptualization, and active experimentation. If our goal is to help adults come to greater understanding of the Christian faith so that it can become a real resource for them as they seek to live faithful lives, we need to provide learning opportunities in a variety of formats. We need lecture classes and adult forums for reflective learners and those who prefer abstract conceptualization. Some classes may be characterized by more personal interaction among learners or more hands-on activities to satisfy those who prefer concrete experience. The active experimenters may learn best by participating in direct service or mission opportunities, which can also be excellent learning experiences. There is a discussion of teaching methods in chapter 4.

Schedule, level of knowledge, meaningfulness, and learning style—all of these must come into play in the process of creating teaching and learning opportunities for adults in the church. What all of this means is that it is no longer possible to offer a one-size-fits-all plan for adult education. Churches need to consider a range of opportunities meeting at different times, in different locations, and made up of a variety of formats. Some may be classes that meet weekly in traditional classrooms on a continuing basis to study the Bible. Some learning opportunities may be designed to meet for a particular number of sessions—ten, or six, or even two—to explore an issue of concern or one book of the Bible. Or we may design learning experiences that meet for just one day or every evening for a week. Study groups may meet at the church, in someone's home, over breakfast at a local restaurant, or even at some-one's workplace. Classes may be taught by laypersons, the pastor, or resource persons from the community who bring special expertise. They may take the form of forums for fifty or sixty people, or small groups of eight to ten people, or one individual meeting once a month with the pastor to learn more about prayer. Teaching and learning in the church may happen any time of the day, any day of the week. The possibilities are limited only by our imaginations.

All of this means that planning for adult education is more chal-lenging than ever before. Planning must be contextual. The particular mix of teaching/learning opportunities will look different in every con-gregation. Those charged with the responsibility for adult Christian education in any particular church must attend to the needs and inter-ests of the people for whom they plan and the resources available to them in the church and community. Many large churches will be able to draw on a wide range of expertise and resources to offer a rich selec-tion of learning experiences. Smaller congregation can plan educational opportunities that build on their unique strengths. Many small churches are characterized by strong relational connections among members. Small groups or one-on-one mentoring relationships may work well here. Small churches may also concentrate on building up the collection of books and tapes in their church library so that persons can study on their own when classes are not available.

Sara Little has suggested that the appropriate image for thinking about planning adult education these days may be a spiderweb.[5] Traditionally, we have often used the image of a staircase to shape our planning, imagining that educational experiences are to be planned sequentially, each building on the previous one and preparing for the next. The movement is forward and upward until the learner arrives at a certain level of knowledge. While this may still work to some extent in some contexts, the realities of modern life affecting patterns of partici-pation in Christian education may mean that this image is no longer the most helpful one. The spiderweb suggests an alternative way to think about planning. A web is an interlocking network of opportunities and experiences that draw on available resources in the congregation and the larger community in order to address the variety of issues and concerns brought by members that are appropriate to Christian education in the church today.

This may feel like an awesome task, but it is not impossible. Each congregation's web will be formulated differently using different components. And we can learn from each other. In the next section of this chapter, we will look briefly at a range of teaching/learning possibilities already being used in congregations across the country. Let this menu of learning experiences stimulate your thinking as you create an education web for the adults in your congregation.

It is appropriate at this point to thank the many individuals who spent time telling the writers about adult education in their congregations. Their ideas and illustrations make up much of what is shared in the following pages.

ELEMENTS OF THE WEB

Sunday School

I'm a little embarrassed to tell you that our Sunday school is going great. It's the heart and soul of our adult education. We have more adults than we ever did. That's when our members have time for education, and entire families spend the morning here. . . . Sunday school is an important tradition we will not give up. (Faith Church, Tennessee)

After hearing her colleagues talk of their frustrations with Sunday school and the alternatives that worked, Martha wasn't sure her Sunday school success would be appreciated. But in many congregations today, the traditional Sunday school for all ages provides a lively base for Christian education. No apologies are needed. Life in the traditional Sunday school requires planning and work to continue its health, because tradition doesn't mean stagnation.

"Traditional Sunday school" is a little hard to define. Most congregations have a long history of some Christian education program on Sunday mornings; however, some churches never had Sunday educational activities. The Sunday schools of most congregations have modeled themselves after the public schools with separate classes for different age groups, sometimes grouping adults by ages also. At the same time, there have always been churches whose Sunday schools have taken the one-room-school approach, or an intergenerational approach, or have ignored adults altogether.

The tradition of Sunday school has sometimes included classes of adult learners that have remained together for decades, with new groups forming as members reach adulthood. Other Sunday schools have offered adult forums and discussion groups, a variety of short-term electives that resembled a university model, or one ongoing class meant for all adults. Obviously, within traditional adult Sunday school there is much variety. Every one of the models mentioned has been found to be an exciting, perfect match in some churches, yet frustratingly lacking in others. There's nothing magical about one particular model. Instead, every congregation seeks a model that fits its situation, while not assuming the model will always fit.

> At Faith our adult discussion was held in the pews of the sanctuary, but we decided to move to the fellowship hall around tables. There weren't many children in Sunday school, so the adults needed and wanted good space for discussion. As the numbers of children increased, the adults wouldn't give up their tables in the fellowship hall, but they were ready to provide money to add on to our church, so now we have a building that's good for everyone. (Faith Church, Tennessee)

> Our Sunday school grew so big we almost killed it. We decided to change it, and people hated the change. So now we're back to our old traditional look, and it works for us. Sure, we make improvements all the time, but we have a traditional Sunday school, and we love it. (All Saints, Wisconsin)

Weekday Education

Some congregations have found that education events during the week are far more satisfactory for adults. Some of these weekday programs look like a Sunday school, just held on another day. Other adult education activities, however, are extremely diverse in subject matter, length and duration, leadership, and scheduling. What those activities have in common is their intention to provide growth and learning among adults seeking to live lives of faith.

> During vacation Bible school several adults came to help with refreshments and recreation and tasks like that. They enjoyed

studying as a class when they weren't busy. They studied other denominations, then visited those churches in the following weeks. (Trinity, Virginia)

Small Groups

In one sense, a majority of the educational opportunities we offer in the church are small groups. Robert Wuthnow, who has done extensive research on the small group phenomenon in the United States, reports that twenty-nine percent of all persons who indicate they are a member of a small group describe that group as a Sunday school class.[6] Many of the councils and committees in which people meet to do the work of the church could also be classified as small groups. But many churches throughout the country are also organizing intentional small groups to draw people together for prayer, fellowship, spiritual nurture, and support. These groups are also often characterized by some type of study.

It has been suggested that there are three basic types of small groups.[7] The first is groups whose primary focus is spiritual growth, sometimes referred to as *discipleship groups*. Study is usually a primary emphasis in these groups. Some concentrate on Bible study, others consider issues of concern to members such as racism or evangelism. The second type of small group is *support and recovery groups*. These are made up of people who gather together because of common life experiences—divorce, parenting, or grief, for example. While the emphasis here is on nurture and support, these groups may also engage in intentional study of the Bible or other resources as a part of their time together. The third small-group type might be called *ministry groups*. These are usually task oriented. Church councils and committees might fit here, but so would groups that organize around a particular mission focus, such as working in a soup kitchen or planning a hunger walk. Again, study is not the primary agenda for this type of small group, but it surely may be a part of what the group does as it seeks to understand its task

While helpful, these categories don't exhaust the possibilities for small groups. In an urban congregation in Ohio, the pastor met monthly for eleven years with a group of members to read books together, most of which focused on spirituality or spiritual growth. Usually, they spent two months on each book.

Some of the books we read were really challenging to our members, Dietrich Bonhoeffer's *Cost of Discipleship*, for instance. But they stuck with them. And through the reading, the group's

members began to talk about their own life experience. The books
we read opened up real opportunities for sharing. (Peace, Ohio)

Like most educational opportunities, small groups can meet at a
variety of times during the week. Small groups can serve many functions
in the life of the church and in the lives of its members, but one role they
often play is educational.

Ecumenical Learning Experiences

In many locations, churches of various denominations are working
together to develop educational opportunities for their members. By
cooperating ecumenically, congregations are able to offer experiences
that would not be possible otherwise. Eight congregations in the Detroit
area—Catholic, Episcopal, Lutheran, Presbyterian, and United Church
of Christ—have offered the Lay Theological Academy every year for
seven years. The academy is planned by a board of directors consisting
of three lay members from each congregation and the pastors as ex-offi-
cio members. Courses are offered on a variety of topics related to faith
and life. Some courses last only for a day or an evening; others run two
to four weeks. Classes meet in each of the participating churches, many
taught by the pastors of these churches. However, each pastor intentionally teaches in a congregation other than his or her own as a way to
encourage his or her members to attend a class at another church. Other
courses are taught by persons from the community—professors at local
seminaries or colleges, counselors, or others with particular expertise.
Each congregation made an initial financial contribution to join the
group. Nominal fees are charged for each course.

> The Lay Theological Academy is intended to supplement the edu-
> cational programs already going on in each parish, to enhance
> what we are already doing. It's not intended to replace that. There
> are some real benefits to each church. We can do things together
> that no church can do alone, like bring in big-name speakers. The
> Academy also encourages us to mix with others in the body of
> Christ, to overcome the parochialism we are all guilty of. We have
> a lot to learn from each other. That may be its biggest gift. (Pastor,
> St. Paul's Church, Michigan)

Cooperative ecumenical programs like the Lay Theological Academy
offer special benefits to smaller congregations by expanding available
resources and providing a larger pool of learners for course offerings.

Theologian-in-Residence

Many congregations contract with faculty members from colleges or seminaries to spend extended periods of time in their churches to teach and to interact with members in a variety of ways. If there is not a college or seminary nearby, the church may invite someone to come full-time for a week. During that time, the resident theologian may participate in worship and Sunday-morning classes, teach a series of studies in the evening during the week, or meet with groups during the day or over a meal. Churches for whom there is a nearby college or seminary may arrange for a professor to be involved with the congregation in various ways for as long as a year. In this case, the theologian-in-residence may teach a long-term class or series of classes, preach several times, lead retreats, or provide any number of other educational experiences.

This possibility does require a significant financial contribution from the congregation. For churches with limited financial resources, it offers another kind of opportunity for a group of churches to work together to share a resident theologian for a week or longer. Events could be scheduled at each of the cooperating congregations. The theologian-in-residence program allows members of local congregations to stretch their thinking through conversation with someone who is doing significant work in biblical study, theology, or ministry in the church.

Building Education into Other Programs or Meetings

Because the demands on people's time seem to be steadily increasing, it makes sense to take advantage of those occasions when people are already gathered at the church to include a period of study. Many congregations are devoting a designated amount of time at monthly meetings of their congregation's governing board or council to study, led either by the pastor or a member of the board. One pastor stops in the middle of the business meeting to take a study break.

> I'm afraid that if I began the meeting with study, too many members would decide that they didn't need to arrive until it was time for the actual business meeting. By placing the study session in the middle, I am trying to say to our members that this is important, too. I am concerned that we spend too much time at our meetings worrying about boilers and leaky faucets, and not enough time thinking about what our work as a church really is. I use the study time to do that. Next year we will be working through a book on

the theology and mission of the church written for laypersons.
(First, Ohio)

This congregation is a new church development in a rapidly growing
suburban area. Many of its members come from other denominations.
The worship committee also spends a portion of its monthly meetings
studying the worship book. The same pastor says,

> Because so many of our people come from other traditions, they
> don't know why we do things the way we do. I think it is especially
> important for the worship committee to understand why our
> worship is structured the way it is so that when questions come
> up from members of the congregation, they will know how to
> respond.

When this pastor is asked why he spends time in business meetings
on study, he says, "I tell people, 'I can understand why some of you cannot be here at Sunday morning classes. You have obligations at work
and family, or you travel, and it's often difficult to get here. But, it is
important to study the faith. This is a time when you are already here.
We aren't asking you to come out another night for another meeting.
It's appropriate to take some of this time to learn about what it means
to be the church.'"

Mission/Service Projects as Education

Many adults in congregations are involved in mission or service projects. While many of these may take place in the local community, often
they involve travel to other parts of this country or even to other countries. The primary focus of these experiences is to carry out the mission
of the church, and they also provide rich opportunities to engage people in what has been called the "pedagogy of obedience." That is to say,
we come to understand more deeply the meaning of the gospel by living
it in mission to God's people.

Mission projects open up a wide variety of possibilities for learning.
If the project takes the group to a location in another culture, wonderful opportunities may present themselves to learn about that culture
and its people. Work projects in low income areas may prompt questions about the nature and causes of poverty in our country and about
the church's role in alleviating suffering. But learning in these situations
is not automatic. It must be built into the experience. Plan a period
of study ahead of time to prepare the group for the mission project.

Set aside a certain amount of time each day during the project itself for study and reflection. And, after the project is over, call the group back together to explore questions raised by their experience.

Many persons in the church report that their participation in a mission project sponsored by their congregation left them with a deeper understanding of their own call to ministry in the world and a renewed sense of commitment to their faith. One pastor tells of her experience with mission projects in her congregation:

> I think these experiences reconfirm the truth of the gospel for our people. We rediscover that it is in giving that you receive. People seem to find real joy in serving and in being part of the body of Christ. The bottom line is that in our summer work camps to Appalachia, people live out the teachings of Christ and discover that it works. (First Church, Pennsylvania)

Intergenerational Learning

Intergenerational learning refers to gathering a variety of ages (usually three or more generations) for learning together. It's how much of daily life works: families are intergenerational, Sunday worship is intergenerational. However, there are few places where different age groups gather to study together, bringing the insights and questions of different generations. Not every topic is best explored this way (young children may not benefit particularly from a study of the Apocrypha, for instance) but some topics may be enriched by this diversity (for example, youth, young adults, and older adults together exploring issues of life and death). Intergenerational learning does not mean that everyone must be doing exactly the same thing at all times; however, much of the learning will be cooperative. An intellectual discussion will exclude many children, and simple yet creative activities will not totally satisfy the adult seeking depth of understanding. However, carefully prepared activities that enable several persons of different ages to explore, talk, create, and share can lead to genuine and enjoyable growth and insight.

St. Philip is planning a new Sunday morning look that combines worship and education in a highly interactive, intergenerational approach:

> We are booming right now with lots of people with religious backgrounds who have abandoned church. They don't care whether the service follows this order or that book, but they want something significant for their lives. We may start with the lectionary, but a

thematic approach may be even more age-inclusive. Worship will include much prayer and singing, and the Word and Sermon will be a time for faith formation. It won't look like the average sermon. It may be very interactive, and we'll make sure it includes children. We'll also include resources . . . ideas, questions, or whatever, for taking Sunday life into life at home. (St. Philip the Deacon, Minnesota)

Intergenerational learning will initially require more planning than expected. A planning team that first learns about intergenerational learning, then commits itself to designing and implementing good education can ensure that this will truly enrich the lives of participants.

Women's Groups, Men's Groups

It may be that more adults gather for study through organized women's groups in the church than through any other single means. Through long tradition such groups have emphasized study, including Bible study, as well as service. Many church denominations provide excellent study resources and leadership helps plus regional and national gatherings that are largely educational.

In recent years there has been a renewed interest in organized men's groups within congregations, and more and more resources are directed toward these groups. Often focused more on service opportunities, these men's organizations are giving increasing attention to study opportunities as well.

Do not underestimate the educational opportunities provided through these organizations. Many churches could enrich adult education simply by supporting their learning potential. In addition, the resources prepared for these groups, including magazines and study materials, can be used in other groups and settings.

Church Publications, Newsletters

Martha looks forward to receiving her monthly denominational magazine. Since her husband's illness, this reading, as well as with her church's newsletter, has kept her connected with the church.

I can't get to church often, but I still feel like I'm a part of things. I work every puzzle, read every article, and soak up the news of my church. The people in these readings become my spiritual partners. (Martha, Virginia)

A recent denominational magazine contained a Bible study, several articles about Christian family life, stories of individuals and churches living out their faith, news of the denomination around the nation and world, and more. Reading the magazine is a condensed version of sitting in the local library studying the Bible, faith, Christian living, and the church.

Congregational newsletters also can be much more than local news. Include crossword puzzles and word games as a fun way to encourage review and learning. Articles about current church questions, issues, and events stimulate thought. Questions posed for reflection about a movie or recent event can challenge individuals and families to talk about faith. Indeed, church bulletins, bulletin boards, hallway artwork, and displays can all be used thoughtfully to stimulate learning and growth.

Retreats

Retreats are not just for youth and they are not just for fun. Many congregations find retreats of twenty-four to seventy-two hours to be perfect opportunities for adult learning through sharing, reflecting, and experiencing. A little distance from the telephone and from daily responsibilities can give better perspective to life issues, helping us integrate faith and life.

> Each fall a congregation member who is a psychologist leads a retreat specifically for "men at midlife." I thought there might be three or four interested men, but twenty came the first year and demand that it happen every year. (First Church, Ohio)

New Hope Church, New York, has an annual family retreat that includes times for families to be together and other times for adults-only discussion. While not actually a retreat, four families at Christ Church, North Carolina, responded to the invitation to vacation together as an experience in Christian community. Each day included Bible study and a discussion around the question, What have we learned today about living in a family?

Unique to retreats is the informal, inviting setting and the extended time period. The setting encourages adults to relax away from the pressures of daily life, to get away from the routine. This often enables us to regain perspective, to review life, to look at things differently. The many hours of a retreat allow thinking, feeling, and sharing at levels impossible in fifty minutes of class time. Together, the setting and duration of retreats make them incredibly rich as learning opportunities.

New Member Education

The first weeks and months in a new congregation can set a pattern for learning and participation. Many congregations provide a number of classes for new members, suggesting that they are committed to understanding and growth. Other congregations find unique ways to help visitors and new members learn about Christianity, the church, and the congregation.

> In our small congregation we have only a few new members each year. This lets me, the pastor, spend a lot of time with each new member family and individual, creating a personalized approach to meet each one's needs. I also connect each new member or new family with a current member to be a personal "welcoming committee" and to introduce them into the congregation. (St. Mark, Michigan)

> Every week we have many visitors, several inquiring about membership. So, every Sunday we offer a one-time "Introduction to Christ Church" during our education hour. A few of our friendliest, most articulate members meet with anyone wishing to hear more about our church and our ministry. If they want more, they are encouraged to come to our adult membership class. (Christ, North Carolina)

Adult catechumenate is a concept becoming more comfortable and valuable in many Protestant congregations. This process of Christian initiation is meant to revitalize those persons new in the faith and, at the same time, the whole congregation. It is more like an apprenticeship in the faith or a mentoring experience than a course of studies.[8]

The Church Library

Vast potential, vastly underused and underrated—that might describe many church libraries. The public library has been described as the greatest adult education in the United States, but most churches have not nurtured the educational potential of their libraries. While valuable for reference work, teaching resources, and study of doctrine, some church libraries become the source of learning through the pleasure of reading. Libraries today include far more than books: audiotapes, videos, media kits, computer software, study groups, and reading clubs. However, it takes vigilance on the part of the library committee to maintain a current and vital collection and to prevent the library from becoming the final resting ground for "gifts" of resources that are out-of-date, irrelevant, and/or of poor quality.

> We have a core group of adults that are kind of like vultures. When new books come to the library they are gobbled up right away. We refer to our library as a family library. We sponsor some reading groups and classes during the year and each summer organize a family reading program to encourage everyone in the family to read from the church library. (Our Savior, South Dakota)

> We don't have many books on our shelves. In fact, we only have a few shelves. But our few books are always being read. We are a congregation of mostly adults. They find books that are meaningful for themselves, buy and read them, then pass them along to others through our church library. Every book comes with a personal recommendation. (Karen, Arizona)

Many church denominations have formed library associations that offer valuable help in organizing and revitalizing church libraries and resource centers.[9]

The church library need not compete with other local libraries, but may focus its attention on the special needs and interests of the congregation. Provide a book list or display to accompany the current sermon series. Highlight several books related to an upcoming event: commemoration of a saint, the anniversary of a significant person or event in history, adult class study of an issue. Point to resources on topics into which adults always want to dig more deeply: parenting, Christian lifestyle, devotions, world religions. Organize a night to see a video and discuss it.

> Our library gets more active use from adults than children right now. Our many members in a nearby retirement home make good use of the library. In fact, we've really increased the library because these members appreciate it and remember it with gifts and memorials. (First, Iowa)

Prepared Programs

Individual churches, denominations, and non-denominational groups provide a vast array of study programs available for purchase and implementation by congregations. Every church mailbox regularly receives brochures describing these programs. Denominational materials are predictable in their doctrinal basis, but it may take some effort to understand the theological foundation for other offerings. Talking with persons who have used the resources and carefully previewing the material can help ensure that it is a good match for your church. Careful planning can bring together eager adults and excellent resources for growth in faith.

Drama

Preparing, performing, and watching plays and musicals have afforded some adults new knowledge, new insights, and new personal growth in faith.

> Drama used to be only for youth in our church, now the adults are involved. Our Bible study group actually wrote some dramas and used them as sermons during Lent. The kids in the church would come up afterwards and talk to the adult in role: "Why were you so mean to Jesus?" (Trinity, Virginia)

> Our entire congregation was involved in learning and presenting a musical based on Luther's Small Catechism. Even as a lifelong church member, I'd never known the Catechism like I do now after singing it thirty times. (St. Paul, Ohio)

> A group of adults from our church sees a movie or play every month. Then we come back to someone's home for dessert and guided discussion. I'm always amazed at how I learn about faith and daily life in a discussion with other Christians. (Sue, Virginia)

New Technologies

Every day we learn of new technologies and their potential for education. Computer software, interactive video, on-line learning—their potential for Christian education is just beginning to be developed. To reach neighborhoods, some congregations—and clusters of congregations—can use free local cable TV access. Study groups in homes permit members to invite neighbors, too. Some cable systems also allow groups to call in to a phone number, which they alone have, permitting dialogue among groups and leaders. In some cases, linking by satellite or telephone lines can tie into programs offered by churchwide and ecumenical groups. Videotapes of major films, focused on key discussion themes, offer opportunities to gather members and guests in homes. These same principles can be applied to develop learning groups at workplaces and other sites, such as homes for the elderly.

Young adults might provide leadership in using the World Wide Web for distance education. Many may know how to search the web for information: biblical, theological, ethical, ecumenical, and more. Resources of the World Council of Churches, the lutheran World Federation, the ELCA, and other denominations are accessible, and searchable on the Web. Courses are already available from seminaries and colleges and may be offered by congregations as well. While such courses are often taken by individuals, they could also be taken by groups, permitting discussion and building of local community. Computer conversation, or "chasts," allow interactive communication with resource people around the world—with sound and sight.

For some this technology presents the threat of unfamiliarity; for others it represents the most exciting educational opportunity of the century. One thing can be predicted: this new technology will change adult education. In the church we must determine how we will use, misuse or refuse to use this technology to the advantage of our congregations.

Several principles may help the church think about how to use the newer media. First, the primary medium of the gospel is always the people of God, gathered around Word and Sacrament and scattered in service in the world. Second, all media (including print, with which we are most familiar and comfortable) need to be used carefully to undergird the community of faith, never to substitute for it. Third, each medium is a gift from God to be claimed creatively. For, as in other areas, we are called to explore freely how to use each medium and be ready to acknowledge our mistakes.

STORIES OF FOUR CONGREGATIONS

As you have just read, the possible elements of the web of adult education seem almost endless. No congregation uses them all. Instead, every church must consider its own context, resources, needs, priorities, and traditions to plan and construct its own ministry of adult education. Here are the stories of four congregations and their adult education. The stories cannot do justice to the total educational ministry, but they provide a snapshot, a look over the pastor's shoulder, into the congregation. These four stories are offered as encouragement to planners and leaders of adult education to imagine new opportunities for learning in their own settings.

All Saints Lutheran Church, Oshkosh, Wisconsin

All Saints is a young, growing mission church of about 300 members in Oshkosh, a "blue collar" congregation of busy families. Pastor Catherine Mode explains, "We have a few small groups, but we aren't that sort of church. A phrase that describes us better is, 'Go with what we've got . . . and only for a little while.'" For All Saints, that means adult education that emerges from the needs, interests, and current experiences of members. Sunday school includes a popular adult forum, but the most meaningful adult education has been generated from the "grassroots."

A deaf man came to All Saints, and the congregation was motivated to work toward deaf ministry. Several study sessions were held in simple signing: "Signs of Hospitality" and "Signs of the Faith." But Pastor Mode was unsuccessful in generating adult Bible study until a group of men wanted it and sought her help in starting it. They met every Wednesday in Lent at 6:30 A.M. Families created through adoption developed a "Family Mosaic" program that meets regularly, and now others with similar needs and interests are drawn into the group.

Three women in their mid-forties wanted to talk about the changing bodies and changing lives of midlife. They contacted others of their age in the church and the group met for nine months.

"If we think they need it, they don't come. Our adult education must arise from the grassroots. It's important, then," says Pastor Mode, "that I never miss an opportunity. I must recognize their readiness and empower them. All too soon the moment is gone." As an experienced church educator, Pastor Mode has particular skill in taking advantage of those times of educational readiness and responding effectively, but it requires constant vigilance and much flexibility. "I must always be ready to step aside from my agenda for a teaching moment."

For Your Reflection. Sometimes we need to learn things in which we express no interest. We may not even know we need to learn them. In a total program of adult education it is important to balance the study of "things we need to study" with the study of "things we want to study," if that does not happen naturally. Consider your own congregation. Is there opportunity to learn those things the church understands to be vital for Christian growth? Is there opportunity for adults to influence the topics of study? How can we make more attractive the study of those things vital for Christian growth?

What is happening today in your church that provides a moment of readiness for learning?

Church of the Holy Redeemer Lutheran Church, Brooklyn, New York

The Church of the Holy Redeemer shares a context with many inner-city churches. It sits in the midst of a high-crime, high-drug area and has experienced decline since its heyday in the late 1960s. When its very survival was threatened and worship attendance dropped to twenty, the congregation lowered its resistance to change. Its new pastor, Stephen Marsh, brought a renewed challenge to growth toward self-sufficiency by the year 2000. Receiving eighteen new members recently brought membership to ninety, eighty-nine of whom are African American, largely from the Caribbean.

Twenty percent of the surrounding neighborhood consists of children under age ten, therefore much creative attention has been directed by very able leadership toward renewing children's Christian education. Pastor Marsh has focused attention on adult education, combining an emphasis on Bible study and ethnic cultural identity as a strategy for developing leadership within the congregation. He currently leads all Bible studies and new member classes, but is preparing for a time when adults feel confident and willing to teach other adults.

New members participate in a four-session course led by Pastor Marsh on Sunday mornings. These sessions include histories of Christianity, Lutheranism, Holy Redeemer Church, and the African-American church. There is genuine excitement in learning how a person of color can be both Lutheran and connected with his or her own culture. That theme is present throughout all educational opportunities at Holy Redeemer, reflecting the rejuvenation Pastor Marsh experienced in exploring his own cultural roots within his Lutheran context.

The other opportunity for more traditional Christian education for adults happens on Wednesday evenings. Pastor Marsh and the church council challenge people to come to these weekly Bible studies, "a good place to learn a lot of things." Every church council member stands before the congregation to say he or she will be coming to Bible study weekly and will struggle toward tithing. Last week fifteen adults came to Bible study, twenty-five percent of Sunday's worship attendance. Two additional weekly Bible studies begin this fall, providing alternative study times for members.

Much adult education, however, is less traditional. Every Church Council meeting begins with thirty minutes of Bible study. Every meeting of a ministry group (committee) begins with fifteen minutes of Bible study. The women's ministry group meets for fifteen minutes of Bible study before worship and continues its monthly meeting after the Sunday service. September brings a month-long emphasis on Christian education, combining Wednesday and Sunday education with special events, last year culminating in an African festival.

Pastor Marsh has recognized the necessity and opportunity of providing leadership for adult education at Holy Redeemer. How has he done this? He uses sermons as teaching times, makes Bible study part of all congregational life, "talks up" education opportunities, and teaches, teaches, teaches. He is committed to bringing the Bible to life within the African cultural heritage and within his current African-American context. Adult education at Holy Redeemer is leadership development, challenging the congregation to become biblically literate, to study regularly, and to join the pastor in teaching.

For Your Reflection. Identify four new opportunities for "less traditional" adult education to happen in your own congregation, such as Bible study at the beginning of church council meetings.

In what ways could a threatening situation lead to renewed Christian education in your church? Does a current crisis offer potential for renewal?

Christ Lutheran Church, Downey, California

The life of Christ Church reflects its changing context. The 1980s saw increasing cultural diversity in an upper-middle-class community. "My daughter's kindergarten class spoke seventeen different languages," says Pastor Kathleen Richter. After the 1992 civil unrest, forty families left the congregation, followed more recently by others who have left because of earthquakes and fires. The reactionary separation into ethnic groups has left Christ Church about ninety percent Anglo, with some members of Asian and Hispanic heritage. "We're smaller than before (about 125 at worship), but we are growing again, including the return of some of those who had moved away."

Pastor Richter, a public-school teacher in her first profession, loves to teach, and leads the adult Sunday school class. Her favorite class, however, is the Wednesday-morning Bible study. About twenty women and men, many retirees, gather faithfully and study hard. "They're as good as any seminary class, except that they don't know Greek. They enjoy studying and are not afraid to ask questions, press for answers, and hear truth." One recent study of 1 Corinthians led to a six-month digression into church history. That led to one retiree borrowing every book on Luther in the pastor's library.

There are other educational opportunities offered occasionally, and they seem to generate interest: Sunday evening forums, weekday evening Bible studies, discussion groups at the annual congregational meeting. Christ Church is a congregation of adults who love to study and learn, but most are not leaders and teachers. "Our members have many gifts and are generous with their time, but they are not teachers. I've adapted to that, partly because I love the opportunities to teach."

Encouragement for adults to learn comes constantly. The annual stewardship drive includes the opportunity to commit to adult learning. New members are expected to study regularly, and they usually follow through with that commitment. Even so, Pastor Richter reflects that "we may not expect enough of our members" in growing and learning. The city of Downey sits next to communities where large, well-publicized churches demand much of members and members respond enthusiastically.

The power of video as a learning tool for all ages has been confirmed by experiences at Christ Church. "Most videos are terrible, but when done well, people get the message. Seeing someone struggle faithfully on a video is more meaningful for members today than reading about it in a book. It's important enough that I recently took a video production class. We have to take it seriously."

For Your Reflection. What use do you make of video in adult education? How can you increase its effectiveness as a resource? List six ways to help your congregation become one that "loves to study and learn."

Christ Lutheran Church, Charlotte, North Carolina

Over two thousand members, multiple staff, adequate budget, wonderful facilities—what could be better? Every congregation, regardless of size, has its own struggles to provide the best possible adult Christian education among its members. The need to plan, implement, and evaluate creatively never ends.

Charlotte, North Carolina, in the midst of the Bible belt, is home to hundreds of Protestant churches, many even larger than Christ Lutheran. This congregation is blessed with many resources, including competent and willing lay leadership.

There are groups meeting at Christ Church every day of the week, many times throughout each day. You may engage in group Bible study at 7:00 A.M., 11:00 A.M., or 7:00 P.M. Most educational opportunities are led by laity, but every clergy and staff leader offers studies that evolve from their own interests and expertise. Pastor Marilyn Ascarza, for instance, focuses much energy on spiritual direction and spiritual renewal through individual and group study and special events. In addition, there are many retreats aimed at particular groups within the congregation, invited lecturers and presenters for weekend seminars, and fifteen women's groups that meet monthly. Last summer four families vacationed together for an intentional experience of Christian community, learning more about family living.

The core of adult Christian education at Christ Church, however, consists of the Sunday-morning education events and "Wednesdays Together." Pastor David Misenheimer is candid: "We were unhappy about Sunday school attendance among adults. A lot of adults participated, but they were only a small percentage of the number that could have been there. We realized we were perpetuating old patterns that didn't work anymore, so why expect them to work in the future?" The new pattern for Sunday-morning adult education is small groups—thirty of them offered this year, scattered among three separate education hours simultaneous with worship services. Groups are offered around common concerns: groups for choir members, parents of various age groups, singles, marriage enrichment, grief recovery, personal growth, midlife transition, new members, etc. Each group, then, explores Sunday's Gospel lesson through their own life experiences.

"Wednesdays Together" attract over 400 members of all ages for a meal (prepared in the church's cafeteria), followed by youth events, meetings, rehearsals of many music groups, and educational opportunities. Included is a study for Sunday's group leaders led by one of the pastors about the upcoming Gospel.

While clergy and other staff teach frequently, most study events are led by carefully chosen lay leadership. The staff, however, serve a vital function in identifying and empowering that leadership, helping to ensure good results.

> There's lots of staff leadership in front-end planning. After all, we know the congregation. We spent an entire staff day on identifying potential groups and another day identifying strong group leaders.

For Your Reflection. In your congregation, what can staff and lay leadership do to help ensure the success of education initiatives? (See chapter 3 for further discussion of the topic of motivation for adult education.) Are you expecting patterns that don't work well now to work better in the future? What can you do to help them work better? Is it time to find a new pattern?

FINAL NOTES

What can we learn about adult Christian education from these congregational stories? The "web" of Christian education is different in each of these congregations, yet there are commonalities.

Each pastor has a high commitment to adult education and is a teacher and educator. The role of each pastor does differ, however. Some do almost all the teaching themselves: Pastor Marsh has a strategy for leadership development and Pastor Richter teaches because teaching is not a gift demonstrated by members. Pastor Misenheimer teaches, but spends more energy strategizing and planning. Pastor Mode is diligent to find the "moments of readiness" for learning and then empowering laity to respond. All these pastors have found effective ways to be a leader in education, and that commitment shows.

Adult education in each congregation is highly contextual. It takes into account the societal and economic situation that surrounds it, whether that be a blue collar community in Wisconsin, a threatened ethnic congregation in Brooklyn, a suburban California community changed by riots, fires, and earthquakes, or a suburban Bible Belt church filled with energetic, professional families. The adult education program in these churches will not, should not, and cannot look the same.

For adult education to fit its setting, constant attention is required, because the context continues to change. Christ Church, Charlotte, recognizes its old patterns are no longer effective. Christ Church, Downey, always looks for the educational opportunities within existing church activities, such as the annual meeting. Holy Redeemer knows the need to integrate cultural heritage and theology. All Saints keeps nurturing grassroots initiatives.

Each congregation uses a planning strategy that works for itself. In each case, however, the pastor can describe the planning method and his or her own place in that planning, giving a rationale for that role. Intentional thought is given to the needs, possibilities, and implementation of adult education opportunities. It doesn't happen without energy.

Finally, for some churches Sunday school remains the core of education and is enhanced by other opportunities. For other churches, weekday programs and other events provide the core of the education web. There is no one right way to accomplish adult Christian education, yet each church has sought and found a balance that works today. Tomorrow requires further planning.

chapter seven

Making the Connections

Norma Cook Everist
Susan K. Nachtigal

Adult education cannot be contained in the Christian-education wing of the church; it cannot be isolated from the rest of the church's mission and ministry. In this chapter we explore connections. Ministry in daily life is not only connected with adult education; the experiences of daily life become a central component of the curriculum itself, so that all of our arenas and relationships can be transformed for ministry. Likewise, learning leads to mission, and mission in turn leads to further learning. Learning can never be an end in itself. The Holy Spirit calls us to faith so that our hearts and minds might be in Christ Jesus. Education is part of our spirituality and spirituality is enriched through education. As a learning community we gather for worship as the Word becomes flesh in us, transforming us once again for daily growth and service. Ministry in daily life, mission, and spirituality are connected to and part of the content for adult education. In this chapter we deepen our understanding of how adult education can enhance our whole life in the church.

CONNECTING EDUCATION AND MINISTRY IN DAILY LIFE

Truck and Engine Company 14

As a group of adults arrived at Truck and Engine Company 14, their host, a fire fighter, greeted them, apologizing that he really didn't know what he could teach these congregational leaders. There were no chairs, so the group stood, and looking around, asked questions. What happens here? What is God doing here? Two and one-half hours later, as the "fire cat" meowed to be let in, the evening had seemed too short for making all of the connections between faith and world that they had begun to explore.

At a time when the church grapples with its theological authority and mission in society, when Christians struggle with ethical issues in a complex world, and when adult Christian education is frequently confined to Sunday morning, we need to ask how to connect adult education with ministry in daily life.

All stages of the life cycle and all of the adult's past and present experiences are important resources for adult education. We find many such experiences beyond the walls of the church building. The adult is more than the volunteer at the usher's post, the committee meeting, or in the choir loft. Those activities are not unimportant, but the Christian's vocation encompasses more than the volitional part of one's life.

All stations in life—whatever occupies one's time, work, relationships, or leisure—provide experiences for theological reflection and discernment. Our vocation, our ministry in daily life, becomes part of our adult education curriculum. The question is how to make these experiences accessible to one another, and to our own cognitive and emotional reflection as well. How do we befriend those experiences when we are not the gathered people of God, but busy being the church in the world?[1] How do we "do theology" in the many technical languages of computers, medicine, agriculture, sports, or advertising in which we live and work each day?

Adults may resist a lecture. Or they will attend lectures, read books, and listen to sermons, but disconnect those from the "real issues" they face each day. But once adult learners take responsibility for their own learning, gain skill in theological reflection, and learn to appreciate sharing their worlds with others in the church, they also listen to sermons in a totally new way. They begin to hear Scripture with new ears, ready to receive new insights for their own connecting with the adult learning project they are pursuing.[2]

Some leaders in the church worry that such independent learners may misinterpret or distort the faith and become heretical. There is greater danger in adults not engaging the faith at all, dispensing with and despising adult education in the church, turning more and more to theologies of the worlds in which they live upon which to base their ethical decision making. Left alone, each of us will turn gospel into law and become heretical, making gods of ourselves. But members of the Christian community bring with them the biblical and theological traditions in which they have been steeped. They become the supportive corrective to one another. In the midst of discussion and reflection, the pastor and other lay leaders, listening carefully, will have opportunity to speak the appropriate biblical word and share a deeper theological insight that relates to the discussion at hand. Such teaching is, in many ways, more difficult than delivering a prepared lecture, but it is also more intriguing.

The fireman in Syracuse spoke authoritatively about the difference between a truck and an engine company, and about the mission of each. He reflected that fire fighters were respected in this inner-city community. A group member saw the activity of our protector God. One person, using a petition of the Lord's Prayer asked, "What is evil in this place?" The questioner had expected an answer such as "fire" or "death," with which the fireman was well acquainted. But, no, those were parts of life. He answered quickly, "Unnecessary death," and told of a fireman being killed on an arson call, and of children dying because of a landlord's negligence in meeting building codes.

With greater subtlety and clarity, this small group of Christians moved beyond interest, and even admiration, to insight and mutual support. Except for the fire bell going off early in the visit, as if on cue to draw people to the "lesson," the night had been a quiet one. The fireman raised the large door to let the cat in, as he shared once more the importance of the community of fire fighters. "It's hard for others to understand how close we get because we have to depend on each other." He now knew he had a broader community of those who understood— at least a little—people from his own congregation. They prayed together, his prayer, in that place, and the evening was complete.

Doing Theology Daily

On Tuesday afternoon, who or what are the gods that you trust above all things? In the middle of the night, what do you fear above all things? On Sunday afternoon, who or what do you love more than all? Those are your gods. Luther's "We are to fear and love God so that . . . ," which begins the catechetical responses to the Ten Commandments, points to perpetual, permeating human questions. No matter what one's station in life, everyone has a propensity to take other, less worthy gods. "That to which your heart clings and entrusts itself, is, I say really your God."[3]

In keeping with adult education theory, and cognizant of the human condition, we do well to begin with the situation of the participants in their worlds. It is not so much a matter of remembering or forgetting Sunday's sermon by Wednesday. Each moment one lives a theology. The key is discerning which theology, and how it is or is not the theology of the baptized.

Having begun with the experiences and dilemmas of adult human life, Christians can turn once more to the catechisms. Suddenly they

take on life, our life. One woman, upon reading Luther's words on the
Seventh Commandment in the Large Catechism, said, "When, again,
was that written?"

> Stealing is a widespread, common vice, but people pay so little
> attention to it that the matter is entirely out of hand. If all who are
> thieves, though they are unwilling to admit it, were hanged on the
> gallows, the world would soon be empty, and there would be a
> shortage of both hangmen and gallows.

> Far worse than sneak-thieves, against whom we can guard with
> lock and bolt . . . [are the others against whom] no one can guard.

> These are called gentlemen swindlers or big operators. . . . They sit
> in office chairs and . . . with a great show of legality they rob and
> steal.

> Those who can steal and rob openly are safe and free, unmolested
> by anyone, even claiming honor from men. Meanwhile the little
> sneakthieves who have committed one offense must bear disgrace
> and punishment so as to make the others look respectable and
> honorable.[4]

Human sin and God's mercy permeate every aspect of life. Adults
who have begun to see their daily lives as part of a Christian curriculum
can recognize alienation and rebellion against God, the thicket of
human sin resulting in broken relationships and a sick society. God's
grace is always a surprise: God's merciful, unconditional love, centered
in the forgiveness of sins, empowering people for radical servanthood in
the world.

If human beings are always living by some theology, then discernment of those popular theologies which are the basis for daily decision
making is an essential task for the Christian seeking to connect
Christian education and daily life. We can think of slogans, bumper
stickers, daily sayings, and advertisements that capture popular theologies. People are quite able to come up with many. We could select
one, any one, and together reflect and theologize on it. Whether it's
"Be number one" or "You deserve a break today," further examination
shows the desperate need to prove oneself, to "get what you can."
Significantly different from passively listening to a lecture or sermon is
the participant's own discovery and discernment process which in turn
equips them to "do theology" in the vernacular. Soon people are seeing
for themselves that "I deserve" assumes that others may "deserve" to wait

on me night and day, or that God's sabbath rest is a gift, a needed gift that I sometimes put off until I'm no good to anybody.

Strategy for Adult Learning. Ask an adult group to call out messages they receive each day. Record them on the board and then ask the group to choose one with which to work. Ask the group to delve into the meaning behind the words, creating a corresponding column entitled "Christian Theology" and noting the contrasts. For example, the group chooses the advertisement, "Call toll free! This offer ends soon!"

Messages We Receive	Christian Theology
Call toll free! This offer ends soon!	God is eternal; we live in God's time.
Hurry up! Do it when we want you to do it.	The creator God comes to and cares for us. Jesus came to be part of our lives. The Spirit lives within us.
Call us!	Redemption *is* absolutely free. God gives us love and all blessings and wants us to be all we can be.
It won't cost you anything! *(We want to sell you something.)*	Christ includes me and everyone else in the Christian community.
You may be left out.	Christ calls us to invite everyone into the Christian community.
If you act now, you can get something others don't have. *(They will be left out.)*	God alone knows my deepest need.
We have what you need.	Christ frees us from all who would make decisions for us;
You have the freedom to buy; let us decide how to satisfy your wants.	Christ frees us to serve so that everyone will have what they really need.

Living with Christianity

The paradoxical nature of much of Lutheran theology tempts people to simplify into legalisms and moralisms. But adults—unlike children, who are at a concrete-thinking developmental stage—can benefit from struggling with the subtleties of paradox. In such documents as Martin Luther's "A Treatise on Christian Liberty," we hear,

A Christian is a perfectly free lord of all, subject to none.

A Christian is a perfectly dutiful servant of all, subject to all.[5]

People need to share their own bondages, as well as the Christian liberty that comes from the cross and resurrection. They can explore how this liberty empowers them for servanthood that the world simply does not comprehend.

Christian liberty is not, as many Christian adults reason, to be equated with the freedom of religion. Foreign to the culture, but basic to Christians, is the forgiveness of sins. For Luther, vocation is life organized around the forgiveness of sins. As certainly as God's grace lifts people infinitely above everything that everyday duties could give, "just that certainly the call does not take us away from these duties but more deeply into them, in order to serve the neighbor, . . . who is everyone."[6]

One example of liberation for vocation arose in an adult group discussion. In pairs people had shared their own experiences of bondage and freedom. Returning to the large group, one older woman said, "I'm a pink lady," going on to explain that meant a hospital volunteer.

My husband lay ill in that hospital for two months. After his death I couldn't go back there. But then someone invited me to volunteer with her. I didn't want to, but she urged me. It was a long time before I was able to go by room 309. But now I can go in and can ask if the person in that room needs anything.

In her own words she described her own alienation, perhaps even her rebellion against God. Through the ministry of her friend, which she at first resisted and then accepted, she was called to a new vocation. But it was only through the forgiveness of sins, perhaps including her own unarticulated inability to forgive her husband for dying, that she was released from her bondage for servanthood, manifested in seeing what her "neighbor" in room 309 needed.

Using Luther's concepts of station and vocation, and relating them to creation and redemption, people can consider their myriad roles and occupations: mother, son, neighbor, citizen, client, manager, friend. Luther contends that everyone, by virtue of creation, has one or many stations, roles, relationships in life, and that one is not intrinsically more holy than the next. Although Luther's world was vastly different, that concept remains true. By virtue of the forgiveness of sins, Christians are called to vocation in their stations. By the power of the Spirit, we live out our vocations. What is my vocation to my young adult children? How is it different from when they were toddlers? What is my calling as a potential client of two competing insurance plans? Do I need further education to faithfully use my gifts? What is my vocation as personnel director in relation to someone who is not carrying their work load? What theology informs my decisions? Luther's treatise says we should not allow people to walk all over us, but yet we should be servants. How can I live out the gospel without abdicating the power of my position?

Strategy for Adult Learning. Invite adults to list their own arenas of daily activity and relationships (stations). In pairs, discuss these. Next, discern the Christian callings (vocations) at this particular time in the arenas and relationships listed. Discuss these callings in pairs. Listen well to each other. Remember that Christ's death and resurrection free us in the forgiveness of sins to accept no one but Christ as Lord and to serve one another. An example:

Erik's Callings

Station	Vocation
Husband	To support, encourage, help
Father of three grade-school daughters	To love and let go
Mid-level manager (under-employed)	Erik struggles with questions here
Neighbor	To know, care, and ? . . .
Son	To respect, listen

Station	Vocation
Brother (younger brother killed five years ago)	To remember, and to move on
Volunteer on stewardship committee at church and as a "big brother"	To be responsible To have a vision To be a consistent role model
Citizen (town, state, nation, world)	What role?

In doing this chart, Erik's education partner might ask, "How do you see your calling to be a parent changing now that your daughters are no longer pre-schoolers?" or "Since you had to change jobs due to corporate downsizing, how much has your own struggle affecting your family? What does the freedom of forgiveness mean to you in this situation?" or "You've been spending a lot of time in your local community. Are there new arenas that need your gifts?" Imagine that Erik, through prayerful reflection, discerns that his calling in relation to his parents may be changing, too. He may be letting his perception of their judgment keep him locked into few occupational choices. He hears that he is free in Christ to receive them as parents, not gods, and then realizes maybe he hasn't been listening, just assuming. He intends to keep clarifying his callings.

Individuals need the Christian community to help them discern with clarity their vocations of radical, powerful servanthood, rooted in the forgiveness of sins. Connecting daily life with the tenet of our biblical and theological faith is powerful adult learning in the Christian Community.

Connecting Faith and World

When we begin with the arenas of the worlds in which we live, the curriculum is always relevant. The connecting process, therefore, is designed never to be above or below an individual adult's learning level. The content is their adult lives as they connect with the Word of God. Such teaching and learning is open, profound, inviting—not coercive or intimidating—yet passionate. In addition to discussion, we can include journal keeping, role play, film, even mime. Going to one another's living and working spaces produces particularly profound insights. Learning is real and relevant. We need each other in the Christian learning community to help us discern vocation, gifts, and mission.

Connections learning groups have met in many places across the country for the past dozen years.[7] In Oakland, California, a few years ago, a group visited a metropolitan newspaper, the workplace of their host. They toured the building from the bottom to the top, where they sat in the man's office. As a newspaper publisher, this Christian had thought through the implications of the faith decision to purchase a paper in Oakland, which existed in the shadow of San Francisco. He struggled with hiring practices and civic responsibility. The themes of his faith were gifts, justice, stewardship, and the challenges of the gospel. He knew who he was and the responsibility and power he handled. He drew on the strength of his local congregation more than many in his public world or his congregation had previously realized.

Another group visited a mall where one person was a security guard. The mall is the public square of today, although it is privately owned and the activity that unites it is consumerism. Another learning group went to a downtown public library in Colorado Springs, Colorado, asking hard questions about what it means to care in one of the few remaining truly public places: "Can you become the *de facto* child-care agent, or the place where the homeless wash up? If you can't do it alone, then what catalytic action in the community is called forth?"

One adult learning group, in visiting a college sports information director at her place of ministry in daily life, learned that she sends out stories to hometown papers—not just of the stars of major sports, but of the wrestlers and the second-string players who volunteer to tutor junior-high children. Christian learning colleagues saw how she appreciated the diversity of gifts in the body of Christ rather than succumbing to the primary sports goal of "making it to the big time." She was living her Christian faith and they helped her articulate her working theology.

In each of these places, people who at first said they had little to say, but could "show people around," soon heard their learning companions asking them, "What is God creating here? What is God forgiving here? How is God shaping community here?" Without exception they found themselves using the images of that world and the terminology as well. The farmer who had to supplement his farm income by driving heavy road-repair equipment felt guilty about not "thinking about God more." Others encouraged him, noting that moving the earth and "making the road straight" had biblical precedent. A woman who described each child she helped in her morning and evening job as crossing guard was reminded by others that the phrase she used, "crossing the children," reminded them of Baptism.

Adults learn much by simply being with their brothers and sisters in Christ in *their* worlds. Over the course of time, sharing pain and joy becomes very real. Pastors and diaconal ministers, whose call is to help bridge church and world, can play a significant teaching and leading role in helping adults become adept at the theological role of connecting faith and daily life. Whether we meet in the firehouse or the church fellowship hall, we need to help people connect the Scriptures and the catechisms with their ministries in daily life.

CONNECTING EDUCATION AND MISSION

Learning Leads to Mission

We should not be surprised when the Christian learning community fails to connect with Christ's mission of reconciliation, because our society measures educational success individualistically. The objective, at least tacitly, is to get an "A," to be the best.

We may admire academic pursuit for the sheer joy of learning, a worthy goal that delights in God's gifts of curiosity, knowledge, and skill. But when the learner is buried beneath the weight of acquired treasures of learning, God's grace cannot be multiplied in the world. Likewise, when learners have as their ultimate goal winning in what they perceive as educational competition, their own accomplishment becomes their mission. This is often at the expense of their brothers and sisters in Christ in the learning community.

On the other hand, and perhaps this is more frequently the case, there are Christians who reject learning. They close their minds and hearts to the stored wisdom of the ages and to God's guidance. They may be engaged in doing, but it may not be God's mission they pursue. They may be highly motivated and even adequately effective for a while, but their ministry will be shallow. They will thirst for wisdom and not even recognize that thirst.

For some, Christian education is considered peripheral, soft, less than real. They believe that the church, even Christianity itself, is not only an anachronism, but inadequate for the public world today. This stance, adopted in frustration, will produce apathy or a heretical mission that competes with, in order to conquer, the outside world.

We begin by believing in the radically good news that we dare not compete to conquer. Rather, we believe God creates us for interdependence and reconciles us to each other in Christ for community and for service. We therefore expect that all members of the body of Christ will engage in lifelong learning as the only way to center their lives in the midst of alternative missions of demanding demigods.

Adult learning will be shortsighted if it doesn't believe Christ has invited the entire church to walk, speak, and serve in the world. Education dare not be measured in pages finished, books completed, people in attendance. Most people now agree that learning cannot be measured in memorization; learning needs to lead to meaning and understanding. But even the latter, if it is an end in itself, is meaningless. Education is measured in mission.

Letty Russell says that "education is involved in the whole of church life, and ceases to be education when it is taken out of the context of the witnessing community." When "the community is not a *witnessing* community, those who are being nurtured in the community receive 'mise-ducation' or a gift of education that has already been turned into a stone."[8] We are called to give our students bread and not a stone. That bread will become part of each person's body, and we together become part of the body of Christ so that we are energized for witness and service.

The congregation that is not engaged in outreach also will be merely a stone. Fed on the bread of life, stuffed full, but not exercising its energy in ministry, this learning community will no longer hunger for the Word. Unchallenged, people will assume the task of critic, a role that can become habit forming.

A sponge already filled with water can hold no more. But when a sponge is wrung out, wiping tables, it will soak up fresh water when placed in a basin. So, too, the congregation—cleansed, filled, and serving at all kinds of tables—will be eager to be filled again with the water of life.

Strategies for Adult Learning.

• Explore the ways your own educational experiences may have been deadening, competitive, or only for individual achievement. Brainstorm ways your congregation's adult education program can be cooperative, life-giving, and have service as its goal.

• Identify three mission goals of your congregation. Discuss specific adult education possibilities that would more fully equip people to engage in these missions.

• At the end of an adult education session, take time to ask each other, "If what we have said here about the gospel is true, what radically new word and action does it have for our lives next week?"

• At the next session, ask each other how your mission and ministry in the world went, and what new questions that raises for your learning together this time.

The Gift of Ministry

The Christian learning community is grounded in one uniting act—baptism into the incarnation, death, and resurrection of Jesus Christ. All enter on the same ground, yet differently gifted. No one has special advantage; no one needs remedial education. Christ gives us the gift of eternal life, which means the goal has already been achieved. Being immersed in this living truth permeates every other endeavor, so nothing is irrelevant; the private and public arenas are bridged. What God has already done and is doing cannot be kept secret, so there is no need to prove one knows more than another. The gift is open and for all, so there is no need to push to the head of the line or win the prize. We are given the ultimate reality of God's unconditional love, and this is always also the gift of Christian community. "We welcome you into the Lord's family. We receive you as fellow members of the body of Christ, children of the same heavenly Father, and workers with us in the kingdom of God."[9] This is the welcome the learning community confesses during the Service of Baptism.

New Christians are carried by the community of faith, which confesses with them the Creed. Each new Christian is given the gift of ministry. We are called to witness to Christ, minister in his name, and engage in Christ's mission in the world. We often hold the mistaken belief that children are the learners and adults the workers in society and the church. We actually confess that all are already in ministry from the moment of baptism and, therefore, all are lifelong learners. The community enters into the cross-shaped mission of Jesus Christ.

We participate in the mission of the living God when we engage as learners in biblical study. Luther says the Scriptures are so shallow a young child can wade in them and so deep a grown person can drown in them. We inquire into the way the Scriptures functioned for the first community, and we allow the text to nurture, shape, and transform our community. We recognize our own context for mission, realize that we are both *interpreted by* the text and *interpreters of* the text. We honor the reciprocity between text and experience, allowing mutual questioning to become the foundation for action.

We are interconnected with the people of God of all times and places. The classroom is always crowded with all the saints. Where two or three are gathered in the name of Jesus, Christ the teacher is present; also present are all others in whom he incarnates himself. Learning in the Christian community is always global and always historic. The task is to become acquainted with these unknown brothers and sisters in Christ through story, and through vicarious and actual experiential learning.

Strategies for Adult Learning.

• Survey your congregation's education and ministry opportunities. Identify the education opportunities according to the age group for which they are intended—children, youth, or adults. Do the same for ministry opportunities. Challenge the congregation to offer at least two educational opportunities for each age group and ministry opportunities open to all ages.

• Explore ways adults in your congregation are already part of local and global missions. Gather some resources for your congregation that will help connect you more directly with brothers and sisters in God's mission from another part of the world.

• Welcome new members to your faith community by asking what ministry and mission activities they are already part of or might like to join, and what educational opportunities they will choose. Help them see how the two can be connected. Challenge each other!

Mission Leads to Learning

Curriculum always deals with God and God's people in this time and place. Our task is to set a trustworthy learning environment in which people can be invited to bring their brokenness, their alienation, their grief, and their guilt to a place that is safely bounded by God's unconditional acceptance and love.

The gospel speaks to actual people in response to their actual lives. Our task is to help each other ask, "What is my mission, and what are the value systems, the beliefs, the very gods on which that mission is based?"

Jennifer is an insurance agent. Her mission is to make a living to support her family and to provide her customers with good services to meet their financial needs, now and in the future. Her goals are to make as many contacts as possible, to respond to phone calls, to sell insurance. Behind these goals are values and judgments. Should she work for a fraternal or commercial underwriter? Should she become a licensed financial advisor? Would that increase her income? Would it serve her clients more fully? These are all questions of understanding one's mission.

There are ethical concerns. "How do I guide people to make their own decisions, providing options but not opinions?" Jennifer wonders, if she holds back her counsel for fear of projecting her own ideas on someone else's decision about what level of risk fits their own temperament.

There is the question of clarity of role. Do people perceive Jennifer as an insurance agent, a financial advisor, or a tax consultant? Her clarity of identity and respect for others and her relationship with God shape her clarity of mission.

Behind these questions are belief systems such as how we weigh needs of the present against those of the future, personal financial well-being as compared to what we leave our loved ones. What do we believe about the importance of the well-being of the individual and of the whole society?

These beliefs inform how we see our daily work, over mission. We may want to help a client discover investment possibilities without undo tax burdens. One insurance agent used the biblical phrase "Render unto Caesar that which is Caesar's." "But not more" was implied.

Deeper still are our gods, of security or risk, or adventure. In an earlier day people questioned whether purchasing insurance showed a lack of trust in God. While that issue is rarely heard today, the basic question of trust in family, in self, in the community, in God permeates our decisions and our mission. Who or what are our gods? Each day as Jennifer engages in her mission to meet her goals, all these deeper issues are at work. A Christian adult learning community can help people reflect on their mission and more clearly know what they believe. Then our witness and our work can be a mission of faith and service in Christ.

Mission does lead to learning! Inevitably we act our way into new ways of believing. People are lifelong learners. We must engage adult Christian learners in reflection upon their mission, their beliefs, and their gods so that all are constantly reestablished at the root in the life-giving mission of Jesus Christ in which we have been baptized.

The society in which we live is not a Christendom, but the language of our daily world is deceivingly similar to that of Christianity. The gods and goals are disguised as our Judeo-Christian heritage. The temptation is to hide out in private ghettos of ethnic Christianity, abdicating the public world to the civil faith. Our call to mission is exactly the opposite, to proclaim that God is still all-powerful. People hunger for communal mission; they want to do something, in the name of something, together. Translating this energy to real, crying needs is not easy. Our challenge is to call our neighbor to a mission of life in the gospel rather than to a mission of death.

Rooted in Christ's incarnation, we can send each other forth knowing that Christ already lives in each neighborhood. Reminded of the creator God's ongoing work, we will seek to replenish the earth, whether that be in South Dakota or in the South Bronx. Believing that the Spirit is at work in ways beyond our present reality, we can dare to envision people working together who are different in gender, race, and class. This will take no small amount of courage when economic and growth statistics say such neighborhoods don't grow and don't become economically viable. Confessing our belief in the God who creates, redeems, and empowers, we can be involved in our daily missions, creating, caring, reconciling, and building community in cross-shaped ways. One cannot help but be a learner when one is engaged in Christian mission.

Strategies for Adult Learning.
• Take time to listen to the "missions" in which each person in your group is engaged in daily life. Ask each other probing questions to learn about the goals, values, belief systems, and gods behind those missions. Reflect together using the Bible and the Creeds on how the gospel can inform and transform our outlook, attitude, and actions.
• If you do not have one, begin an adult forum to discuss the issues of the public world that affect us all. You may want to meet somewhere in your community other than the church building. Invite others to come to learn, and be ready to learn from them. Delve into the Scriptures; share your faith. Challenge each other to make a difference in the public (social, commercial, political, cultural) world, whether that be through individual (even divergent) or communal efforts.
• Walk or drive around your neighborhood and look and listen for needs. Talk to people. Ask questions. Then meet as a congregation, or as an ecumenical or interfaith committee, to design strategies for education and mission that seek to meet those needs by empowering people.

CONNECTING EDUCATION, SPIRITUALITY, AND WORSHIP

Traditionally, we think of education as being aimed at the mind. Education is that process through which the student's mind acquires information and the skills to read, write, speak, listen, observe, analyze, order, and apply data. Through these educational means the mind is opened to see, understand, and make sense of life in this world.

Christian education is a similar process, but it takes wider aim at body, mind, and spirit. When developing Christian education in congregations, we want to use our heads as we plan and implement programs. We want our endeavors to make sense, to be logical, and to be intellectually challenging. However, Christian education is a unique discipline because it has as its goal the involvement of the whole self. Christian education values knowledge and intellect but, just as important, it includes the foundation of a Christ-centered reality that seeks to inspire the soul.

Foundations

There are three writings that help us understand this larger aim of Christian education: St. Paul's writings in the book of Philippians; Luther's explanation to the Third Article of the Apostles' Creed, written in his Small Catechism; and Canticle 13 in *Lutheran Book of Worship*. As you prepare to teach, or as you train other teachers to teach, read through these passages again and again. Read them silently and read them aloud. Slow down and ponder words that seem to stand out. These words are the means through which the Spirit works in us and for us. In Philippians, St. Paul writes:

> If there is any encouragement in Christ, any consolation from love, any sharing in the Spirit, any compassion and sympathy, make my joy complete: be of the same mind, having the same love, being in full accord and of one mind. Do nothing from selfish ambition or conceit, but in humility regard others as better than yourselves. Let each of you look not to your own interests, but to the interests of others. Let the same mind be in you that was in Christ Jesus, who though he was in the form of God, did not regard equality with God as something to be exploited, but emptied himself, taking the form of a slave, being born in human likeness. And being found in human form, he humbled himself and became obedient to the point of death—even death on a cross. Therefore God also highly exalted him and gave him the name that is above every name, so that at the name of Jesus, every knee should bend, in heaven and on earth and under the earth, and every tongue should confess that Jesus Christ is Lord, to the glory of God the Father (Philippians 2:1-11).

In these verses, St. Paul is urging us to do more than simply use our heads. He is calling us to think the way Christ thinks, to have the mindset that Christ has. Such thinking reaches far beyond the function only of our minds. This thinking reshapes our whole outlook on life. It reaches into and transforms our self-perception, our relationship with our neighbor, and our understanding of life before God.

Martin Luther discusses this paradox of the Christian mind in his Small Catechism. For the Christian, having this mind of Christ is beyond our construction, our comprehension, or our conjuring. This mind cannot come to us through rigorous thought, higher learning, or scientific proof. Luther wrote about this great irony in his explanation of the Third Article of the Apostles' Creed, "I believe in the Holy Spirit":

> I believe that by my own understanding or strength I cannot believe in Jesus Christ my Lord or come to him, but instead the Holy Spirit has called me through the gospel, enlightened me with his gifts, made me holy, and kept me in the true faith, just as he calls, gathers, enlightens, and makes holy the whole Christian church on earth and keeps it with Jesus Christ in the one common, true faith. Daily in this Christian church the Holy Spirit abundantly forgives all sins—mine and those of all believers. On the last day the Holy Spirit will raise me and all the dead and will give to me and all believers in Christ eternal life. This is most certainly true.[10]

Think about Luther's explanation as compared to running. Running is a popular sport in North America and it is commonplace to hear of races being run locally, regionally, or nationally. What is typical in each of these races is that the runners' bodies are in prime condition, well trained, and ready to run the marathon miles. What is not typical is to see a marathoner who does not have sight in his eyes. And yet, one morning, an unsighted marathoner was seen running alongside a guide runner. Together they held the same pace, allowing the unsighted runner to keep his hand on the shoulder of his guide. What was particularly moving was to see, periodically, the guide runner reaching up and placing his hand on that of the unsighted runner's in order to secure its position squarely on the guide's shoulder. The guide ran the entire race with the unsighted runner; throughout he continued this securing gesture.

How long do we try to run the marathon with our own mind's eye rather than through the vision won for us by the Christ? How many times do we blindly endeavor to be guided by our own strength and intellectual resolve rather than rest in the security that comes from being squarely situated in the love, grace, and mercy of God.

God's invitation to us is to live the vision even when we cannot see, to listen to the call of the gospel, to receive "this mind that is ours in Christ Jesus" even when we cannot understand, and to live not only according to the information we accumulate and comprehend through education, but also by the depth of inspiration we receive from the Spirit.

Christian education has a soul purpose: to move to the depths of our being, to strike our hearts, and to create in us the fullness of "the mind of Christ."

Canticle 13, based on 2 Timothy 2 and set to music by scholar and composer Lucien Deiss, also expresses this deeper way of knowing:

Refrain: Keep in mind that Jesus Christ has died for us and is risen from the dead. He is our saving Lord; he is joy for all ages.

1) If we die with the Lord, we shall live with the Lord. If we endure with the Lord, we shall live with the Lord.

Refrain

2) In him all our sorrow, in him all our joy. In him hope of glory, in him all our love. Refrain

3) In him our redemption, in him all our grace. In him our salvation, in him all our peace.

Refrain[11]

Sometimes it is difficult for our minds to comprehend what these words mean because the Lord is not physically at our side. From all appearances we are not "with the Lord." Reliance on logic and a tendency toward self-sufficiency sometimes prevent us from resting our sorrow and joy in God. But here the Word of God has a way of collapsing time. We don't need to return to that time when Jesus was physically present on earth in order to experience his presence. Nor do we need to invent extraordinary experiences to help ourselves believe that the gifts that Jesus Christ won for us are really true and relevant to our lives.

Instead, by the power of the Word, all of life—past, present, and future—is lived in the presence of God's eternal now. We don't only teach that God in Christ Jesus died for us a long time ago, and then rose again. We teach also that God now dies with us, lives with us, and endures with us in all things. We don't only teach that Jesus died for our sins and that someday, when we die, we'll go to heaven to experience the everlasting grace of God. We teach also that today is the day of salvation, and that joy, redemption, grace, peace, and all the other gifts mentioned in this canticle are a part of our blessed life now. In this time-collapsing work of the Word everything that God in Christ Jesus accomplished then is immediate to us now.

From an educational standpoint, this is important because we will never prove that we are in Christ or that Christ is with us. However, God does for us that which we cannot do for ourselves. The Word made flesh makes a home in our flesh, and moves us to believe the unbelievable. The Word made flesh moves us in our fleshly lives to think the unthinkable, to inspire the dispirited, and to fathom the incomprehensible. This canticle is the Word moving through words, and in its singing we are teaching the saving acts of God to ourselves and one another.

In all three of these selections we can see that as we live in the knowledge of Christ, the finitude of our knowledge is exposed. We were empty, until Christ emptied himself for us. We lived unto death, until Christ died for our life. The truth about our own understanding and strength reveals to us the limitations of education aimed at our minds alone. Education centered in Christ is aimed at the transformation of the whole self, so that the mind of Christ might live in us and teach us all things. In short, this paradox of our faith and this wonder of Christian inspiration is summed up in that familiar benediction: "May the peace of God, which passes all human understanding, keep your hearts and minds in Christ Jesus unto life everlasting. Amen" (based on Philippians 4:7).

Spirituality as Education Aimed at the Heart

It would not be enough just to read the above passages in a single reading without slowing down to meditate on each phrase and draw connections to our own lives. Nor would we cull the depths of each passage without reading it over and over again, allowing it to sink deeper and deeper into our being.

As we read these passages, we can take them into ourselves by imagining their characteristics. Words come to life when our sensate and tactile selves are engaged in interpreting them. Words come to life when we feel the emotions they represent. Given the context of Christian education, spirituality is education aimed at the heart so that the heart can appropriate the fullness of the experience the words are trying to convey. Spirituality is the process of receiving information at the center of ourselves where, by the power of the Holy Spirit, it is given new life and new meaning.

In our hearts words are more than words when we

taste them,
smell them,
touch them,
see them.

Words are more than words when we

feel them,
trust them,
love them,
believe them.

Words are more than words when they

identify us,
convict us,
forgive us,
comfort us.

Spirituality is education carrying all this information to the heart because the heart is the place where education becomes flesh. Our hearts are the place where education becomes connected to us and to the Spirit of Christ alive within us. In our hearts the words and means used to educate us are translated into words and means that inspire us.

This process could be illustrated in the way the human heart functions: Blood in need of oxygen is carried to the heart through the veins. Once the blood arrives at the heart, the heart and lungs work together to oxygenate the blood and turn if from dark to bright. Then, the oxygen-rich blood is pumped out of the aorta into the rest of the body.

Education is like the blood flowing into the lungs and heart. It is in need of vital oxygen. Once reaching the heart and lungs, words and information are enlivened and given new meaning, allowing inspired, Spirit-enriched education to flow out of our hearts and serve the rest of the body.

Word in Creation

In Genesis, as the Word proceeds out of the mouth of God, creation begins to happen. Those words in Genesis 1, "And God said let there be . . . and it was so . . . and behold it was very good," are familiar to each of us. The Word of God was spoken and the sun, moon, stars, seas, land, plants, animals, and human beings were made. It is clear from the Genesis account that the Word of God, if it wills, has the power to move heaven and earth.

There are a number of ways in which Christian educators can teach the creation story. First we can teach that everything that lives, moves, and has its being comes from God. Then, we can proceed to teach the order of creation and the particular events of each day of creation. Then, we can marvel at the mighty deeds of God and give thanks that God is all-powerful and able to do such creating out of nothing.

But the challenge of completing the Christian education task requires the teacher to bring this story closer to each student's heart. How can we connect the contents of this story with the life-sustaining movement the Spirit wants to make in the hearts of those students? How can we move this story from being a series of external words spoken *to* the students into being the living Word at work *in* the students? This is not to suggest that we are trying to do the Spirit's work for the Spirit, but rather that we are taking seriously God's promise to work powerfully through our words, expressions, and articulations. Teachers must tackle the important task of putting the Word into words that teach and inspire students.

In recalling what was said above about the Word's ability to collapse time, perhaps one place to begin teaching this story is with another story. For example, remember the story of the Upper Room on that first evening of the resurrection of our Lord? The disciples were huddled together in that little dark hideaway because they were afraid. Everything for which they had been working, and the one for whom they had been working, was gone. Their hopes for a new life in the Messiah were over, and they were left with nothing: nothing to say, nothing to do, nothing to be. But then Jesus, the Word made flesh, came and stood among them. He repeatedly said to the disciples, "Peace be with you," and showed them his hands and side. The text in John 20:20 says that they "rejoiced when they saw the Lord." Then Jesus "breathed on them" the Holy Spirit and left.

Creation out of nothing isn't just about the creation story. It is the story in the Upper Room where the disciples were nothing, and the Word came to them and offered something mightier than their devastation, more courageous than their fear, and more true than their minds could reason. The Word was God in the flesh offering his wounded hands and side in order that, beginning one night in a small room, all isolation and terror, all meaningless hatred and presumption, all injury and death might be destroyed. Out of nothing the Word created again: light and life never to be overcome.

Can we not, in the collapse of time that is the Word's way, begin to realize that this story is the Word addressing us, even now, as we are confronted by the isolation and the nothingness of our lives? Can we not, through the flesh that is the means for the Word, hear for ourselves the words of Jesus spoken to us now, "Peace be with you"? And can we not, from those very lips, receive in our flesh the breath of life that is the Holy Spirit? Over and over again we are created out of nothing. In believing the depth and breadth of this story, and also this truth about our life in Christ, Christian education is accomplished and spirituality is sustained.

The Word Made Flesh

Looking at the creation texts in Genesis and the story of the Upper Room in the Gospel of John leads us to the prologue of that same Gospel.

> In the beginning was the Word, and the Word was with God, and the Word was God. He was in the beginning with God. All things came into being through him, and without him not one thing came into being. What has come into being in him was life, and the life was the light of all people. . . . And the Word became flesh and lived among us, and we have seen his glory, the glory as of a father's only son, full of grace and truth. (John testified to him and cried out, "This was he of whom I said, 'He who comes after me ranks ahead of me because he was before me.'") From his fullness we have all received, grace upon grace (John 1:1-4, 14-16).

This Gospel text is imbued with the same language and imagery that is used in the Genesis 1 creation account. John uses this language and imagery to connect the One of whom he speaks with the One who, by the power of the spoken Word, creates at will. Every time the Word was spoken, life came into being. So great was the power of the Word, John writes, that the "Word was with God, and the Word was God."

Not only did John believe in the creative power of the Word, but that the Word became flesh (Ephesians 2:15 and Colossians 3:9-10). This was in order that, in the flesh, all the power of God would dwell. In the flesh of Jesus, the new humanity would be created. In the flesh of Jesus, God would fulfill all the law and the prophets. In the flesh of Jesus, the Word of salvation would be spoken. And, in the flesh of Jesus, God would choose forever to dwell in our flesh.

And so, here the power of God resides in the flesh of humanity. This Word made flesh is the place of convergence where heaven and earth are knit together in a single peace: sin meets grace, death meets life, time meets eternity. And not only are heaven and hell united in the Word made flesh, but also, our fragmented, truncated, isolated ways of learning, living, and loving are redeemed and knit together into God's gifts of forgiveness, wholeness, and new life. Of course, this convergence between heaven and hell and between the fragments of our lives doesn't happen only once. It happens over and over and over again. And this convergence doesn't happen out there somewhere, in a lofty stratosphere. No, for the sake of Christ, it happens in our world, in our bodies, in our minds, in our spirits.

Because this meeting of Word and flesh happens in us, it is imperative that we don't limit its occurrence to the Christian education classroom or the Sunday morning pew. Instead, the movement of the Word made flesh, ever uniting Christ's life with our death, is studied in the classroom, praised from the church pew, but also, always and everywhere, abiding in us. In the service of Holy Baptism we say to the newly baptized, "You have been sealed by the Holy Spirit and marked with the cross of Christ forever."[12] It is the power of the Word made flesh that makes these words mobile and true. The Word carries the cross wherever our flesh travels and speaks to us the inspiration or the Spirit-in-us-ness that we need and for which we yearn.

Likewise, the Word speaks to us in the Holy Eucharist. It's not just that we learned about Holy Communion years ago in confirmation class and still can recite the liturgy by memory. It's not just that we have learned the meaning of "real presence." It's not just that we go to worship each Sunday and receive the sacrament as frequently as possible. While these are important, the work of the Word is more than the compilation of learnings and good habits. Instead, the liturgy of the Eucharist connects us with salvation history and the long line of believers who have fleshed out God's presence throughout the ages. In our hearing of the words, "Take and eat, this is my body, take and drink, this is my blood," the Word is reaching for us again. And then in the Eucharistic blessing, the Word that was body and blood poured out for us in the meal is sent to go with us, to converse with us, to encourage us, to guide us, and to hold us along the way. "The body and blood of our Lord Jesus Christ strengthen you and keep you in [God's] grace."[13]

The church calls the Word and sacraments "means of grace." Such wording is reminiscent of John's words: "From his fullness we have all received, grace upon grace." Spirituality is education aimed at the heart, proclaiming to us again and again, in words, the coming of the Word, whose Spirit lives in our hearts by faith.

Strategies for Adult Learning. Making the connections between the Word made flesh and the substance of our daily lives is not just a theoretical or theological exercise. It is the very process through which God gets "fleshed out" in our everyday words, actions, and attitudes. One of the tasks of Christian education is to take those things that we do routinely and fill them with meaning. For example, here are some connections between our life of education and our action of worship:

• *Learn to pray the Lord's Prayer with a specific person or concern in mind.*

> Our Father in heaven,
>> hallowed be your name in *Timothy* today,
>> your kingdom come in *Timothy* today,
>> your will be done in *Timothy* today,
>> on earth as in heaven.
> Give *Timothy* today *his* daily bread;
> Forgive *Timothy his* sins
>> and lead *Timothy* to forgive those who sin against him.
> Lead *Timothy* not into temptation,
>> and deliver *Timothy* from evil.
> For yours is the kingdom, and the power,
>> and the glory in *Timothy*,
>> now and forever.
> Amen.[14]

• *Learn to live the lectionary.* The Word of God wants to do its work in us, and the best way for that to happen is to read it. For every Sunday in the church year there are three lessons and a Psalm designated. The Word would have more room to work in our lives and to teach us the godly life if we connected with these readings on Sunday and on every other day of the week. Providing each church member with the weekly readings for preparation and meditation not only teaches the Scriptures to the congregation, but also transforms their lives of worship. Some parishes may wish to invite members to read each lesson every day. Others may wish to focus on reading the Gospel text or the Psalm once every day. The point remains the same in each case—reading the word shapes the Word in us.

• *Learn to pray the catechism.* As we learn the Ten Commandments, the Creeds, the Lord's Prayer, and other foundations of our Christian faith, they need to become more than mere words. In order for the Word to speak through these words, we need to do as one prayer suggests; read, mark, learn, and inwardly digest them. Consider the number of ways in which we could, through prayer, unpack the symbols that these words represent. Through prayer and meditation, sight and sound and other senses are awakened and the words become alive to us. For example, in the morning when we pray the beginning of the Creed, "I believe in God . . . ," do some exploring and ask some questions. What do I see when I pray the word *I*? What is my sense of the word *believe*? How will I give sight to God today and in whom will I sense God's presence. A book such as Donald W. Johnson's *Praying the Catechism* (Evangelical Lutheran Church in Canada, 1995), is most helpful when it comes to making connections between the life of education and the action of worship in the parish.

• *Learn to live the liturgical year.* There is depth and richness ready to be tapped in learning the liturgical year. Not only are there treasures to be found in learning the history of the liturgical year and its evolution over time, but there are life-enhancing, life-educating parallels that can be drawn from simply giving the church year an interested glance. Using the liturgical year in worship, we live and weave together the component parts of our lives. The moods, seasons, colors, and themes provide a means through which we can learn the fullness of Christ's life, even as they provide some with the means to offer back to God the fullness of our life in Christ.

There are a number of ways in which a parish might make connections between education and worship using the liturgical year as a tool. For example, on the first Sunday in Advent, a congregation might have a parish event in which there is a combination of activities that includes both educational and ritual aspects of Advent. Making candles, advent calendars, advent wreaths, and Jesse trees are just a few ways to engage adults and children in the educational aspect of Advent. Then, through the singing of Advent hymns and the praying of a devotional liturgy, the educational aspect of Advent is deepened and experienced through worship, prayer, and the ritual of lighting the first Advent candle.

CONCLUSION

In this chapter we have connected the task of adult Christian education with the life of the whole congregation and the life of the whole person. Ministry, by its very nature, is connected to daily life, the world, mission, Christian spirituality, and worship. Adult Christian education is vital because it provides an integral setting in which we can explore these arenas and connect them to the foundations of our past, the promised hope of our future, and the real circumstances of the present. This process is, again and again, Christ giving himself for the sake of the world, and the church giving itself for the sake of Christ. There are no limits as to where we, through Christian education, might reach in faith. Thus, teaching is central to the life of the church and *making the connections* lies at the heart of the matter.

chapter eight

Organizing for Adult Education

Norma Cook Everist
Susan K. Nachtigal

PLANNING TOGETHER

The process of planning a program of Christian education for adults in the church involves a multitude of perspectives, considerations, and choices. There are as many possibilities in planning adult education as there are persons within the congregation. Thus, the key is planning *together*, interweaving the many ideas, interests, and personal inclinations of leaders and adult learners to create a vital adult education ministry. This does not mean that we plan to do everything in the same way, but rather that the same gospel mission is held by each of us. Centered on this gospel mission, we are held together to do our work: women, men, laity, clergy, associates in ministry, diaconal ministers, deaconessess, and teachers. The foundational strength of any adult education program lies in bringing together a wide variety of individuals, ideas, approaches, skills, and subjects, so that even while our differences abound, we move ahead as a community.

Getting Started

Some people believe that planning Christian education should focus on the examination and selection of suitable curriculum materials. Others feel that the emphasis should be on recruiting and training teachers, regardless of the curriculum. Still others believe that concern over curriculum and teachers is secondary to providing a comfortable, well-equipped, safe, and confidential environment in which adults are able to participate, discover, and learn. Clearly, any of these emphases would be incomplete if left to stand alone. But, together, these begin to create a necessary foundation for adult Christian education in the parish. Following are some questions for the planners of adult learning to consider.

What kinds of curriculum resources meet our needs?

For each resource considered, ask:

• Is the subject clearly and fairly conveyed in an interesting manner?
• When, where, and by whom was the material written?
• What are the theological assumptions of the material itself?
• What level of biblical, theological, and historical understanding does the material assume?
• Does the course outline require a long-term or a short-term commitment from the students?
• Is each lesson self-contained or are the lessons formatted to build a sequence from one week to the next?
• Does the curriculum invite both teacher and student participation?
• Is there room in the material for questions, discussion, and exploration?
• Does the course require homework?

Who will teach?

• What kind of gifts and sensibilities does teaching this course require?
• Who has interest and previous experience in this subject?
• Does this course require a single teacher, a team of teachers, a lay and clergy team, a pastor, an associate in ministry, a deaconess, or a diaconal minister?
• What kind of training, guidance, and additional resources will the teacher(s) need?

Where will the class meet?

• How many rooms in the church building are suitable for adult education classes?
• What size are the rooms?
• What are the pros and cons of adult education held in the nave of the church building?
• Which rooms are set up with teaching and learning equipment such as table, chairs, chalkboard, maps, screens, or video?
• Which rooms are more casually arranged with sofas and easy chairs?

• How does the subject and the manner in which it will be taught match the mood and physical arrangement in which the class will meet?

Planning Styles

There are a number of different planning styles that influence adult education. We all know leaders whose style is to plan ahead in detail while others prefer to let their classroom agenda unfold as the year progresses. Some leaders prefer to follow printed curriculum exactly as it is presented, while others customize their curriculum as they go along. Some teachers need and appreciate training, while others are more effective teachers with less direction and more latitude. Some leaders function best in the middle of an unkempt, creative mess, while others are undone by such chaos, preferring a place for everything and everything in its place. But finally, together, these preferences combine to create a cadre of responsible teachers able to touch our lives, each in his or her own unique way.

When planning for this diversity in teaching style, consider the following:

• Which goals and parameters are helpful and necessary for all teachers?

• What are you doing to help all teachers appreciate and learn from one another's unique gifts and teaching style?

• Do particular teaching styles lend themselves to teaching particular groups of adult learners?

• How are you intentional in nurturing the faith of the teachers and in encouraging them to pray for support and for one another?

• For those who plan ahead, are the materials, information, and calendar details made available soon enough to help them do so?

Planning for Content

Similarly, there is a variety of perspectives regarding appropriate educational content. In recent years, many adult Christian education leaders have framed their content as either focused on Bible or focused on life-related topics. Advocates for Bible study observe that even though the Christian tradition is enmeshed within the North American culture, many Christians do not know the contents of Scripture, much less the story of God's saving love offered in Jesus Christ. Conversely, there has been much discussion to the effect that the church and its traditional teachings have become boring and irrelevant, suggesting that what Christian educators need to do is encourage political, social, ethical, and theological dialogue. Forums, topical studies, and discussions of day-to-day life issues often catch adults' interest more than the subjects traditionally offered. This either/or tendency to focus the content in a single direction illustrates the importance of careful planning in adult education. All of these subjects together provide a responsible mix of material ready to address the mix of our lives.

Bible, church, world, and experience provide four cornerstones for adult education. None of these arenas exists in a vacuum. It is the goal of adult Christian education to compare, integrate, and weave together these avenues through which God addresses us.

Consider these questions as you plan for content:

• If planning a Bible study, how will the class explore where Scripture intersects with what the church teaches, the way the world is, and the way the learners experience life?

• If planning a course about worship or other aspects of corporate church life, what are the scriptural roots and the contemporary connections for what we say and do? For example, in the Communion liturgy, what is the connection between communion bread and bread for the world? How does this bread connect with each person's experience of daily bread? What does the "feast of victory" mean for the church, the world, and each of us?

• If planning a course with a focus on a life-related topic, how will the adult learners discover what is written in the Bible and the other important documents of our church that relate to it? How do these compare with civil documents and contemporary societal values?

• If planning a course about faith and daily life, how will the class find out what the Scriptures say about work, play, and our baptismal vocation? How will they discern those things in their world that encourage or get in the way of their daily expression of faith and love of God?

Planning with Perspective

Given these variables in approach, style, and content, it is clear that planning adult Christian education in the congregation can be a formidable task. To unite a congregation and help it move toward the same goal is challenging, but the task need not be overwhelming. Instead, the challenge can be the very means through which a congregation becomes inspired, integrated, and intentional in its mission and ministry. Individual differences in approach, style, and content show a congregation the many means through which our loving God communicates with us. Variations in perspectives and approaches to planning Christian education provide fertile soil for the practice of Christian love toward one another, as well as the achieving of our common learning objectives with one another. Through planning together, listening to one another's interests and concerns, honoring one another's unique contributions, and cherishing one another's gift of faith, we set up an educational ministry communicated not only through our words, but also through our deeds.

The Role of the Professional Christian Educator

Among the laity and clergy, there are some who have been called to serve as professional Christian educators: diaconal ministers, directors of Christian education, teachers, principals, professors, associates in ministry, literacy program directors, English as a second language coordinators, and others. Some of these individuals serve in institutional settings, while others serve in parishes or church-related schools. In any case, these important Christian educators lend their expertise in creating bridges between church and society by bringing people's needs to the life of the church, and by bringing the mission of the church to people in their everyday lives.

Professional Christian educators have been trained and are in a unique position to teach the church how to translate Scripture, theology, and methodology into words, relationships, and actions that help people learn and apply to their lives the saving grace of God in Christ Jesus. Often, Christian educators are the best equipped to teach our Sunday school teachers as well as to teach those who are involved in educational ministry in the larger community. As the church continues to broaden its understanding of ministry, the role of the professional Christian educator will continue to emerge as vital to the ministry of adult education in the local parish in the surrounding community.

The Role of the Laity

Energetic, interesting, and life-changing adult education requires the laity of the church also to be involved in the leadership of this ministry. There are several reasons for this:

• Leaders of adult education are called to move beyond planning *for* people and talking *at* members. Even the phrase "involving adults in planning" can sound as though the initiative is external to the participants, as though clergy and other leaders were cooking up something to goad laity into being a part of the program. In effective planning, those committed to adult Christian education, both clergy and lay, avoid manipulation in which delegating becomes, in effect, relegating and abdication.

• Adult education begins with living out what we believe during the planning process as much as teaching what we believe in the classroom. Mutual conversation and learning are as important in our planning as they are in the articulation of our theology in a classroom. The way we treat one another and the practices we employ in our planning speak volumes regarding the content we plan to teach in the classroom. How much better it is, for the sake of our life together, when the laity are called into leadership positions in planning.

• Adults need to lead in the planning of their own learning because it is their lives and experiences that create the context for the classes; it is their needs and hopes that must be addressed and served. The lives of adults—professional and non-professional, old and young, new member and longtime member, privileged and underprivileged—provide the depth and breadth of the class.

Some may say that this emphasis on lay leadership emerges from present thought focused on inclusivity, participation mandates, and a nonhierarchical orientation. While it is true that these concerns may paint part of the picture, there is a deeper reason for lay leadership in planning adult education. The encouragement of lay leadership is a direct expression of what we believe about God's relationship with us and our relationship with one another. It is in the life of the church that laity are reminded that they *are* the church, the body of Christ, the communion of saints, the priesthood of all believers. Wisdom, understanding, knowledge, fear of the Lord, and joy are at the heart of the baptismal calling and at the heart of educational ministry. This calling and this ministry beckon the laity to lead and, at the same time, provide the laity with the gifts necessary to accomplish the task.

The Role of the Pastor

Everything said above about Baptism and the laity is true for clergy as well. However, the clergy hold a public office that bears specific responsibilities. The pastor needs to be an inspiring, visionary, caring leader in the educational ministry of the congregation. To establish a process in which the laity are fully engaged in planning adult education does not dismiss the pastor from his or her leadership responsibilities. In fact, it could be said that the more a group is engaged, the more the pastoral leader is needed. The pastor's role is not a matter of working oneself out of a job, nor is it one of abdicating his or her responsibilities. Instead of saying, "Here's the book; see you next spring," the pastor has very specific responsibilities to ensure meaningful adult learning in the life of the parish.

The pastor's "response-ability" to the call helps provide the glue for Christian education in the church. As the spiritual leader of the community, the pastor has four unique opportunities to shape educational ministry:

Presence. This includes being interested in, supportive of, and walking alongside others without fostering their dependence. The ability to respond to parishioners as the Spirit works in them is critical. For example, the pastor can listen to individuals as they express directly and indirectly their interests and needs, encourage them to articulate their own faith questions, and challenge them to discover and develop their own unique contributions. In addition, the pastor needs to be a presence in the teaching ministry of the parish in order to give it visibility and public affirmation. That is to say, *the pastor teaches,* and those classes are important and carefully chosen.

Integration. This includes helping the people of the congregation make connections between body, mind, and spirit by moving them toward feeling in their hearts what they clarify in their minds and articulate with their lips. For example, the pastor can provide intentional opportunities for prayer and meditation beyond weekly worship, devotional reading materials, or the study of particular parts of Scripture. Furthermore, the pastor is in a unique position to relate the movement of the Spirit working within the church catholic, integrating and translating that movement in the local church. The pastor can convey to the local congregation relevant issues being considered by the church at large.

Setting the tone. This includes creating a positive work environment that respects the time and efforts of the teachers and fosters their growth. At the very least, the pastor can ensure clear methods of operation, including regular teachers' meetings, timely communications, procedures for acquisition of materials, clear calendar management, and other administrative essentials. In addition, the pastor can discourage idle gossip and mean-spiritedness, and encourage support for and celebration of one another.

"Wording" the gospel. Finally, the pastor must have the ability to respond to the movement of theology and the need for theology to press in and be applied to everyday life. As the pastor takes on the public dimension of Word and Sacrament ministry, he or she takes on

the responsibility to communicate, to make clear, to lift up, and to point to all the ways in which the Word and the presence of God are moving in the life and the people of the congregation. This might be called "wording" the gospel.

Rather than relying on the pastor's ability to be novel or entertaining, education in the life of the parish is directly related to the pastor's ongoing proclamation, application, and incarnation of the gospel in the life of that congregation.Clearly, all of this education does not take place only in a classroom. It also takes place in the manner in which the everyday routines of the church are carried out to fulfill its mission. It is an expression of the pastor's understanding of being "under call" to a congregation: by serving, by understanding Christian spirituality, and by expressing the incarnational theology we believe. When the pastor finds himself or herself teaching in the classroom, he or she has first undergirded those classes with a parish environment that expresses what is now being taught in the class. Thus, the pastor is sometimes a teacher in the classroom, but always a teacher through proclamation and deed in the entire life of the congregation.

Although the pastor is deeply involved in guiding the Christian education program, this is not to say that the pastor is solely in charge. Instead, the pastor and other planners and teachers of adult education in the congregation form a team that is defined by lively exchange, challenging dialogue, provocative questions, and a rapport of mutual love and respect. There is joy in realizing that as clergy and laity work together, they are vitally connected to the continuous unfolding of salvation history and that the ministry of planning education is forwarding the mercy and grace of God in their time and place.

The Planning Process

Intentional planning that makes use of many individuals' varied interests and skills is paramount to a successful adult education ministry. The product of time spent in preparation will be an energizing and meaningful adult education program. One way of making this task enjoyable and productive is to form an adult education planning team.

As the team begins its work, ask each of the teachers to choose a phrase from the ones below to complete this sentence: Planning to me means . . .

   • dreaming up ideas and envisioning what we can do together in the future;

   • organizing the work that needs to be done;

• purchasing and pulling together the materials that we will need next Sunday;
  • being ready and able to change course whenever necessary;
  • deciding what to do differently next time;
  • looking at the program from some distance with perspective.

Of course the answer is "all of the above." However, in doing this exercise, the planning team could learn some things about each other and how they might work together to do the ministry most efficiently and effectively. These differing approaches help team members see how they need each other in the task of planning. Together, they cover the spectrum far better than any one could alone. As a planning team, members will work with all the types of planning:

  • Long range
  • Short term
  • Last minute
  • At the time
  • Right after
  • Next time

Long range. How far ahead do we need to work? Some people prefer the preliminary dreaming stage best. However, this stage includes more than just dreaming; it also means reviewing past trends and looking into the future for the broader needs of the congregation and its neighborhood. This stage comes long before (four to six months) the beginning of a program year and allows time to discuss the vision for the future of adult education in your church.

Short term. All planning requires organization: deciding who is going to do what and when, ordering the tasks, making specific assignments, acquiring materials, finding appropriate meeting spaces, specifying to whom each worker is accountable, notifying members of upcoming courses, and other endless details that are specific to the event. The success or failure of an event hinges on these activities. Many great ideas never reach fruition because careful execution of this stage is overlooked.

Last minute. This includes tending to the details that couldn't be done earlier, such as getting out the equipment, making the coffee, unlocking the doors, and setting up the tables and chairs. When recruiting help for this stage, it is important to specify what the term *last minute* means, since some people will arrive thirty minutes before, while others arrive only five minutes early. In any case, it is clear that this stage will go much better if short-term planning has been done carefully. Also, this stage will be done in a gracious and inclusive manner if long-range planning was a time of broad-minded thinking. For example, as you unlock the doors before the event is not the time to say, "We should have invited everyone on the block to this event. Why didn't we think of that sooner?"

At the time. This stage involves thinking on one's feet and making decisions in the moment. All of education is a wording of God's Word and the embodiment of God's presence as the Holy Spirit moves and acts in the hearts of the speaker and the listeners. Thus, the teacher and the participants will want to honor what is developing in the moment, and be ready to change course at any time, gradually or abruptly. For example, in the midst of discussion, the leader is constantly watching, weighing, deciding, "Should I wait for a few more responses or move on? Should we probe this question more or, instead, make a connection to the prior point? Is this segment becoming too repetitive and do we need to pick up the pace of this discussion?" This is planning in process and education in action. Some rely on making their decisions only in this stage, saying, "I don't use curriculum; I just want to be open to whatever happens." Ironically, that plan is not to plan. All teachers need to learn to plan effectively, for those who plan well in the earlier stages are actually more, not less, ready for effective impromptu teaching in the moment. See chapter 4 for specific ideas for this type of planning.

Right after. This stage pertains to that time immediately following the session when one has the opportunity to straighten up the room, put the materials away, and do whatever miscellaneous tasks are left. Sometimes this aspect of planning is overlooked or avoided. This is also the time to make some notations about the learners and what concerns need to be addressed before the next session. For example, "Bob hasn't been here for several weeks; give him a call" or "This session went well because . . ." or "Remember to make copies of the June 1 news article for next week."

Next time. This stage brings planning full circle. The planning team should plan to meet one or two weeks after a course or event in order to critique it. It is not necessary to meet after each session of every course or during the middle of events that are happening in succession, but education planners in the parish too often overlook this opportunity to gain new insight. While the event is still fresh in your minds, it can be helpful to discuss these questions: Who wasn't a partner in this process? Who are we not reaching? What went especially well, and why? What did we find to be unworkable and unhelpful? Do we need an entire overhaul? Which gifts were used and which not used? There is more about evaluation later in this chapter.

INVITING, SUPPORTING, AND RECOGNIZING TEACHERS

Inviting Persons to Teach

If we think about the things that most capture our interest and to which we want to give our treasured time and energy, they are the activities that hold meaning and require investment. The movement of the Holy Spirit in the life of the church calls us not to simply mark time or casually check off a list of activities and programs one by one. This ministry of education is more than "fill the bill" and "Thank goodness we found someone to do that for this year!" The ministry of Christian education is the "Word made flesh"— through whom God has promised to work mightily to bring light and life to God's people.

The person recruiting teachers for upcoming courses needs to discover and utilize those who will be gifted teachers, rather than simply completing their task of finding enough teachers. The individual's response to the invitation to teach is also more than a simple yes or no. Being response-able means he or she is serving out of a sense of mission and baptismal calling, rather than a feeling of guilt or the inability to say no. The seriousness with which this invitational task is carried out sets the tone for the importance of the educational endeavor that lies ahead.

When inviting teachers to teach, it is best to do it in person. It is important that expectations be clarified, perhaps preparing a brief written job description, sometimes called a teaching covenant. Whether verbal or written, be sure to ask the following clarifying questions, preferably within the planning team, before your conversations with potential teachers:

• Why are we doing this work?
• What are the specifics of the task being asked of this teacher?
• What kind of commitment are we expecting and for how long?
• What support do we promise to this person?
• Who holds the interest and the gifts to plan and carry out this task in the most effective way?
• What kind of maturity of faith does teaching require?
• How is the Spirit trying to speak to us and shape us in the planning and the doing of this ministry?

These questions, and others you may think of, provide the backdrop necessary for an educational endeavor to have depth, definition, focus, and meaning.

Supporting Teachers

Preliminary and ongoing support and education is vital for preparing and sustaining those who are going to teach in the congregation. This help enables teachers to be response-able in their ministry. We support and educate teachers by proclaiming and teaching the gospel to them in a way that makes them able to respond. Instead of inviting teachers to teach and then leaving them in a vacuum, everyone is well served to talk about the sure foundations on which we stand. The foundations of Scripture and tradition, doctrine and history, church, Word and Sacrament make us response-able. Our God-enabled response helps us to see that we are the revelation of Christ's body, wounded and raised now, and what we do is the continuance of God's work. This power invites teachers to do more than teach a class; it invites, supports, and educates teachers to be part of a mission. This power operates from the inside out, from the very love of God poured out for the sake of the world. This power makes teachers response-able. This power anchors what happens before the question of the classroom even arises. With the support and learning that comes from this serious and joyful reality, the classroom becomes a setting in which God works and changes lives.

In addition, there are important and ongoing ways of supporting the ministry carried out by those who teach in the parish. Classrooms need to be properly equipped. Supplies, curricular materials, and additional resources need to be organized and easily accessible. The pastor has an opportunity to be supportive by visiting the classrooms from time to time, or by being a welcoming presence before or after class. Carefully scheduled events and advance discussion and notification regarding changes in the schedule help support the teaching endeavor. Communication is key, as is including teachers in ongoing decision-making processes.

Recognizing Teachers

The recognition of teachers helps us not only to say "three cheers and thank you" for the ministry they do on our behalf, but equally important to publicly lift up these ministers in prayer and thanksgiving. Recognition during worship isn't for showing off the teacher's good works, but rather for the sake of gathering together in the midst of worshiping God and giving visual and intentional focus to the ministry that we hold as vital, life giving, and life sustaining.

Specific ways of recognizing the work of the entire adult-education ministry team include:

- installation of the team during worship;
- notes of appreciation and encouragement as appropriate;
- acknowledgments in church newsletter and other communications;
- year-end thank-you letter;
- year-end celebration and wrap-up;
- listening to their evaluation of the planning process and program;
- providing educators with a subscription to an educational ministry magazine or journal.

EDUCATING THE EDUCATORS

The Need for Education of Adult Educators

One may assume that teachers of adults do not need teacher training. After all, adults already understand what it is to be an adult; adults don't need any special methods; in fact, teaching adults isn't really teaching, just discussing. Each of these assumptions has "false" written all over it. As we have seen in chapters 2 and 3, adults are fascinating people with a variety of learning styles, constantly changing in stage of faith throughout the life cycle. We need to learn about how people at each stage of adulthood view God, themselves, and the world, and about how they grow and learn. We need to give close attention to the methods we use and continue to grow in our range of teaching styles. Teachers of adults are also adult learners. Honor their hunger to learn even, and especially, while they are teaching.

Teachers need preliminary and ongoing interaction and education so that they can understand, appreciate, and be challenged by the task at hand. Rather than inviting teachers to teach and then leaving them in a theological and spiritual vacuum, we need to help them grow in their knowledge of the scriptural, historical, spiritual, and ecclesial foundations on which they stand. We all need to appreciate that we are part of the long history of God's work among God's beloved people and that we are the revelation of Christ's body, wounded and raised. All of this is a tethering, anchoring, or grounding that we need before the question of classrooms even arises. Without this serious and joyful work, the classroom task is drastically diminished. Educators of adults need continually to be learners of the Word. Steeped in all facets of Christian faith, of methods, and of adult learners, teachers will be challenged and equipped to enjoy their important responsibility.

All of this sounds well and good, but who has time for teachers' meetings? It's hard enough to persuade teachers to teach, much less expect them to have time for meetings. The scenario often goes something like this:

It's mid-August and the adult education program—in fact the Christian education program in general—has only half the teachers we need. We are desperate, so we call a few more people: "It's not hard, it's just adults, you know. It's not a very big group and most often not everyone is there anyway. I'll drop off the book for you. What's that? You won't be home tonight? Well, I'll just put it outside your front door." We think to ourselves, "Whew, another one down. Now, who else can I call?" Weary when the task is done, or "sort of" done, we hope no one has problems halfway through the year.

In this scenario, not hearing from teachers is good news. This may be an extreme example, but most leaders in Christian education can relate to this scene. Actually, the answer to chronic problems of teacher shortage is to do the exact opposite of what one might expect. We need to recommend, even insist that teachers in the Christian learning community not teach unless they are continuously engaged in their own ongoing growth in faith and teaching skill. If we do not feed the teachers, they will not have strength to feed others. By expecting as little as possible in order to recruit, we set ourselves up to receive those phone calls in February: "I can't come next Sunday; could you find someone to take my place? In fact, for the whole month?" We need to take a leap of faith and do that very thing that no one has time to do: increase the challenge by requiring that teachers of adults be equipped for their teaching ministry.

When we expect very little of our teachers, they live down to our expectations. We need to challenge teachers both with the demands of the task and the promised power to do the task. The teacher's faith formation is the greatest resource the teacher has in teaching. The task in educating the educators is to help teachers wear the Bible, be their theology, live their spirituality, do their methodology, and make connections with their own faith development.

A Teacher Education Enrichment Program

In order to keep growing we need ongoing help in a number of areas. An effective teacher education enrichment program should include all of the following on a regular, if not precisely equal, basis:

- Bible
- Theology
- Spirituality
- Strategies (methods)
- Adult life-cycle development
- Administration

Bible. Many adults feel inept as biblical scholars. They may read the Bible regularly, but may not have been exposed to critical skills of reading and interpreting texts nor to significant historical and contextual information. A faithful sharing of the Bible in a believing community is core; biblical background and tools can enhance our belief and faithful service.

If there are a number of classes, and not all are using the same series of Bible texts, how can one have a joint session for teachers? That question assumes that teacher enrichment means only being told exactly what to teach on a given text. Our growth will necessarily increase our ability to teach biblically.[1] Even if the adult education class we teach is on a contemporary topic, we need to be prepared to refer to biblical texts or, for example, to place a current movie in dialogue with a biblical text.

People who teach adults need regular study of the Bible, personally and in a community. We need an overview of the entire Bible and various means of interpreting the Scriptures. We need to explore the socio-historical context that will help open up differing voices in the text, connecting that context with our context today. We need not fear the thorny questions, even those of biblical authority. If we move together into the text at deeper levels, the Spirit can help us grow in interpretations for our day.

Theology. We never read the Bible without employing some theological interpretation. That's why individuals and church bodies can come to such radically diverse meanings from reading the same text. Neither do we watch a news broadcast without interpreting the news. Each of us has a working theology, cast perhaps in plain, everyday terms. Each of us has an ethic, a set of values, a world view, concepts about God that we use to make meaning in our world. We, therefore, need to reflect on our working theology and to grow in understanding of Christian theology and our church traditions.

Together teachers could study the three articles of the Creed, pursue Luther's teaching on law and gospel, or the varied relationships of Christ and culture. Teachers might bring an experience from class and discuss theological understandings of the questions posed there. Or the group might start with a specific topic, such as death, the church (ecclesiology), sin, forgiveness, or Christian freedom. As adult educators become more thoroughly grounded in these and many other topics of Christian theology, they will be more competent and confident to engage in class discussions.

Spirituality. Adult educators need to be people of faith who have a deep and lively trust in God. Too often teachers are stressed out by the end of the week and have a hard time finding strength for the teaching task. Their own struggles may leave them in doubt about eternal life or the power of God over the forces of evil. Teachers need permission to share their own doubts. Teachers addressing their spiritual issues may then be able to encourage their adult learners to speak about their own faith struggles.

As teachers of adults in the parish, each time we meet we need to take time to tend to each other. We may go around the circle, asking how our teaching is going, how we are doing. In listening well to one another, we will be prepared to pray specifically for each other's needs. We may share in leading devotions, in challenging each other as we continually discern our gifts, in holding each other accountable for our own faithful witness in the world, and in praying for one another during the week.

One may say this is just what we do in the adult class we each teach. Good! But while leading we sometimes become preoccupied with leadership tasks. Teachers need time away from leadership tasks, when we can simply be nourished in our own faith.

Strategies (methods). We have seen in chapter 3 the many adult learning styles present in any learning community. We often teach others in the way we like to learn. Obviously that limits our teaching and somewhat handicaps the participants. How do we increase the number of methods we know how to use and with which we feel comfortable?[2] We can do so by modeling them for one another in our community of teachers. We can also share experiences and examine together what happened, why something worked, and why something else fell flat.

Such honest sharing will not come quickly or easily; we need a trustworthy learning space to try methods, such as role-play, case study, debate, experiential learning. Soon we will eagerly await coming together, seeking wisdom in a colleague group where we can not only grow in skills, but have fun doing so.

Adult life-cycle development. Adults continue to change throughout the life cycle. Using the resources of a local education professional, psychologist, computer, books, and tapes, we can learn about the fascinating world of adulthood. Sometimes we know people in the congregation so well that we forget they and we are always changing. Being aware is the first step.

As we invite participants to think about this with us, we welcome insights from them about themselves. We could role-play how adults at different stages might respond to a question or perceive a doctrinal position. God doesn't change, but our perceptions of the world, relationships, and God grow and change. As a young adult I may be searching, reviewing, and beginning to own my beliefs as distinct from my family's. In the middle years I may be struggling with questions of ultimate worth, but be open to renewed commitments. In older adulthood, I may question the world around me, but be more clear on how I can wisely be a blessing to others. In the adult faith community we can learn to be curious rather than judgmental about each other's stage of life.[3]

Administration. This component is placed last not because it is least important, but because it is the component churches are most likely already doing. After all, we have to attend to details of where and when classes meet in order to proceed at all. But one might be amazed at how often we ignore such details, again assuming that with adults it doesn't matter all that much.

Knowing the accurate meeting time and having enough chairs do matter. While youngsters might cry and teenagers might act out, adults for the most part will have learned to be gracious—they simply won't come back. Adult learners expect that a class will begin promptly when it was advertised to start. They also expect a certain level of comfort—chairs big enough, lights bright enough, a place quiet enough so that real learning can take place.

The group of teachers of adults can serve as an administrative task force, doing overall planning, tending to details, evaluating and broadening their mission. This is not all they should be doing, but neither should it be neglected. Rather than having one meeting a year to do all of this, the group will do well to regularly review the physical learning space, communication strategies, and outreach potential. They also can review sources of conflict before such problems become so large that they hinder the program. Administration and conflict management, tended to regularly, will set the stage for vital adult learning.

An Example

The adult education team at St. Matthew's Church decided to commit ninety minutes once a month to growth and mutual accountability in their teaching. Finding a time when they were all free was tough, but they decided they would enjoy a time together after work on Tuesdays, yet not going too late into the evening. They discovered they could all meet from 5:45 until 7:15, if someone could pick up food and bring it to the church. (Your adult education team might decide on Saturday mornings from 10:00 to 11:30, or over Sunday brunch.)

Each time they meet they devote the first fifteen minutes to asking each other, "How's it been going with your group?" They have learned to eat while talking informally, yet intentionally, sharing in a random but inclusive and comprehensive way. The group has quickly become honest, sharing both the frustrations and the exciting surprises. They often give specific suggestions on methods and note biblical and theological issues to discuss later. They look forward to this time when they can caringly hold each other accountable for growth in teaching.

The group then moves into the first of two twenty-five-minute specific growth segments. It's not a lot of time, but doing two segments means they are growing in a balanced and planned way. This year they decided to work through John's Gospel, both to study in depth a Gospel in its entirety and to develop skill in watching for biblical themes.

Every other month, during the second twenty-five-minute segment, the group has a session on adult life-cycle development. Ann, a leader of a koinonia group, wants to do some reading in this area and has volunteered to lead this time, assisted by the director of Christian education.

On alternate evenings, the team members demonstrate teaching methods for each other. Most of the teachers have been using the lecture/discussion method with the adult groups. It is tried and true, comfortable and predictable. The same learners each week speak up, and the same learners don't. The education team members plan to learn roleplay and case study.

The administrative side has gone fairly well. But the team does brainstorm twice a year on how to include more adults in the congregation and how to reach out into the neighborhood.

After their third meeting, Brian said, "Hey, we're forgetting something, our own growth in faith." The group quickly agreed but seemed a little embarrassed. Some members felt they were not quite as "spiritual" as others, or even as spiritual as some of the participants in the groups they led. They decided to spend one evening reflecting on their own spiritual journeys and then they invited in a resource person to present types of spirituality. From then on, each evening they ended with five to seven minutes of prayer and nurturing each other spiritually.

After five sessions, the group was excited about how much they had learned. Carrie suggested they expand the time to two hours. It sounded like a good idea, but they concluded some people might then skip a session or leave early. They needed to make commitments they could reasonably keep and to use the time extraordinarily well. A couple of other people from the congregation heard about this group and asked if they could join, thus expanding the cadre of potential teachers of adults. The pastor has discovered that this group is one that feeds the pastor as well, enjoying the refreshing partnership.

Educators' Retreat

To give the adult education team a longer time to grow personally and in their teaching task, consider planning a yearly retreat. The congregation, as part of the commitment to this leadership responsibility, might fund travel and accommodations. Construct a possible agenda to include these topics:

Biblical. For example, study John 1. "Beginning" links us to all of salvation history. All that was made was made out of the relationship within the triune God, each part of creation in relationship with the other.

Theological. For example, focus on incarnation "and the Word became flesh." The historical body/soul separation is still deeply embedded in our culture and in the life of the church. The group could discuss why it was so essential for God to enter this world in the form of an infant. Martin Luther's Christmas sermons would be a good resource.

Spiritual. For example, emphasize the word *abiding.* The group could explore the word *abiding* and how it relates to those whom we love: spouse, children, dear friends. In times of solitude and during quiet walks, people could experience God's abiding presence.

Methodological. For example, explore prayer partners. The group could spend time in prayer and then develop a prayer-partner strategy for themselves back home and, more broadly, for their classes.

Developmental. For example, investigate faith history. The retreat setting gives long, uninterrupted time for people to share their faith journeys and life-cycle stages, including their perceptions over the years of what it has meant to be "spiritual enough" to be a leader and teacher in the church.

Administrative. For example, discuss what it takes to help spiritual growth and learning happen warmly and comfortably for the adults we teach. They might work on at-home worship resources.

A retreat can give the educators time to build community with one another and to discover the radical nature of grace. Regular meetings sustain growth. Whether the number of educators of adults in your church is two or twenty, taking time to nurture the nurturers—to educate the educators—is essential.

REACHING OUT

Adults are coming! The adult education leaders are excited about their teaching task. Now we can rest!

That's exactly the time to recall the Great Commission, Matthew 28:18-19: "All authority in heaven and on earth has been given to me. Go therefore and make disciples of all nations, baptizing them in the name of the Father and of the Son and of the Holy Spirit, and teaching them to obey everything that I have commanded you."

We may become so cozy in our congregation study group, so confident in our preparation that we leave no room for the Spirit to surprise us with grace. Are we ready to be an Acts-of-the-Apostles people on the move, living epistles, living letters of invitation to the neighborhood?

Beginning with Outreach

Most congregations believe they are friendly and inviting, but people outside may not experience us the same way. How can we be the hospitable people God intends us to be?

We need to commit ourselves to the premise that all of the congregation's education is parish education—that is, adult education for the entire neighborhood, whether that be forty square blocks in the city, a suburban subdivision, edge city,[4] or a county township. We are sent out to the entire world and we have particular responsibility for the neighborhood in which we are rooted.

We dare not let the neighborhood be a mere afterthought; the people in the neighborhood will recognize that. Rather than thinking after our planning is done, "Oh, and we could also put up posters in the area," we need always to begin with the question, "How is Christ commissioning us to "Go . . . teach. . . ." in this endeavor?

Beginning with the concept of *neighborhood parish* will change the way we design adult education. We can begin by walking and driving around the area. Who is there? Who is not there? Who is there but not readily seen? We need to engage in conversation throughout the parish neighborhood, listening for issues and interests, needs and change. We will want to gather perspectives of members who live and work in the community, speak to community leaders, seek out newcomers to the area. Are there divisions? What other faith communities serve this neighborhood? There may be a need for basic or life-change education in the neighborhood. We have an educational ministry of sharing the gospel in the world; we have a ministry of education, helping people to secure knowledge and skills to be able to work.

Strategies for Adult Education Leaders.
• Discover and discern your congregation's parish "neighborhood." Where and what is it?
• Regularly contact area people and institutions to listen, invite, and network.
• Make a plan that ensures every educational ministry opportunity includes parish outreach.
• Consider initiating an ecumenical or inter-faith approach to outreach ministries in education.

Connecting with Ministry in Daily Life

Adult Christian education assumes that the lives and worlds of individuals are connected with each other. By beginning with the parish concept, it is easier for adult education planners and participants to envision the scope of adult education as it connects with ministry in daily life.

Not all congregation members live and work in the neighborhood, however *neighborhood* is defined. Rather, we live, work, spend leisure time, and relate to friends in many neighborhoods. Some of these directly intersect, others may seem totally disconnected from life within our faith community.

How do we help people see their daily lives as part of the curriculum? The decisions we make each day, and the principles and values upon which we base those decisions, are starting places for thinking about God and grief, life and forgiveness, hope and challenge. How is Christ already present in the neighborhoods in which I live and work?

Adult Christian education dare not be confined to one hour a week in the church basement. There are formal and informal ways to be growing in Christ when we begin from our arenas of daily life.[5]

Strategies for Adult Education Leaders.
• As leaders, visit parishioners in places of work, leisure, and volunteer service.
• Invite people to bring the issues of their daily worlds to the planning process for adult education.
• Design and use resources which give people the insight and skill to theologically connect faith and daily life.[5]

Growing with the Congregation

Having begun with the assumption that all education is parish education, we need to look at the congregation with new eyes. We need a
corollary assumption, that every adult in the congregation is to be
involved in adult education. All are learning something, growing and
going somewhere. All of the New Testament images of the church
portray the people as either growing or dying: vine and branches,
fig tree, body of Christ. No one remains absolutely the same. So the
question is not, "Who is an active participant in adult education?" but,
"How are adults in this congregation growing? What are they learning
and what are they teaching?"

Likewise, we must not assume everyone knows of the adult education opportunities simply because they are in the bulletin, and that all
are invited and included. Keep telling people by bulletin, by postcard, by
Internet, by word of mouth, by any means necessary. There is no better
means than personally inviting people to come with you. Go visit people who have never attended an adult class and discover their needs and
interests. Design some offerings for individuals, small groups, and large
gatherings. Think about unlikely pairings, such as young adults and
older shut-ins. Plan for groups of people with similar needs, such as
those recently bereaved.

When one part of the body of Christ is growing, its relationship to
the rest of the body is changed. If three members go to an area workshop, they come home enthusiastic, assuming others will be excited to
try all the new ideas these three learned. They may be unprepared for
the apathetic reception they actually receive. Keep telling, connecting,
informing the rest of the congregation and the community about the
adult education that is taking place. Tell with a listening ear so that people ask, rejoice with, and learn from one another.

Strategies for Adult Education Leaders.

• As a congregation, emphasize that all adults are adult learners.
Make this a part of sermons, newsletters, bulletin boards, and personal
conversations. Systematically ask each adult, "How do you plan to learn
in the Christian community this year?"

• Multiply the adult education opportunities you offer, using a variety of approaches, leadership, methods, times, and locations.

• Create opportunities for groups in the church to tell other groups
what they are doing and learning.

Connecting Globally

All parish education is global education. Whether through Internet, World Wide Web, business travel, relatives back home in Guatemala, vacation trips, or mission partners, all of us are part of many intersecting communities around the world, individually and collectively. We are created and made new to be part of God's interdependent world.

John Wesley said, "Don't make the parish your world; make the world your parish." The world is our parish whether or not we know it. The mission field is our front door, not some foreign place far away. And that formerly far-away place is connected with every aspect of our daily lives. We have much to learn from the people of the world, much also to learn about Christian faith and life. How does your congregation take its place in the global community?

In times of economic and political shifts, nations and their people grow fearful of the neighbor. We have Christ's mandate to go into all the world—not to conquer, nor even to compete, but to learn from one another and to learn how to live with one another in God's economy of justice and God's community of peace. That's an educational challenge. We need not be afraid.

The ways to keep connected, and the numbers of people with whom we are connected, multiply daily. We are part of each other's lives instantaneously. We may feel our knowledge and our computers are out of date before we know how to use either effectively. How will we welcome these new possibilities and responsibilities? How can we learn to use them for adult education? How far can we journey on the information highway? The issue is not just new tools for Christian education, but also discernment of our Christian calling in this new kind of global community.

"Go, therefore . . . " sends us forth on all highways, some that may not have been invented when we started our own faith journey. Matthew 28:18-19 is preceded by the eleven disciples already on the move, going to Galilee to the mountain to which Jesus had directed them (28:16). When they saw Jesus, they worshiped him. They also doubted. In the midst of focusing on Jesus, joining him on his journey already begun, on this side of the cross and resurrection, we have a challenge and a promise: "And remember, I am with you always, to the end of the age" (28:20).

Strategies for Adult Education Leaders:

• On a map, have congregation members plot out all of the ways they, their families, their businesses, and your church are connected around the world. Talk about learning possibilities.

• Design a study and action group to brainstorm and implement ways to creatively use electronic communication for adult Christian education in a global mission perspective.

• Use newspapers, magazines, television news, and features, as well as computer connections, to provide resources for an adult study group to study the shifts in global economics and politics. Talk about your own fears and hopes as well as Christ's challenge and promise.

Reaching Out in Many Ways

How, then, do we develop a comprehensive adult education ministry outreach strategy? There are many ways. Each congregation will do best to create its own. One approach is the familiar Who? What? Where? When? Why? and How?

Who? Who are the adults in your church? Who are the adults in your parish neighborhood? What are their ages and stages in the life cycle? What is their range of interests and occupations? What varying ethnic and racial groups are represented? What is the range of economic class? Who might be in your neighborhood, but not yet visible? How can you reach them?

What? What kinds of adult education events and experiences are possible in your setting? Review chapter 6 for ideas, and list possibilities in these categories:

• Sunday morning and midweek offerings;
• koinonia groups or other small groups;
• ecumenical lay schools of religion;
• learning opportunities with denominational groups—conference, district, synod, or churchwide;
• learning opportunities with church councils, committees, task forces, or other groups that meet regularly.

Where? Where is the most unlikely place for adult education to happen? Go there and find possibilities. Walk and drive around the neighborhood and explore: the park, the mall, a cafe, hospice center, library—let your imagination lead you. Where within the congregation might people meet? Nooks and crannies of the building? In members' homes, workplaces, family gatherings? Nursing homes?

When? Is Sunday at 10:00 A.M. the only time? What about 7:30 A.M.? Thursday afternoons at 5:15? Noon hours? Once a week? Once a month? Three weekends a year? Every Saturday for a month?

Why? Because God's people are created to learn, designed to develop their faith. Why would young adults want to think about vocation and relationships? Why would older adults want to consider economic issues and the concept of hope? Why would middle adults ask their faith community questions about meaning and identity? Why in the world do we care about one another? How could adult education opportunities connect with these questions?

How? Consider the vast range of adulthood, the variety of ways adults learn, and devise multiple methods to teach and learn. How do you like to learn? What are ways you know how to teach? How might you increase your skill in other methods? How can you connect with others who want to learn as you do?

Once the adults in your church catch the vision that all are learners and all can reach out, allow the creativity and enthusiasm to carry you further than you dared dream. The Spirit moves where the Spirit will.

EVALUATING

"Learning is measured in mission," wrote Letty Russell some twenty-five years ago.[7] Styles of education, instruments for measuring growth, and attitudes toward grading have all changed in the past twenty-five years, but the statement remains true. In the Christian education community, learning is not for its own sake, nor is it for greater understanding of the Bible or theology alone. Learning is for the sake of mission and ministry.

But how can one measure that? The Spirit blows where the Spirit will. Faith is a gift. Can we be responsible for another person's coming to faith? Moreover, how can we by our own power carry out ministry in the world? We can't, but we can communicate, understand, and be responsible to one another. God created us to learn and grow, and to become the full human beings we were created to be. We cannot know completely what our fullness encompasses, but we can recognize its absence when we are not using and developing our God-given gifts, or are even, perhaps, rejecting them.

As we learn and grow together through adult education, it is important for us to be diligent in evaluating our work so that we can build on our strengths and bolster our weaknesses. Generally, evaluation of adult Christian education can be divided into four categories:

Planning process. Did we allow adequate time for planning? Were the right people involved in the planning? Were appropriate materials used? Were there multiple opportunities for adults to connect with one another?

Program results. Did the expected number of people attend? Were the meeting places adequate? Was the targeted audience reached?

Content. Was the information presented in an interesting and meaningful manner, using commonly understood vocabulary? Were there offerings that included different styles of learning? Was the knowledge base of the participants enhanced?

Long-term effects. Did the experience lead to a change in the behavior of participants? Were the participants moved to be diligent in prayer and devotion? Has there been an expression of these changes evident in the church's life?

Objectives

The first three categories listed above are more easily evaluated than are the long-term effects, because they have objectives that are short-term and measurable. Objectives for our education programs need to be SAM: Specific, Attainable, and Measurable. A learning community needs to know what they seek to accomplish, then evaluate if the goals have been met and how the learning is making a difference.

Let's look at an example of how our learning can be measured in mission *and* be evaluated specifically. Trinity Church offered a twelve-week series on "Parenting our Parents." In the planning stage for this course, the adult education team wrote the following objectives, using them to guide the details of their planning. After the course was complete, the team met again to review the effectiveness of this adult education opportunity in light of the objectives.

Trinity Church, Parenting Our Parents

Cognitive objectives:
- to understand the physical, mental, and emotional aspects of aging;
- to become acquainted with community resources for the elderly;
- to learn about the services provided by the parish nurse.

Affective objectives:
- to grow more aware of our own love and fears in regard to our parents;

• to trust Jesus' promise to be with us to the end of the age;
• to appreciate our parents' faith history;
• to enjoy time spent in prayer and devotion with our parents.

Action objectives:
• to be able to refer to a listing of home care alternatives;
• to become a more skilled listener;
• to arrange for regular in-home celebration of Holy Communion;
• to develop a network of persons for mutual support.

The adult planning team gathered information for their evaluation in several ways:

• surveying participants two weeks after the course, and again six months later;
• making a home visit to the parents involved to gauge their perception of growth in relationships and faith;
• reviewing arrangements for and participation in in-home celebration of Holy Communion;
• questioning the parents about their level of satisfaction with the information and services provided by the parish nurse.

After completing the initial evaluation, it is important to use the information to modify the process or program in order to improve it. For example, if you were part of the adult education team at Trinity, your evaluation may proceed in several ways:

• If you learned that the parents were unclear that the parish nurse would make home visits, the team might help the nurse rework the information materials and seek other ways to help people learn of the services.
• If you learned that parents and children have a difficult time praying together, the team might offer additional group meetings on prayer, providing an encouraging guide for common prayer.
• If you learned that family members have a difficult time listening to one another, you could provide appropriate training and guidance to improve listening skills.
• If you discovered that care-giving children felt isolated and weary, you could find ways for the congregation to uphold these members in prayer and with respite services.

Long-term Effects

Once the immediate results have been measured, and corresponding changes made, the evaluation turns to long-term criteria. These criteria are the cornerstone of planning a comprehensive program of adult education. The following questions are examples of ones that can be used for ongoing adult education team discussions about growth and educational mission:

• How is our adult Christian education ministry built on our baptismal calling to live in God's unconditional love?
• How do we assist individuals in using the gifts of creation and of faith to serve others?
• How are individual's gifts being discovered and their skills developed?
• How do we reach out to others beyond the walls of this church building?

CONCLUSION

In the gift of sanctification, the Holy Spirit makes us holy through Jesus Christ. What else is there to know or do or accomplish? Nothing. We already have salvation as a gift; we don't need good grades, certificates, or rewards. Instead, we are free to grow in Christ through risking, stretching, and daring to care more about others.

Education is the process of unwrapping and using the gifts God has given. The organizational tasks of planning, recruiting teachers, supporting teachers, training teachers, reaching out, publicizing, and evaluating are simply the good stewardship of these gifts. We are free to use and give away God's loving gifts, for there will always be enough. We can freely serve others and tell them God loves them. Clearly, learning is measured in mission.

Notes

chapter one
The Gospel Calls Us

1. Gerhard Kittel, ed., article on *didasko* in *Theological Dictionary of the New Testament* (Grand Rapids: Eerdmans, 1964), 2:138.
2. Robert L. Conrad, "Roots of Christian Education in North America," in *Education for Christian Living*, ed. Marvin L. Roloff (Minneapolis: Augsburg Publishing House, 1987), 22-23.
3. Recently a similar model has been revived in Roman Catholic and other circles.
4. Martin Luther, preface to the Small Catechism of 1529, in *A Contemporary Translation of Luther's Small Catechism: Study Edition*, trans. Timothy J. Wengert (Minneapolis: Augsburg Fortress, 1994), 73. All references to the Small Catechism are to this edition, unless otherwise noted.
5. Ibid., 74.
6. See Richard Robert Osmer's excellent seventh chapter in *A Teachable Spirit: Recovering the Teaching Office in the Church* (Louisville: Westminster/John Knox, 1990).
7. The Search Institute study in 1990 showed that "most denominations have much greater success in including children than high school youth and adults. . . . A major task is to increase the involvement of high school students and adults in formal Christian education" (Search Institute, *Effective Christian Education: A National Study of Protestant Congregations: A Report for the Evangelical Lutheran Church in America* [March 1990], 53). See also Loren B. Mead's call for congregations to build adult education and expand the network of capable teachers (*Transforming Congregations for the Future* [Alban Institute, 1994], 60).
8. See James D. Smart, *The Teaching Ministry of the Church* (Philadelphia: Westminster Press, 1954).
9. See Malcolm Knowles, *The Modern Practice of Adult Education* (New York: Association, 1971).
10. For example, Leon McKenzie, *Adult Religious Education: The Twentieth Century Challenge* (Mystic, Conn.: Twenty-Third Publications, 1975) and *The Religious Education of Adults* (Birming-ham: Religious Education Press, 1982).
11. For example, Joan Marie Smith and Gloria Durka, eds., *Aesthetic Dimensions of Religious Education* (New York: Paulist Press, 1979).
12. See especially Thomas Groome, *Christian Religious Education: Sharing our Story and Vision* (San Francisco: Harper and Row, 1980) and

Sharing Faith (Harper, 1991); also Daniel Schipani, *Religious Education Encounters Liberation Theology* (Birmingham: Religious Education Press, 1988).

13. James Fowler's stages of faith form the basis for this approach.

14. Brueggemann's *The Creative Word: Canon as a Model for Biblical Education* (Philadelphia: Fortress, 1982) uses biblical canon as a model for Christian education. Brueggemann argues for a core in Christian education curriculum that combines an authoritative core (the character of Torah) with education that is a disruption for justice (as in the prophets) and that which reflects reason and passionate trust in God (the character of the Wisdom literature). Sara Little, in *To Set One's Heart: Belief and Teaching in the Church* (Atlanta: John Knox, 1983), argues for education on the basis that "beliefs which engage the thinking powers of the person as they emerge out of and inform faith, sustained, reformed, and embodied by the faith community, can be an important factor in bringing integration and integrity to life" (p. 9).

15. Kay Kupper Berg, "Christian Literacy, the Core Curriculum, and the Urban Church" in *Urban Church Education*, ed. Donald B. Rogers (Birmingham: Religious Education Press, 1989), 50-59.

16. Richard Robert Osmer, *A Teachable Spirit: Recovering the Teaching Office in the Church* (Louisville: Westminster/John Knox, 1990), 16-18.

17. Martin Luther, the Large Catechism, in *The Book of Concord*, trans. and ed. Theodore G. Tappert (Philadelphia: Fortress Press, 1959), pt. I, 23. All subsequent references to parts of *The Book of Concord*, except the Small Catechism, are taken from this edition of that work and are cited by part (pt.) or article (art.), and section number.

18. Apology of the Augsburg Confession, arts. II, 3; IV, 33.

19. Augsburg Confession, art. IV, 1-2; Solid Declaration, art. III, 25.

20. Augsburg Confession, art. XX, 28; Solid Declaration, art. III, 13, 16.

21. See Paul Tillich, *Systematic Theology* (Chicago: University of Chicago Press, 1957), 2:166.

22. For Tillich's educational methodology, see Margaret A. Krych, *Teaching the Gospel Today: A Guide for Education in the Congregation* (Minneapolis: Augsburg, 1987).

23. Large Catechism, Shorter Preface, 2.

24. Small Catechism, 75.

25. Large Catechism, Longer Preface, 7-8.

26. Gerhard Ebeling, *Luther: An Introduction to His Thought*, trans. R. A. Wilson (London: Collins, 1970), 70.

27. Large Catechism, pt. IV, 37.

28. If we are ever tempted to doubt God's promise of mercy, we must respond with "But I am baptized! And if I am baptized, I have the promise that I shall be saved and have eternal life, both in soul and body" (Large Catechism pt. IV, 44).

29. The Augsburg Confession, article IX, 1-2, states that "Baptism is necessary for salvation, that the grace of God is offered through Baptism, and that children should be baptized, for being offered to God through Baptism they are received into his grace."

30. See Jean Piaget, *Six Psychological Studies*, trans. Anita Tenzer (London: University of London Press, 1968), 8-70.

31. See the *Confirmation Ministry Task Force Report*, approved at the August 1993 ELCA Churchwide Assembly, which uses Baptism to call the church to lifelong learning.

32. In "To the Christian Nobility," Luther says, "A cobbler, a smith, a peasant—each has the work and office of his trade, and yet they are all alike consecrated priests and bishops" (*Selected Writings of Martin Luther, 1517-1520*, ed. Theodore G. Tappert [Philadelphia: Fortress, 1967, 266). And, in "The Freedom of a Christian," Luther writes, "Not only are we the freest of kings, we are also priests forever, which is far more excellent than being kings, for as priests we are worthy to appear before God to pray for others and to teach one another divine things. These are the functions of priests, and they cannot be granted to any unbeliever. Thus Christ has made it possible for us, provided we believe in him, to be not only his brethren, co-heirs, and fellow-kings, but also his fellow-priests" (*Martin Luther's Basic Theological Writings*, ed. Timothy F. Lull [Minneapolis: Fortress, 1989], 607).

33. Jürgen Moltmann, *The Spirit of Life: A Universal Affirmation*, trans. Margaret Kohl (Minneapolis: Fortress, 1992), 192-3.

34. Ibid., 183.

35. Gerhard Ebeling, "Word of God and Hermeneutics" in *Word and Faith*, trans. James W. Leitch (London: SCM, 1963), 326.

36. Paul Tillich, *Theology of Culture*, ed. Robert C. Kimball (New York: Oxford University Press, 1964), 204-6.

37. See Martin Stallmann's approach to church education in "Contemporary Interpretation of the Gospels as a Challenge to Preaching and Religious Education" in *The Theology* of *Rudolph Bultmann*, ed. Charles W. Kegley (London: SCM, 1966), 236-253.

38. The ELCA *Statement of Purpose* declares that it shall "nurture its members in the Word of God so as to grow in faith and hope and love, to see daily life as the primary setting for the exercise of their Christian calling, and to use the gifts of the Spirit for their life together and for their calling in the world" (4.02e). Many other denominations express similar purposes.

39. Martin Luther, "To the Councilmen of All Cities in Germany That They Establish and Maintain Christian Schools," in *Martin Luther's Basic Theological Writings*, ed. Timothy F. Lull (Minneapolis: Fortress, 1989).

40. Martin Luther, "A Sermon on Keeping Children in School," in *Luther's Works*, vol. 46 (Philadelphia: Fortress, 1967).
41. Wolfhart Pannenberg, *Systematic Theology*, vol. 2, trans. Geoffrey W. Bromiley (Grand Rapids: Eerdmans, 1994), 275.
42. Augsburg Confession, art. V.

chapter two
What Teachers Need to Know About Adults Today

1. Dean R. Hoge, Benton Johnson, and Donald Luidens, *Vanishing Boundaries: The Religion of Mainline Protestant Baby Boomers* (Louisville: Westminster/John Knox, 1994), 12-14.
2. Robert N. Bellah, Richard Madsen, William M. Sullivan, Ann Swidler, and Steven Tipton, *Habits of the Heart: Individualism and Commitment in American Life* (Berkeley: University of California Press, 1985).
3. Tex Sample, *U.S. Lifestyles and Mainline Churches* (Louisville: Westeminster/John Knox, 1990), 11-13.
4. Ibid., 15-16.
5. Ibid., 26-28.
6. Ibid., 39.
7. Ibid., 45-54.
8. Tim Celek and Dieter Zander, *Inside the Soul of a New Generation: Insights and Strategies for Reaching Busters* (Grand Rapids, Mich.: Zondervan Publishing House, 1996), 20.
9. Ibid., 53.
10. Kevin Graham Ford, *Jesus for a New Generation: Putting the Gospel in the Language of the Xers* (Downers Grove, Ill.: Intervarsity Press, 1995), 37-39.
11. Ibid., 170.
12. Ibid., 221.
13. Celek and Zander, 134.
14. Ibid., 152.
15. Sample, 59-61.
16. Ibid., 63.
17. Ibid., 70-80.
18. Ibid., 88ff.
19. Ibid., 94.
20. Ibid., 117.
21. Ibid., 133.
22. Merton Strommen, Milo L. Brekke, Ralph C. Underwager, and Arthur L. Johnson, *A Study of Generations* (Minneapolis: Augsburg Publishing House, 1972), 133.

23. Search Institute, *Effective Christian Education: A National Study of Protestant Congregations: A Report for the Evangelical Lutheran Church in America* (Minneapolis: Search Institute, 1990), 22.

24. Ibid., 3.

25. David Keirsey and Marilyn Bates, *Please Understand Me: Character and Temperament Types* (Del Mar, Calif.: Prometheus Nemesis Book Company, 1984), chap. 4.

26. See Lawrence Kohlberg's *The Psychology of Moral Development* (San Francisco: Harper and Row, 1984), for a detailed explanation of the stages.

27. Carol Gilligan, *In a Different Voice* (Cambridge: Harvard University Press, 1982), 174.

28. See James Fowler's *Stages of Faith* (San Francisco: Harper and Row, 1981) for his definitive work on faith development.

29. Karl Ernest Nipkow, "Stage Theories of Faith Development as a Challenge to Religious Education and Practical Theology," in *Stages of Faith and Religious Development*, by James W. Fowler, Karl Ernest Nipkow, and Friedrich Schweitzer (New York: Crossroad, 1991), 97.

30. Gail Sheehy, *Passages* (New York: E. P. Dutton and Company, 1976), 84ff.

31. Daniel Levinson, *The Seasons of a Man's Life* (New York: Alfred A. Knopf, 1978), 90. See also *The Seasons of a Woman's Life* (New York: Alfred A. Knopf, 1996), 25.

32. Sharon Parks, *The Critical Years* (San Francisco: Harper and Row, 1986), 97.

33. Sheehy, 138ff.

34. Daniel Levinson, *The Seasons of a Woman's Life*, 118.

35. Ronald Duska and Mariellen Whelan, *Moral Development: A Guide to Piaget and Kohlberg* (New York: Paulist Press, 1975), 46.

36. Ibid., 48.

37. Ibid., 47.

38. James Fowler, *Stages of Faith* (San Francisco: Harper and Row, 1981), 174ff.

39. Ibid., 184ff.

40. Robert L. Conrad, "Christian Education and Creative Conflict" (Ph.D. diss., Princeton Theological Seminary, 1975), 87-127.

41. Levinson, chaps. 14-15.

42. Evelyn Eaton Whitehead and James D. Whitehead, *Christian Life Patterns* (Garden City, N.Y.: Image Books, 1982), 219.

43. Duska and Whelan, 47.

44. Fowler, 201. There is a debate as to whether the final stages of Kohlberg's moral thought and Fowler's religious belief actually exist. The empirical data are very slight.

chapter three
Principles of Adult Learning

1. Eugene C. Roehlkepartain, *The Teaching Church: Moving Christian Education to Center Stage* (Nashville: Abingdon Press, 1993), 78.

2. Linda J. Vogel, *Teaching and Learning in Communities of Faith* (San Francisco: Jossey-Bass, 1991); Norma Thompson, "Adult Religious Life and Nature" in *Changing Patterns of Religious Education* (Nashville: Abingdon, 1984), 274.

3. Malcolm Knowles, *The Adult Learner: A Neglected Species*, 4th ed. (Houston: Gulf Publishing, 1990), 54.

4. Ibid., 54

5. Leon McKenzie, *The Religious Education of Adults* (Birmingham, Ala.: Religious Education Press, 1982), 116-119.

6. Ibid., 120.

7. A. Roger Gobbel, "Christian Education: An Exercise in Interpreting" in *Education for Christian Living*, ed. Marvin L. Roloff (Minneapolis: Augsburg, 1987), 139.

8. Malcolm A. Knowles, "A Theory of Christian Adult Education Methodology" in *Christian Adulthood* (Washington, D.C.: U.S. Catholic Conference, 1982).

9. McKenzie, *The Religious Education of Adults*, 113.

10. Knowles, *The Adult Learners*, 52.

11. Joseph Davenport III, "Is There Any Way Out of the Andragogy Morass?" *Lifelong Learning: An Omnibus of Practice and Research* 11, no. 3 (1987): 17.

12. Knowles, 53.

13. Malcolm Knowles, *The Modern Practice of Adult Education: Pedagogy Versus Andragogy* (New York: Association Press, 1976).

14. Knowles, *The Adult Learner*, 54.

15. *Lutheran Book of Worship* (Minneapolis: Augsburg Publishing House and Philadelphia: Board of Publication, Lutheran Church in America, 1978), p. 121.

16. Knowles, *The Adult Learner*, 57-63.

17. Eduard C. Lindeman, *The Meaning of Adult Education* (New York: New Republic, Inc., 1926), 6.

18. Ibid., 10.

19. Ibid., 10.

20. Edward Thorndike, *Adult Interests* (New York: The Macmillan Company, 1935), 1.

21. Ibid., 2

22. Leon McKenzie, "The Purposes and Scope of Adult Religious Education" in *Handbook of Adult Religious Education* (Birmingham, Ala.: Religious Education Press, 1986), 20-21.

23. Daniel D. Pratt, "Audragogy After Twenty-Five Years," *New Directions for Adult and Continuing Education*, no. 57 (Spring 1993): 15-23.
24. Sharan M. Merriam, "Adult Learning: Where Have We Come From? Where Are We Headed?" *New Directions for Adult and Continuing Education* 57 (Spring 1993): 5-14.
25. Ibid., 11.
26. John Elias, *The Foundations and Practice of Adult Religious Education*, rev. ed. (Malabar, Fla.: Krieger, 1993).
27. R.E.Y. Wickett, *Models of Adult Religious Education Practice* (Birmingham, Ala.: Religious Education Press, 1991), 50.
28. Stephen D. Brookfield, *Understanding and Facilitating Adult Learning* (San Francisco: Jossey-Bass Publishers, 1990), 121.
29. Ibid., 121.
30. K. Patricia Cross, *Adults as Learners* (San Francisco: Jossey-Bass, 1982), 222-228.
31. Margaret Fisher Billinger, "Adult Learning in Religious Context," in *Adult Religious Education: A Journey of Faith Development*, ed. Marie A. Gillen and Maurice C. Taylor (New York: Paulist Press, 1995), 75.
32. The Smalcald Articles, in *The Book of Concord*, trans. and ed. Theodore G. Tappert (Philadelphia: Fortress Press, 1959) pt. III, art. IV.
33. See Marie A. Gillen and Maurice C. Taylor, eds., *Adult Religious Education: A Journey of Faith Development* (New York: Paulist Press, 1995); and Berard L. Marthaler, *Catechetics in Context*, 2nd printing (Huntington, Ind.: Our Sunday Visitor, 1974).
34. Nancy Foltz, *Handbook of Adult Religious Education* (Birmingham, Ala.: Religious Education Press, 1986), 81-82.
35. Jeanne Tighe and Karne Szentkeresti, *Rethinking Adult Religious Education* (New York: Paulist Press, 1986), 81-82.
36. Vogel, 143-144.
37. Thompson, 273-4.
38. Brookfield, 1-24.
39. Raymond J. Wlodkowski, *Enhancing Adult Motivation to Learn* (San Francisco: Jossey-Bass, 1985), 4.
40. Alan Boyd Knox, *Adult Development and Learning: A Handbook on Individual Growth and Competence in the Adult Years* (San Francisco: Jossey-Bass, 1977), 524-528.
41. Allen Tough, *Intentional Changes: A Fresh Approach to Helping People Change* (Chicago: Follett Publishing, 1982), 51.
42. R. Wade Paschal, *Vital Adult Learning* (Nashville: Abingdon Press, 1994), 32.
43. Kent L. Johnson, *Developing Skills for Teaching Adults*, Teaching the Faith series (Minneapolis: Augsburg Fortress; St. Louis: Concordia Publishing House, 1993).

44. Search Institute, *Effective Christian Education: A National Study of Protestant Congregations: A Report for the Evangelical Lutheran Church in America* (Minneapolis: Search Institute, 1990), 60.
45. Wlodkowski, 7.
46. McKenzie, *The Religious Education of Adults*, 62.
47. Wlodkowski, 8.
48. Walter Brueggemann, *The Message of the Psalms* (Minneapolis: Augsburg Publishing House, 1984), 19-23.
49. Johnson, *Developing Skills for Teaching Adults*, Participant Guide, 6.
50. Search Institute, 6.
51. Robert Bellah, *Habits of the Heart* (Berkeley: University of California Press, 1985).
52. Dick Murray, *Strengthening the Adult Sunday School Class* (Nashville: Abingdon, 1981).
53. Paschal, 52.
54. David L. Silvernail, *Teaching Styles as Related to Student Achievement* (Washington, D.C.: National Education Association, 1986), 28.
55. Cross, 119-120.
56. Paschal, 32-46.
57. Tighe and Szentkeresti, 106-109.

chapter four
Teaching Matters: The Role of the Teacher

1. Richard R. Osmer, *A Teachable Spirit: Recovering the Teaching Office in the Church* (Louisville: Westminster/John Knox Press, 1990).
2. *Sharing the Light of Faith: National Catechetical Directory for Catholics of the Unites States* (Washington, D.C.: United States Catholic Conference, 1979), 4-5.
3. *Sharing the Light of Faith*, 113.
4. Walter Brueggemann, *The Creative Word: Canon as a Model for Biblical Education* (Philadelphia: Fortress Press, 1982), 1.
5. James A. Fowler, *Becoming Adult, Becoming Christian* (San Francisco: Harper, 1984).
6. Jack L. Seymour and Donald E. Miller, *Contemporary Approaches to Christian Education* (Nashville: Abingdon Press, 1982); also Seymour and Miller, *Theological Approaches to Christian Education* (Nashville: Abingdon Press, 1990).
7. Eugene C. Roehlkepartain, *The Teaching Church* (Nashville: Abingdon Press, 1993), 112-113.
8. Parker Palmer, *To Know As We Are Known* (San Francisco: Harper, 1983), 113.

9. Mary Elizabeth Moore, *Teaching from the Heart* (Minneapolis: Fortress Press, 1991), 198.

10. Hans-Reudi Weber, *The Book That Reads Me* (Geneva, Switzerland: World Council of Churches, 1995), 37.

11. Palmer, 104.

12. John Westerhoff, *Will Our Children Have Faith?* (Minneapolis: Winston Seabury Press, 1976), 89.

13. Alan Jones, *Exploring Spiritual Direction: An Essay on Christian Friendship* (New York: Harper and Row, 1982), 124.

14. Weber, 26.

15. Ibid., 26.

16. Daniel Goleman, *Emotional Intelligence* (New York: Bantam, 1995), 15.

17. Charles Foster, *Educating Congregations* (Nashville: Abingdon, 1994), 63.

18. Martin Luther, explanation to the First Article of the Apostles' Creed, in *A Contemporary Translation of Luther's Small Catechism: Study Edition*, trans. Timothy J. Wengert (Minneapolis: Augsburg Fortress, 1994), 25.

19. John L. Elias, *The Foundations and Practice of Adult Education*, rev. ed. (Malabar, Fla.: Kreiger Publishing Company, 1993), 37.

20. Ibid., 56.

21. Ibid., 56.

22. Ibid., 57, 63.

23. Ibid., 57.

24. Ibid., 63.

25. Linda Vogel, *Teaching and Learning in Communities of Faith* (San Francisco: Jossey-Bass Publishers, 1991), 106-109.

26. Malcolm Knowles, *Self-Directed Learning* (Chicago: Association Press, 1975), 15.

27. William E. Diehl, *Thank God It's Monday* (Philadelphia: Fortress Press, 1982), XI.

28. Foster, 54.

29. As quoted in Goleman, 234, from a speech at Cornell University, September 24, 1993.

30. Vogel, 157.

31. Foster, 55.

32. Weber, 1.

33. Foster, 60.

34. Knowles, *Self-Directed Learning*, 9.

35. Henri J. M. Nouwen, *Reaching Out: The Three Movements of the Spiritual Life* (Garden City: Doubleday and Company, 1975), 47.

36. Vogel, XI.

37. Osmer, 12.

38. Leon McKenzie, *The Religious Education of Adults* (Birmingham, Ala.: Religious Education Press, 1982), 218.

39. Ibid., 219.

40. Ibid., 218.

41. Vogel, 160.

42. C. Ellis Nelson, *Where Faith Begins* (Atlanta: John Knox Press, 1971), 10.

43. Maria Harris, *Fashion Me A People* (Louisville: Westminster/John Knox, 1989).

44. *Confirmation Ministry Study: A Global Report* (Geneva, Switzerland: Lutheran World Federation, 1995), 49.

45. Clark M. Williamson and Ronald J. Allen, *The Teaching Minister* (Louisville: Westminster/John Knox Press, 1991), 106.

46. Loren Mead, *More Than Numbers* (New York: The Alban Institute, 1993), 43.

47. Vogel, XII.

48. McKenzie, 191.

49. Paulo Freire, *Pedagogy of the Oppressed* (New York: The Seabury Press, 1973).

50. McKenzie, 190.

51. The three impact areas illustrated in figure 2 are adapted from Muska Mosston, *Teaching: From Command to Discovery* (Belmont, Calif.: Wadsworth Publishing Co., 1972) passim. The steps are adapted from Kenneth R. Moore, *Classroom Teaching Skills* (New York: Random House, 1989), 8.

52. Osmer, 19.

53. James Michael Lee, *The Flow of Religious Instruction* (Birmingham, Ala.: Religious Education Press, 1973), 206.

54. McKenzie, 198.

55. The concept of figure 1 is an expansion of Muska Mosston's work in *Teaching: From Command to Discovery*, which is tuned more finely in *The Spectrum of Teaching: From Command to Discovery* by Muska Mosston and Sara Ashworth (New York: Longman Press, 1990). The "Creative Tension" column has been inserted by this author.

56. Malcolm Knowles, *The Modern Practice of Adult Education* (New York: Association Press, 1970), 273ff.

57. Osmer, 14.

58. Elias, 225-226.

59. Knowles, *The Modern Practice of Adult Education*, 15.

60. Roehlkepartain, 31.

61. Ibid., 104.

62. Bruce Joyce and Marsha Weil, *Models of Teaching* (Englewood Cliffs: Prentice-Hall, 1986).

63. Elias, 247.

64. R. Michael Harton, "Working With Educators of Adults" in *Handbook of Adult Religious Education*, ed. Nancy T. Foltz (Birmingham, Ala.: Religious Education Press, 1986), 127.

65. John Westerhoff and Gwen Kennedy Neville, *Learning Through Liturgy* (New York: The Seabury Press, 1978), 122.

66. *Confirmation Ministry Study*, 8, 14.

67. Goleman, 4.

68. Eugene C. Kreider, "Styles of Teaching" page in *Teaching the Bible*, Teacher Education series (Minneapolis: Augsburg Fortress, 1992), 31.

69. The idea is based on R. Tannenbaum and H.W. Schmidt, "How to Choose a Leadership Style," *Harvard Business Review* (March 1958).

70. Weber, 1.

71. See Weber, IX.

72. Osmer, 149.

73. Weber, XII.

74. Goleman, 96.

75. Knowles, *The Modern Practice of Adult Education*, 15.

76. Weber, 37.

77. Martin Luther, "A Simple Way to Pray," in *Devotional Writings*, ed. Gustav K. Wiencke, vol. 43 of Luther's Works, ed. Helmut T. Lehmann (Philadelphia: Fortress Press, 1968), 209.

78. R. E. Y. Wickett, *Models of Adult Religious Education Practice* (Birmingham, Ala.: Religious Education Press, 1991), 66.

79. Roehlkepartain, 95.

80. McKenzie, 212.

81. Ibid., 213.

82. Benjamin Bloom with J. Thomas Hastings and George F. Maddus, *Handbook on Formative and Summative Evaluation of Student Learning* (New York: McGraw Hill Book Company, 1971). See chapter on "Summative Evaluation," 61-85.

83. Ibid., 117-138.

84. Roehlkepartain, 95.

85. David Peterson, *Facilitating Education for Older Learners* (San Francisco: Jossey-Bass, 1983), 281-282.

86. Knowles, 67.

87. Osmer, 14.

88. Michael Fishbane, *Biblical Interpretation in Ancient Israel* (Oxford: Clarendon Press, 1985), 542-543.

89. Olivier Messiaen, program notes for the "Quartet for the End of Time."

chapter five
Content Areas of Adult Education

1. *Lutheran Book of Worship*, pp. 13-41, 179-192.
2. Thomas H. Groome, *Christian Religious Education* (San Francisco: Harper and Row, 1980), 25.
3. Suggested methods for implementing curricular materials are in *Teaching the Bible to Adults and Youth* by Dick Murray (Nashville: Abingdon, 1993) and *Transforming Bible Study: A Leader's Guide* by Walter Wink (Nashville: Abingdon, 1990).
4. Some resources for beginning storytellers:

   Aurelio, John. *Fables for God's People*. New York: Crossroad, 1993.
   Bausch, William J. *Storytelling: Imagination and Faith*. Mystic, Conn.: Twenty-Third Publications, 1991.
   Simpkinson, Charles and Anne, eds. *Sacred Stories: A Celebration of the Power of Story to Transform and Heal*. San Francisco: Harper San Francisco, 1993.
   White, William R. *Stories for Telling: A Treasury for Christian Storytellers*. Minneapolis: Augsburg, 1986.
   Williams, Michael E. *The Storyteller's Companion to the Bible*. 5 vols. Nashville: Abingdon, 1990-.

5. Concordia College, Moorhead, Minn.
6. Stanley J. Hauerwas, *A Community of Character: Toward a Constructive Social Ethic* (South Bend: University of Notre Dame Press, 1981), 1.
7. George W. Forell, *The Protestant Faith* (Philadelphia: Fortress Press, 1960), 6.
8. John B. Cobb Jr., *Lay Theology* (St. Louis: Chalice Press, 1994), 11.
9. Robert Benne's term for ordinary Christians who "become ordinary saints, not because of either their heroic or ordinary deeds, but because of the extraordinary grace of God in Christ that is freely offered to them" in *Ordinary Saints: An Introduction to the Christian Life* (Minneapolis: Fortress Press, 1988), X.
10. Douglas John Hall, *Thinking the Faith: Christian Theology in North American Context* (Minneapolis: Fortress Press, 1991), 58.
11. Maria Harris, *Fashion Me a People* (Louisville: Westminster/John Knox Press, 1989), 16.
12. Ibid., 41.
13. Henri J. M. Nouwen, *Reaching Out: The Three Movements of the Spiritual Life* (New York: Doubleday, 1975), 37-38.
14. *Lutheran Book of Worship*, p. 201.

15. Bruce C. Birch and Larry L. Rasmussen, *Bible and Ethics in the Christian Life* (Minneapolis: Augsburg, 1989), 22.
16. James M. Childs Jr., *Faith, Formation, and Decision* (Minneapolis: Fortress Press, 1992), 6.
17. Some resources for adult member classes:

Erlander, Daniel. *Baptized, We Live: Lutheranism as a Way of Life.* Chelan, Wash.: Holden Village, 1981.
Hall, George F. *Being in the Body of Christ.* Philadelphia: Parish Life Press, 1978. Includes leader guide.
Marshall, Robert. *On Being a Church Member.* Minneapolis: Augsburg Fortress, 1988. Includes leader guide.
Marty, Martin E. *Come and Grow with Us: New Member Basics.* Minneapolis: Augsburg Fortress, 1996. Includes leader guide.
Marty, Martin E. *Invitation to Discipleship.* Minneapolis: Augsburg Publishing House, 1986. Includes leader guide.
Nestingen, James A. *Roots of Our Faith: A Six-Session Course on Lutheran Teaching.* Minneapolis: Augsburg Publishing House, 1979.
Nichol, Todd. *A Study of Luther's Small Catechism for Adults.* Minneapolis: Augsburg Fortress, 1991. Includes leader guide.

18. H. D. Aiken, *Reason and Conduct* (New York: Alfred A. Knopf, 1962), 65-87.
19. The Great Books Foundation has developed a process for discussion called "shared inquiry." Discussion leaders invite discussion by asking questions of fact, interpretation, and evaluation about a particular text or selection.
20. Some resources that offer a broader discussion of ethics:

Benne, Robert. *Ordinary Saints: An Introduction into the Christian Faith.* Philadelphia: Fortress Press, 1988.
Benne, Robert. *The Paradoxical Vision: A Public Theology for the Twenty-First Century.* Minneapolis: Fortress Press, 1995.
Birch, Bruce C. and Larry L. Rasmussen. *Bible and Ethics in the Christian Life.* Minneapolis: Augsburg, 1989.
Childs, James M. *Ethics in Business: Faith at Work.* Minneapolis: Fortress Press, 1992.
Childs, James M. *Faith, Formation, and Decision.* Minneapolis: Fortress Press, 1992.

21. Marc Kolden, *Living the Faith* (Minneapolis: Augsburg Fortress, 1992), 13-15.

chapter six
Exploring Opportunities for Adult Education

1. Those five denominations are Christian Church (Disciples of Christ), Evangelical Lutheran Church in America, Presbyterian Church (U.S.A.), United Church of Christ, and United Methodist Church. In the Evangelical Lutheran Church in America, only twenty percent of the adults who participated in this study reported forty or more hours a year involvement in Christian education.

2. C. Jeff Woods, *Congregational Megatrends* (The Alban Institute, 1996), 60-61.

3. Sara Little, "Rethinking Adult Education," in *Rethinking Christian Education: Explorations in Theory and Practice*, ed. David S. Schuller (St. Louis: Chalice Press, 1993), 102.

4. Nancy T. Foltz, "Basic Principles of Adult Religious Education," in *Handbook of Adult Religious Education*, ed. Nancy T. Foltz (Birmingham, Ala.: Religious Education Press, 1986).

5. Little, 107.

6. Robert Wuthnow, *Sharing the Journey: Support Groups and America's New Quest for Community* (New York: The Free Press, 1994), 66.

7. George S. Johnson, David Mayer, and Nancy Vogel, *Starting Small Groups—and Keeping Them Going* (Minneapolis: Augsburg Fortress, 1995), 13.

8. Walter Huffman, "Catechumenal Ministry: An Introduction" (unpublished manuscript, 1992), 2.

9. For example, the Lutheran Church Library Association, 122 W. Franklin Avenue, Minneapolis, Minn. 55404.

chapter seven
Making the Connections

1. See chapter 1 in *Method in Ministry: Theological Reflection and Christian Ministry*, rev. ed., by James D. Whitehead and Evelyn Eaton Whitehead (Kansas City: Sheed and Word, 1995), for a method of attending, assertion, and pastoral response.

2. See Allen Tough, *The Adult's Learning Projects* (Toronto: Learning Concepts, 1979). Tough says almost all adults undertake one or two major learning projects a year, some as many as fifteen or twenty. The median is eight, involving distinct areas.

3. Martin Luther, the Large Catechism, in *The Book of Concord*, trans. and ed. Theodore G. Tappert (Philadelphia: Fortress Press, 1959), pt. I, 3.

4. Large Catechism, pt. I, 224-231.
5. Martin Luther, "A Treatise on Christian Liberty," trans. W. A. Lambert and Harold J. Grimm (Philadelphia: Fortress Press, 1957), 251.
6. Einar Billing, *Our Calling*, trans. Conrad Bergendoff (Rock Island: Augustana Press, 1958), 6.
7. *An Adult Education Resource: Connections: Faith and World*, a 24-session adult study to be published by Division for Ministry and Division for Congregational Ministries, Evangelical Lutheran Church in America, in 1997.
8. Letty M. Russell, *Christian Education in Mission* (Philadelphia: The Westminster Press, 1967), 13, 37.
9. *Lutheran Book of Worship*, p. 125.
10. Martin Luther, *A Contemporary Translation of Luther's Small Catechism: Study Edition*, trans. Timothy J. Wengert (Minneapolis: Augsburg Fortress, 1994), 29.
11. *Lutheran Book of Worship*, Canticle 13.
12. Ibid., p. 124.
13. Ibid., p. 92.
14. Ibid., adapted from the two versions of the prayer on p. 91.

chapter eight
Organizing for Adult Education

1. See Joseph Marino, *Biblical Themes in Religious Education* (Birmingham, Ala.: Religious Education Press, 1983), and Frederick Tiffany and Sharon Ringe, eds., *Biblical Interpretation: A Road Map* (Nashville: Abingdon, 1996).
2. See Mary Elizabeth Mullino Moore, *Teaching from the Heart: Theology and Educational Method* (Minneapolis: Fortress Press, 1991), and Richard Robert Osmer, *Teaching for Faith: A Guide for Teachers of Adult Classes* (Louisville: Westminster/John Knox Press, 1992).
3. Robert L. Browning and Roy A. Reed, *Models of Confirmation and Baptismal Affirmation* (Birmingham, Ala.: Religious Education Press, 1995). See especially part III on young adults, middle adults, and older adults.
4. Joel Garreau, *Edge City* (New York: Doubleday, 1991). Garreau develops the concept of "edge city" as the new hearth of civilization. Every U.S. city that is growing, is growing with multiple urban cores, beyond suburbia.
5. See Norma Cook Everist and Nelvin Vos, *Where in the World Are You? Connecting Faith and Daiy Life* (Washington, D.C.: The Alban Institute, 1996).

6. See Jack L. Seymour, Margaret Ann Crain, and Joseph V. Crockett, *Educating Christians: The Intersection of Meaning, Learning and Vocation* (Nashville: Abingdon, 1993).

7. An excellent, provocative piece is CBS Reports, "Who's Getting Rich and Why Aren't You?" with Harry Smith, August, 1996. Video and transcript available through CBS.

8. Letty M. Russell, *Christian Education in Mission* (Philadelphia: The Westminster Press, 1967), 9-15.